AN EMPTY PLATE

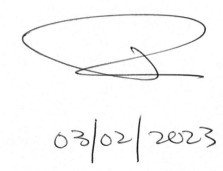

03/02/2023

AN EMPTY PLATE

Why we are losing the battle for our food system,
why it matters, and how we can win it back

TRACY LEDGER

First published by Jacana Media (Pty) Ltd in 2016
Second impression 2017
Third impression 2018
Fourth impression 2022

10 Orange Street
Sunnyside
Auckland Park 2092
South Africa
+2711 628 3200
www.jacana.co.za

ISBN 978-1-4314-2423-8

Cover design Shawn Paikin
Set in Adobe Garamond Pro 11/13pt
Printed and bound by Creda Communications
Job no. 003942

See a complete list of Jacana titles at
www.jacana.co.za

For Hein

Contents

Acronyms and abbreviations

ANC	African National Congress
BFAP	Bureau for Food and Agricultural Policy
CCHIP	Community Childhood Hunger Identification Project
COSATU	Congress of South African Trade Unions
CSI	corporate social investment
DA	Democratic Alliance
DAFF	Department of Agriculture, Forestry and Fisheries
DDS	Dietary Diversity Score
DRDLR	Department of Rural Development and Land Reform
ECC	Employment Conditions Commission
EFF	Economic Freedom Fighters
FMF	Free Market Foundation
GAS	*Gruppi di Acquisito Solidale* (solidarity purchase groups in Italy)
GDP	Gross Domestic Product
GEAR	Growth, Employment and Redistribution
GHS	General Household Survey
GNU	Government of National Unity
HSRC	Human Sciences Research Council
IDP	Integrated Development plan

IES	Income and Expenditure Survey
IQF	Individually Quick-frozen
JMPD	Johannesburg Metro Police Department
LED	Local Economic Development
MSA	Municipal Systems Act (2000)
NAMC	National Agricultural Marketing Council
NCDs	Non-communicable Diseases
NDP	National Development Plan
NEDLAC	National Economic Development and Labour Council
PACSA	Pietermaritzburg Agency for Community Social Action
PHA	Philippi Horticultural Area
RDP	Reconstruction and Development Programme
SAFE	South African Fruit Exporters
SANHANES-1	South African National Health and Nutrition Examination Survey
SASSA	South African Social Security Agency
StatsSA	Statistics South Africa
VUFA	Vukuzenzele Urban Farmers Association

Prologue

Imagine South Africa, 2016

It is 22 years since the dawning of democracy in the Rainbow Nation, but for many South Africans the promise of freedom has been tainted by a terrible deprivation. Every night, millions of children lie awake, unable to sleep from the torment of thirst. At school they faint from that thirst, and their physical and intellectual development is permanently stunted by chronic dehydration. In their dusty daydreams they fantasise about holding a glass of clean water in their hands.

The hospitals are crowded with people sick and dying from drinking polluted water – all they could find or afford. Parents beg in the streets during the day, hoping to earn something to buy a little water, dreading having to return home empty handed. Some families send their girl child up to the local truck stop, hoping she can make enough to stave off the family's thirst for a few days.

What went wrong? What catastrophic event has left South Africa without water and created such suffering? The sad reality is that there is plenty of water – the poor walk alongside gushing canals of water, fenced off with razor wire, out of their reach. The shops are full of water – there are chains of water retail stores and speciality designer water shops. If you have enough money, you can drink until you burst. If you don't, you learn to live with a permanent thirst and, sometimes, you die from that thirst.

The cruellest irony is that South Africa's Constitution guarantees everyone the right to water, but somewhere along the line the government was convinced that 'free' market forces in the provision of water would be in everyone's best interests. There are certainly winners: water-bottling and water-retailing companies are booming – recording profits that run to billions of rands. They bottle enough water for export to neighbouring countries and their shareholders and senior managers increase their wealth every year. These water-processing and retailing companies proudly advertise donations of water to the most desperate that cannot afford to buy their product, and they receive awards for their compassion.

Things are very different for those who work at the water-production facilities: it is hard labour for very little pay – most water workers cannot afford to buy sufficient water for their families on their monthly wage. They are often subject to brutal treatment from their employers – but are ignored by a government that believes that this collateral damage is acceptable in this growing and profitable sector.

Of course there is concern that more than three-quarters of all South Africans cannot afford to buy the water they need: a social grant system has been put in place to ensure that only a small minority actually die from thirst. Beyond this, there is little real sympathy with the thirsty. After all, they could source their own water. There are hundreds of public- and private-sector initiatives that teach the poor how to dig their own wells in the backyards of their shacks in the informal settlements, and thousands of spades have been distributed to assist them to do so. Those that do not dig – well, they have chosen to go without and they do not receive much sympathy from government or the wider public. Poverty-stricken mothers are chastised for not giving their infants sufficient water, and are encouraged to attend educational sessions where the error of their ways is pointed out to them.

Those who protest about the commodification of a basic requirement for life are shouted down and accused of not understanding basic economics. Yes, of course all this suffering is unpleasant, but that is the way things are. Look at how well the water sector is doing, South Africans should be proud of it! There is no place for morality in economics – everyone knows that.

Are you shocked? Are you horrified that such a thing could happen in a democracy in which the government regularly professes to be on the side of the poor? Or are you rolling your eyes at this fantastical nonsense, hoping that you still have the receipt for this book so that you can get a refund?

I have bad news for you, cynical reader. Every word of this story is true, right now, save for one tiny detail: this isn't the story of water in South Africa, it is the story of something just as critical to our survival – this is the story of food.

If you feel like it, come with me. I will tell you a story.
I'll show you something.
(Markus Zusak: *The Book Thief*)

Introduction

Only the poor man feel the pain every time.
(Handwritten sign held by a striking farmworker in
De Doorns, 2012)

In August 2012, a group of farm workers – mostly women
– went on strike on the Keurboschkloof grape farm in the De Doorns
area of the Western Cape, which is about 170 kilometres north-east of
Cape Town. De Doorns lies in the Hex River Valley, an important part
of South Africa's export grape-producing region. After the death of the
farm owner in early 2012, the management of Keurboschkloof was
taken over by South African Fruit Exporters (SAFE), a privately owned
farm-management and fruit-export company. SAFE's website trumpets
their company motto as 'working together, earning together', and their
emphasis on 'mutual trust' between themselves and the 'wonderful
people' on the farms that they manage. The workers on Keurboschkloof
saw very little evidence that SAFE considered them to be 'wonderful
people' or of the company's belief in 'mutual trust'.

Workers on the farm alleged that their salaries had been reduced
since SAFE had taken over. Payslips produced by them for an
investigating journalist indicated that this reduction was as much as
30 per cent in some cases.[1] In addition, many of the farm's employees
had their contracts changed from permanent to seasonal workers under

the new management, effectively reducing both their annual income and their job security. Workers felt particularly aggrieved since they alleged that the previous owner had promised that their conditions of employment would remain unchanged after his death. SAFE defended its actions, suggesting that the seasonal worker rate of R75 per day on the farm (about US$8.80 at the time) should be considered generous against the fact that the minimum wage in the area was R67 per day. (Actually the legal minimum wage in the agricultural sector at that time was R69 per day, a fact SAFE seems to have ignored.) The company also insisted that the changed working conditions (ie, lower wages and the reduction in permanent staff) were necessary to improve 'the effectiveness and performance'[2] of the farm. These sentiments probably more accurately reflected SAFE's guiding business principles than the concept of 'mutual trust'.

The strike at Keurboschkloof struck a chord with other farmworkers in the Western Cape and spread rapidly across the fruit and wine sector, first in De Doorns and then to other areas in the region. By November 2012, the strike had spread to 16 towns and involved thousands of workers. The strike action was marked by a ferocity that caught most observers by surprise: vineyards and orchards were set alight, cars torched and journalists attacked. Three striking workers were killed during the protests and scores of others injured. The anger of the farmworkers reflected their desperation and frustration at their appalling poverty and living conditions on the farms, which had been ignored largely by both government and the wider public. The unfolding of the strike, and the response by both government and employers, highlighted many unpleasant truths about the dominant agri-food system in South Africa. Most notably, it showed who had power and influence and who did not, and the devastating impact of that imbalance on the lives of the most vulnerable.

The central demand of the farmworkers was a more than doubling of their daily wage. The minimum wage in the agricultural sector is set every three years by the Minister of Labour in a wage determination. This set wage amount then escalates by a pre-determined annual amount (usually consumer inflation) for the duration of the three-year determination period. A R69 per day minimum wage ($8.40 at the time) had been set in March 2012 and was not due for revision until 2015. Workers were demanding an immediate increase to R150 per day (about $17.50). But wages, as pitiful as they were, were not the only demand of the striking workers or the only reason for their anger and the violence that marked the strike. Farmworkers – particularly in the Western Cape – are one of the most exploited and badly treated groups in contemporary South Africa. Democracy and post-1994 'freedom' have meant very little to people who are often evicted from their homes, assaulted by their employers and generally live in appalling conditions. They enjoy little support from their government, either the national ANC-led government or the Democratic Alliance (DA) that rules the Western Cape province. The ANC's current strategy for socio-economic development – the National Development Plan (NDP) – refers to the relationship between farmers and farmworkers as 'difficult', a triumph of understatement. Additionally, farmworkers do not benefit from South Africa's generally powerful labour movement. It is estimated that fewer than 3 per cent of farmworkers in the Western Cape are unionised, largely as a result of aggressive opposition by employers, which, although technically illegal, is not countered by government. During the strike, South Africa's largest trade union movement – the Congress of South African Trade Unions (COSATU) – purported to negotiate on behalf of the farmworkers and assumed the lead negotiating role over smaller worker organisations. But COSATU was conspicuously absent after the strike, when workers who were fired for participating tried in vain to get compensation for unfair dismissal.*

As the strike spread across the Western Cape, and increased in violence, government was forced to respond. Initial efforts were focused on persuading employers to negotiate directly with workers, but many employers insisted that the strike was 'political' rather than related to wages or working conditions, and they refused to negotiate. Then, on 15 November 2012, the Department of Labour announced that it would cancel the existing sectoral determination and start a process to review the minimum wage in agriculture. This was overseen by the Employment Conditions Commission (ECC), which was established in terms of the Basic Conditions of Employment Act to, *inter alia*, advise the Minister of Labour on such sectoral determinations.

The outcome of this ECC review would impact all farmworkers in South Africa, not just those on strike. Initial negotiations were conducted between employer organisations and COSATU, acting as the employee representative (despite the fact that most farmworkers

---

* Ironically, it was largely because of the fact that the farmworkers were not unionised that their strike could not be classified as 'protected' under South African labour legislation. This, in turn, meant that they could be summarily dismissed for participating (on the basis of unauthorised absenteeism), without their employers suffering any implications.

across South Africa were not members of COSATU). The most notable outcome of these initial negotiations was that a South African research organisation (the Bureau for Food and Agricultural Policy – BFAP) was appointed to 'provide an agricultural economic analysis' which would form the basis for the wage negotiation. Employers, who had been adamant that they could not afford the R150 wage demand and who wanted some kind of objective assessment to support their claim, suggested this approach. The BFAP is a respected research organisation, comprising mostly academics from two universities in South Africa with prominent departments of agricultural economics. This organisation had additional credibility as an authoritative voice on agriculture since it had prepared the rural development/agriculture chapter of the National Development Plan in 2011.

The BFAP was asked to investigate the impact of higher wages on both employers and employees. Their report was delivered in December 2012 and largely supported the employers' position. Its main finding was that if wages were increased to R150 per day, a significant number of farms would either go out of business or would be forced to reduce their workforce drastically in favour of mechanisation to reduce costs. This was despite the fact that labour is a relatively small part of input costs in commercial agriculture in South Africa. Wages make up only about 10 per cent of total farming costs across the sector, but the generally very low margins in agriculture make farm viability vulnerable to even the smallest cost increases. Wages are a higher percentage of costs for the fruit industry in the Western Cape due to the labour-intensive nature of production, particularly harvesting.

In their report, the BFAP focused on a number of agricultural products, including potatoes, apples and pears – the fifth, seventh and tenth largest employers in agriculture, respectively. For all three of these products, the BFAP was clear that farmers simply could not afford the R150 wage. Prices received for many crops had either declined in real terms over the previous 10 years or had increased only marginally. Input costs such as fertiliser, seed and electricity had steadily increased, meaning that farming margins were falling. Over the previous 20 years, the number of farms in South Africa had fallen significantly, as producers found it more and more difficult to stay in business. This inability to pay a higher wage was what the BFAP termed 'the farmers' dilemma'.

The report also concluded that R150 a day was not in the best interests of the workers, since it would encourage farmers to substitute machines for labour, thereby exacerbating already high unemployment in rural South Africa. The BFAP's calculations suggested that R104.80 per day was the maximum that was possible under current business and market conditions: 'it is evident that if average wages increase by more than R20/day (that is, to around R104.00 per day), many of the typical farms will be unable to cover their operating expenses, and hence not be able to pay back borrowings or to afford entrepreneurs remuneration'.[3] This report was the main bargaining chip of employers, and the central reason why the R150 per day demand was not met. Instead, a new minimum wage determination was set at R105 per day (effective from 1 March 2013), slightly higher than the BFAP report recommended, but well below what labour wanted.

The BFAP report and its commissioning were noteworthy for two important reasons, neither of which received much attention, either at the time or subsequently. The first was the idea (and the general acceptance of this idea) that the 'value' of people in post-apartheid South Africa should be determined solely by their 'value' as inputs into the economy. The only report commissioned by government to provide a basis for the strike negotiations was one that determined the *affordability* of the farmworkers for their employers. This effectively relegated their appalling living and working conditions to some kind of inevitable economic collateral damage. Despite large-scale evidence of illegal evictions and violent treatment at the hand of employers, no regulatory response was considered. The ECC recommended that the National Economic Development and Labour Council (NEDLAC)* should establish an 'urgent' review of the sector, but this has never happened.

The second reason, in addition to considering how a higher wage might affect farmers, was that the BFAP report also assessed how higher wages might improve the living standards of the farmworkers. As a proxy for this they considered the impact of various wage levels on household access to food. A team of nutritionists compiled four possible 'daily food-plate options', based on existing research around food choices and portion sizes. They calculated the monthly cost of each option for a Western Cape family of two adults and two children, using official retail food prices. They then compared these costs to a number of household-income scenarios[4] based on various minimum wages.

The findings were sobering: they suggested that a fairly modest, but still nutritionally balanced, diverse and calorie-sufficient basket of

---

* NEDLAC is a consensus-seeking body, aiming to reach agreement among government, labour and organised business on economic development policy.

food would cost just over R7 000 (about US$814) per month for a family of two adults and two children. This equated to almost R85 000 (US$9 767) in a year. *None* of the BFAP's household-income scenarios, including a R150 per day wage, would be sufficient to purchase this basket of food. The BFAP termed this finding 'the workers' dilemma'. A family with two adults earning R105 per day (the implemented minimum wage) and receiving state child-care grants for each of their children, would be able to afford only *one* of the study's four balanced plate-food options. This was a plate with limited nutritional dietary diversity and containing only about 60 per cent of daily calorie requirements. Given the hard manual labour of most farmwork, they would feel very sharply the lack of these calories.

The ECC report published these findings about the workers' dilemma as part of their final report, but they do not seem to have considered them critically. Government pressed ahead with a R105 per day wage determination in the face of clear evidence that this was not sufficient income to allow farmworkers and their families to enjoy any measure of food security. But the really puzzling thing was that no one asked this seemingly obvious question: Why is it that farmers cannot afford to pay a decent wage because they get such a low price for their produce, but farmworkers go hungry because food is so expensive?

Both the BFAP and the ECC reports were noteworthy for what they did *not* talk about. In the farming world described by both, there appeared to be only two participants – farmers and consumers (farmworkers in this case). Both are in a clear predicament. Farming margins are declining to the extent that additional costs may push farmers out of business. Thus they often cannot afford to pay workers a living wage that would actually enable them to feed themselves and their families. In this version of reality, the policy-balancing act is between the survival of the farmers and the survival of the workers. But this is not the entire picture: in reality, farmers and consumers are only two parts of a much larger agri-food system. It is the other players in this system that set the rules, and who are largely responsible for both low farming margins *and* the inability of farmworkers to feed their families. What was not discussed was not so much the elephant in the room as the Tyrannosaurus looming over the house.

Most South Africans – even in rural areas – do not produce any of their own food or purchase it directly from farmers. Instead, we buy our food from retailers or fast-food outlets or restaurants or informal traders. In addition, a growing proportion of what we eat has been modified from its 'natural' state; processed and flavoured and packaged into something very different from what left the farm. In its journey from field to plate, most agricultural produce passes through a number of intermediaries – wholesalers, processors, distributors and supermarkets – before it arrives as our dinner. The term 'agri-food system' refers to all the activities and participants involved in the production and consumption of our food. When we start to think about the provenance of our food as located in a complex system, we begin to see that every activity and every participant is connected. We also start to see how the farmers' dilemma and the workers' dilemma are, in fact, two parts of the same system, driven by the same system dynamics.

Consider potatoes: the BFAP report paid considerable attention to the current state of potato farming in South Africa. It produced statistical modelling to show that potato farmers simply could not afford to pay workers R150 per day. Why? Because the price they receive for potatoes has been on a downward trend for many years, while input costs are on the up. Farming margins are falling, smaller potato farmers are steadily going out of business, and many of the 30 000 people employed in the sector are at real risk of losing their jobs. And the price in question? About R2.50 per kilogram in the first quarter of 2013. If that seems low with respect to what you remembered paying for potatoes, you would be correct. The average *retail* price of potatoes at the same time was about R9.60 per kilogram – almost four times higher than the farm-gate price. This left farmers with only about 25 per cent of the retail price, out of which to meet all their farming expenses. It is a similar story with respect to apples: an average producer price of around R5.70 per kilogram but an average retail price of around R14.50[5] – 2.5 times higher.

So the 'price' that was used to determine the affordability of the wage increase was not really the 'price' of the potatoes or apples, in that it was not the price that you or I or the farm workers paid. Farmers received only a fraction of *that* price, despite carrying all the risk and expenses of farming. Farmworkers received an even smaller part. In addition, there are no processing costs involved in either of these products before they are sold by the retailer – they are usually just sorted, washed and put in a bag. The farmer generally carries this cost, not the retailer. In contrast to the fragile financial state of many farms, and the dire poverty of most farmworkers, food is a very good business, indeed, for other participants in the agri-food system. While farming incomes decline and farmworkers struggle to feed their families, the profits of South Africa's food retail giants and big processors go up. While farms go out of business and farmworkers lose their jobs, the number of supermarket outlets increases each year. The big four supermarket groups in South Africa now control more than two-thirds of the retail food market.

Much of this profit growth has been derived from a steady increase in the difference between what farmers get paid and what consumers pay for food. A May 2008 article about apple prices had the journalist in question decrying the R4 per kilogram gap between the average farm price and the retail price. In 2013 that gap had risen to almost R9 – more than doubling. The gap has increased for almost every other basic food item over the past 20 years. And this information is not secret: every three months the National Agricultural Marketing Council (NAMC) – a part of national government – releases its *Food Price Monitor*. This reports trends in consumer food prices and some of the corresponding farm-gate prices, and it diligently records the growing gap between the two. The NAMC has also published a number of special investigative reports, illustrating the negative effects of growing supermarket and processor power on rural livelihoods and the cost of food.

So why did the BFAP report (or, indeed, anyone making a representation to the ECC) not mention this? According to the BFAP, wages make up about 10 per cent of farming overheads. Wages could have been doubled – to almost the R150 per day that the workers wanted – if farmers were given an extra 10 per cent for their produce and passed it on. This still would have left a very healthy farm-gate–retail-price gap and the average supermarket seems to be in no danger of going out of business on the basis of paying an extra 25 cents per kilogram for potatoes. The main reason why farmers are unable to pay workers significantly more (and the main reason so many are going out of business) is because the lion's share of the value of their product is going to other participants in the agri-food system. At the same time, the main reason why the farmworkers cannot afford to feed their families is because of the markup on food between the farm gate and the retail shelf in those same supermarkets. The BFAP balanced plate-food options would have cost some 50 to 70 per cent less if most of the components had been purchased directly from the farmers who produced them. And it is not just farmworkers who cannot afford to eat. There is plenty of evidence to indicate that as many as 80 per cent of South African households cannot afford a nutritious plate of food every day, simply because of the retail price of food.

There are clear winners and losers in our agri-food system: farmers and consumers are mostly on the losing side, while big corporates – processors and supermarkets – are on the winning side. This has serious implications for poverty, food security and the future of farming in South Africa. So once again we have to ask ourselves why the 2012 farmworker wage negotiations, and all the surrounding analysis and media attention, failed to ask any questions at all about the workings of this wider, corporate agri-food system. The answer is that, for all intents and purposes, that part of the system that operates beyond the farm gate has been rendered invisible. Of course supermarkets are not really invisible, but their position *in the agri-food system* is. Most people do not make connections between the failure of land reform and the growth of supermarkets and food-processing companies. None of the farmworkers or the associated organisations that made representation to the hearings of the ECC in 2012 highlighted the connections between their poverty and the wealth of corporate food companies. Not one of the thousands of pages issued by the South African government on the causes of and solutions for widespread food insecurity even acknowledges these entities. Instead, they focus on the ability (or inability) of the poor to produce their own food.

A massive multi-billion dollar industry, one that effectively decides who gets to eat and who does not, has successfully made itself invisible, contriving a disappearing trick that would be the envy of Harry Houdini. It has done so with the tacit support of a government that tells us daily it is on the side of the poor. It has been aided and abetted by a host of well-meaning do-gooders and consumers unaware that they have handed over responsibility for their dinner to those least interested in their welfare.

South Africa's dominant, corporate agri-food system is a microcosm of those in many other countries, particularly the European Union and the United States (the so-called North). These countries have also seen a steady growth in corporate control of food markets and a corresponding negative impact on farmers and rural livelihoods. But the growth of the corporate agri-food system in South Africa has also had a particularly devastating impact on the average household. Its negative effects have been magnified far beyond those seen in other countries because of the particular national context – high poverty and unemployment – within which it operates. As consumers in the North find themselves under increasing financial pressure, and rural livelihoods are further eroded, the South African experience may provide a cautionary tale of what lies ahead when we make corporate earnings the critical determinant of who eats and who does not.

The aim of this book is to undo the magic trick and to explain how the South African agri-food system was constructed; to make every part of that system visible. This book shows how it operates and how it has far-reaching and often devastating effects on land, people and poverty. This story is fundamentally about power – who has it and who does not, and why. It attempts to answer these two questions: How did we get to this position, where the financial interests of the few have effectively been deemed more important than the well-being of the vast majority? And how could we go about changing this to build for ourselves a more equitable and just system?

PART 1

The winners and the losers

Our agri-food system has clear winners and losers; but who are they and how did they get to be winners or losers? In the following three chapters, I have traced the history of food in South Africa from the point of view of those who produce it, those who eat it and those who make a living from selling it. This is a story of money, of power, of unanticipated consequences, and of personal and social tragedy.

Chapter 1

Producing food: The lie of the land

My grandparents were farmers, although they were not born to it. Quite the opposite: my grandfather qualified as an architect and my grandmother (a city girl through and through) was a classics student. They met at university and married in 1940, settling into an apartment in downtown Johannesburg. But shortly thereafter my grandfather got the yen to be a farmer rather than an architect; no one quite knows why, but it is an urge that strikes many people. Despite my grandmother's misgivings, they set up a chicken farm about 50 kilometres south of Johannesburg in 1942 and then moved a few years later, to a nearby farm and a different industry – dairy. They lived on that farm until their deaths, a few months apart, in 1996 and 1997

As farmers from the 1940s through to the early part of the 21st century, my grandparents lived through enormous change in the agricultural sector, some of it good, but much of it bad – for farmers, farmworkers and the consumers of food alike.

Divide and rule

The defining feature of this period of history was apartheid and the resulting seizure and re-allocation of black-owned and occupied land by force under the white government. Productive agricultural land – and specifically who had access to it and who did not – was always a point of tension in South Africa. The country had (still has) limited amounts of high-potential agricultural land, as well as water resources for irrigation. The (white) government faced increasing pressure in the early parts of the 20th century from their (white farmer) voters to have preferential access to the most productive land. At that time there existed a successful class of black commercial farmers, who played a key role in supplying food to the rapidly growing towns around South Africa. These farmers either worked their own land or leased and farmed on white-owned land. It was estimated that at the turn of the 20th century, as much as 80 per cent of white-owned land was, in fact, being farmed by black tenants. One of the (but not the only) reasons for the commercial success of these black farmers was because they were able to make use of family labour, thus reducing their input costs. At the same time, these local employment opportunities in family agriculture (either for the market or for family subsistence) made black persons generally unwilling to work on white-owned farms, where they were usually very poorly paid and often badly treated.

Many white farmers, however, saw the problem a little differently, reasoning that it was the responsibility of 'their' government to ensure that they had access to the best land, that they did not have to face 'unfair' competition from black farmers, and that black people were 'persuaded' to work as wage labourers on their farms.[6] This pressure for land and labour for one part of the population, at the expense of another, found a ready audience in a government already keen to follow official policies of 'separate' (that is, unequal) development on racial grounds.

The Natives Land Act of 1913 was a key piece of legislation in both the dispossession of black South Africans' land and the development of our 20th-century agricultural policy. The Act set aside approximately 8 per cent of all farmland as designated 'reserves' and these became the only areas that could legally be farmed by black South Africans. The remaining 92 per cent was for the exclusive use of white farmers. The follow-up legislation in the 1950s, which effectively confined black South Africans to the Bantustans ('homelands') based on these reserves, created significant pressure on that land, making food self-sufficiency impossible for most people forced to live there.

The 1913 Act also made it illegal to sell 'white' land to black farmers, and outlawed the practice of leasing 'white' land to black farmers, or allowing sharecropping by black tenants or workers on such land. The Act thus effectively wiped out most black commercial farmers in a relatively short period of time. The effect of the Act was not just to make sure that white farmers had access to the best land, but also to create an 'incentive' for black people, previously self-employed in agriculture, to be forced into having to look for employment – either on white-owned farms or in the rapidly growing mining sector. As South Africa 'developed', it was becoming a cash-based economy – without sufficient land to produce all their food requirements black South Africans needed money in order to eat. South Africa's modern history of food insecurity was under way.

In addition to preferential access to land, South Africa's white farmers were the beneficiaries of a number of government-financed programmes designed to support agricultural production and producers. There were a number of reasons for this preferential treatment, which required a significant national budgetary allocation. Until the late 1970s, white farmers were a particularly important political group. The way in which electoral areas had been demarcated meant that a relatively small group of farmers had significant voting power. The government was thus eager to keep them happy. In addition, as South Africa became more and more isolated internationally because of her apartheid policies, self-sufficiency became the priority of an increasingly paranoid and defensive state. Food self-sufficiency and national food security was a key focus area.

White farmers generally received guaranteed prices above comparable international prices, had access to a range of inputs at subsidised prices, could borrow money at preferential rates and were well protected against foreign competition. They were also guaranteed labour at extremely cheap rates. For much of the 20th century there was no minimum wage legislated for farmworkers, and it was illegal for them to form or join a labour union. Low wages and poor living conditions were common for most agricultural employees, while some also faced routine physical abuse at the hands of their employers. Farmworkers additionally faced increasing insecurity of employment as a result of increasing mechanisation: hundreds of thousands of farmworkers lost their jobs in the last decades of the 20th century as farms became bigger and more capital intensive. Capital intensiveness increased despite low labour costs, in part because farmers could access cheap finance (courtesy of government) to invest in capital equipment. Losing your job on a farm meant not just losing your income, but also becoming homeless, as most farmers evicted those they no longer employed (and the vast majority of farmworkers lived on the farms).

As a result of all this official support, South Africa's national agricultural production rose steadily during the first part of the 20th century and, in most years, surpluses were produced that could be exported. Needless to say, within a few short decades after the 1913 Land Act, white farmers almost completely dominated South Africa's production of food, making use of the latest technology and inputs. Farms consolidated and became bigger. By the mid-1980s, just 6 per cent of farms produced 40 per cent of agricultural output. The large, white-owned, highly mechanised commercial farm became the symbol of South Africa's successful 'development'.

A key component of agricultural policy during this period was controlled marketing: essentially this meant that government controlled the prices at which agricultural production was sold, as well as the channels through which that produce could be sold. They also controlled the retail price and margins of certain food items along the production chain. The Marketing Act of 1937 was the first important piece of legislation in this regard, and was the response to a 1934 commission of enquiry into agriculture – the Viljoen Committee. This committee proposed state intervention as a way of protecting (white) farmers from the adverse effects of unpredictable weather and market risks, through a system of guaranteed producer prices and surplus offtake (that is, government guaranteed both a price for farmers and that they would buy surplus produce). The 1937 Marketing Act put in place a complex system to control the movement, pricing and quality of almost all agricultural products. The 1968 Marketing Act expanded on this – promulgating schemes for a wide range of products, with each scheme being under the control of a board (such as, for example, the Dairy Board). Boards were mandated to set prices, decide on how and to whom produce would be sold, buy surpluses and set levies to be paid by farmers, which were used to fund the operation of the boards. There was thus an enormously complex (and expensive) set of regulation around the white agricultural sector, principally for the purpose of supporting farmers.

Things were very different in the black 'homelands', where large numbers of people were crowded into relatively small areas, with very limited access to quality agricultural land. There was almost nothing in the way of official farmer support or capital investment into homeland agriculture. All the same, the expectation of the apartheid government was that a significant number of the homeland residents should produce enough food to meet most of their nutritional requirements. The government expected the balance to be made up of food purchased out of wages remitted by those working in 'white' South Africa. As Diana Wylie illustrates in her history of food and politics in South Africa, *Starving on a Full Stomach*,[7] the government was aware of the existence of hunger and malnutrition in these homelands, although they often tried to minimise the extent of the problem. It was also clear that much of their concern was not due to compassion for the victims, but rather reflected a worry that widespread and chronic malnutrition would reduce the productivity of black labour in white industry and thus compromise the economy. Most of the official responses to the shortage of food in black households laid the blame squarely at the feet of black farmers, on their lack of productivity and failure to embrace 'progressive' farming methods. (The 'ignorance' of black people with respect to correct nutrition was the second favourite scapegoat.) The following quote, written in 1945 by a dietician sent out to evaluate conditions around food and nutrition in the Ciskei, is illustrative of the general view at the time:

> The Natives in the Ciskei will never be able to face a bad drought under existing conditions. They are not producing enough food to feed themselves at present; and it is doubtful whether they ever will unless their whole point of view and system of farming is radically changed very soon.[8]

Black farmers were generally viewed as backward and stubborn in their refusal to accept 'modern' farming methods, such as reducing the number of cattle that they held in order to bring down stocking rates to levels determined to be most 'productive'. Those interventions that did exist in homeland agriculture were aimed mostly at the 'betterment' of farming practices, an approach that tacitly implied that the reason why black farmers were not as productive as their white counterparts was because they lacked the necessary skills and commitment to 'proper' commercial farming. The fact that these farmers had very limited access to productive land (the main reason why their cattle stocking rates seemed to be too high – a question of too little land for the cattle, rather than too many cattle for the land) and nothing approaching the support system rolled out for white farmers was conveniently ignored.

This approach was compounded by the general view of small-scale agriculture – that it was not an optimum farming model and could never be as productive as large-scale, mono-culture farming enterprises. This view also held in 'white' South Africa, as the apartheid government's focus on national food security meant that it gave increasing preference to larger-scale commercial units. Many of the farms in the homelands were relatively small, either out of necessity (the shortage of land) or tradition (farms were as large as could be farmed by a family unit), and usually combined the production of a range of outputs – livestock, dry-land crops and vegetables. The prevalence of small, mixed-production farms in the homelands was seen as further 'proof' of the backwardness of African farmers.

The effect of the control boards was not just to support farmers, but also to create – through the single-channel marketing system – a limited number of intermediaries in each value chain. Government also intervened in agricultural markets in terms of prescribing retail margins for many products and occasionally subsidising the consumer price of food. Bread is a good example of how the system worked (and, as we shall see, an even better example of its long-term implications). The importation of wheat was carefully controlled and wheat farmers received a guaranteed price, together with a guaranteed offtake (that is, they could sell all their production at the agreed price). Only a limited number of registered mills had the right to buy wheat and mill flour, and the Wheat Board had the sole power to grant or refuse such registrations. The same applied to bakers: only a limited number had the right to produce bread (to government specifications regarding loaf size and weight, which was strictly monitored) and these registrations were also under the control of the Wheat Board. The government set the retail price of bread (and the various margins allowed from milling through to baking and retailing) and subsidised it – meaning that bread was sold at a lower price than that at which it was produced (after including the various statutory margins) and it was, in fact, cheaper than in many other countries. In terms of bread, therefore, there was an argument to be made that government intervention was probably benefiting consumers.

Over time, however, the complex producer–support system became increasingly unpopular, including among some farmers, who were often unhappy with the restrictions imposed on market access and marketing channels by the various control boards. Many of them believed that they would be better off finding their own customers, rather than being restricted to the single-channel marketing schemes. A clear childhood memory is of my grandfather stomping around his house shouting about 'the bloody Dairy Board', which he perceived as a group of incompetent civil servants that he had to fund out of his farm income (via the scheme levies) with few benefits for his business. There were more critics, however, among consumer groups, who believed that the policy of supporting farmers was making food more expensive than it should have been (it must be said that the main focus was the position of white consumers who believed they were getting a bad deal; there was little general public interest in the hunger being experienced in the Bantustan 'homelands').

There were broader factors at work as well: by the 1980s, white farmers were no longer the political force they had been, and government was thus not under the same kind of pressure to accommodate them as they had been 20 years prior. More importantly, the apartheid state was under severe and increasing financial pressure. Years of sanctions had reduced foreign investment and the ability to borrow foreign money to almost nothing. The cost of the war in South West Africa (Namibia) and trying to keep control of an increasingly rebellious population at home had put the public fiscus under enormous pressure. The economy was slipping into recession, tax revenues were declining and the reality was that the elaborate system of farmer support was just too expensive to continue. The bread subsidy alone made up around 1.5 per cent of the total annual national budget between 1960 and 1980 (although this was down from more than 3 per cent in previous decades).

Freedom comes to the farm

From the mid-1980s, therefore, the South African government started to think seriously about the future of the various marketing schemes and their control boards, and how the cost of these could be reduced, or even eliminated. An added impetus for market deregulation came from the global movement to increase international trade and dismantle domestic protection structures, particularly those around agriculture. If South Africa wanted to rejoin the international economy, it would have to follow suit.

A number of commissions of enquiry were set up in the 1970s and 1980s to investigate the agricultural subsidy schemes, and these mostly recommended a gradual process of deregulation and a withdrawal of government's direct financial support for farmers. The subsidy on white bread was abolished in 1984, although a portion of this money was used to continue a subsidy on brown bread. Government price controls (and the relevant subsidies) for maize meal, dairy products and brown bread were abolished in 1991.

In the midst of significant national political change, the Kassier

Committee was appointed in 1992 to investigate the entire structure of agricultural marketing in South Africa, and it came to some radical conclusions (certainly far more radical than any of its predecessors). The deliberations and recommendations of this committee, together with the ANC government-in-waiting's proposed agricultural policies, are an important factor in understanding how we arrived at the agricultural marketing system we have today. The committee was scathing – to say the least – about the existing agricultural support system, claiming that it was responsible for declining productivity in the agricultural sector, as well as increasing farmer indebtedness and high consumer food prices. The committee was clearly influenced by the changes that everyone knew in 1992 were coming to South Africa, as well as the increasing global dominance of neo-liberal economic thinking that had first become popular under the economic policies of Thatcher in the United Kingdom and Reagan in the United States in the 1980s. This passage from the committee's report is instructive in this regard:

> The Committee concurs with the view that the most fundamental concern in this enquiry should be ethical rather than legal, material or organizational … This implies, in the first instance, a democratic, non-racist and non-sexist dispensation which in turn means equality of outcome in the social and political spheres and equality of opportunity in the economic sphere. This can be interpreted as that the individual is a being in his/her own right and should be permitted to follow his/her own will within the limits set by society, rather than a situation where the individual is considered to be part of society and thus first and foremost is subordinate to the will of the people whereafter he/she can exercise his/her own choices.[9]

In other words, one of the important points that the committee was trying to make was that state involvement in agricultural marketing was not compatible with the 'freedom' that most people envisaged was coming or the supremacy of the individual under neo-liberal economic systems. The devil, as always, would lie in the detail – what would 'equality' look like under a new dispensation and who would enjoy the fruits of 'liberation'?

The Kassier Committee concluded that the marketing schemes had benefited a few farmers at the expense of the wider society. They recommended a radical restructuring of the agricultural sector and the wholesale removal of all the marketing schemes within a short period of time, on the basis that 'there can be little doubt that the liberalization of agricultural marketing will contribute to a more efficient, equitable and sustainable farm sector in South Africa'. The clear implication was that dismantling the marketing schemes would increase competition and thus reduce the cost of food and address food insecurity. The most productive farmers would prosper, the less productive would go out of business, and everyone would benefit. Faith in the free market had never been higher.

The language of 'freedom' and 'liberation' was also used by the African National Congress (ANC) in respect of its agricultural policy proposals: a 1994 Land and Agricultural Policy document stated that the mission of the ANC in respect of agriculture was to 'achieve equitable access to and optimal use of agricultural resources'. A priority of the ANC was to address the history of dispossession of land, and to encourage and support a new class of black commercial farmers. Realistically, they knew that the extensive support that had been made available to white farmers could not simply be extended to black farmers – there was not enough money available. Instead they settled on a programme of land reform, which would make land available to black South Africans for agriculture, and a programme of targeted support for such farmers. The creation of a new class of black commercial farmers was also seen as a key strategy to address rural poverty.

The dominant discourse at the time focused on the history of black South Africans as successful commercial farmers, who had gone out of business because of apartheid. If they were allowed to compete on an equal footing against white farmers – granted the 'equality of opportunity' referred to by the Kassier Committee – they would succeed. A new 'liberated' agricultural system would ensure that the most productive farmers would do well, no matter what their skin colour. The popular language around agriculture was thus of the apartheid crime of exclusion and the 'new' South African remedy of inclusion, via market 'freedom'. After all, free markets are colour-blind.

The ANC's 1994 Land and Agricultural Policy focused on land reform as a means of redressing the injustices of the past (this original emphasis on justice is important, as we shall see.) It also envisaged a more equitable and inclusive agricultural sector, with lots of support for the previously neglected smallholder sector and a significant improvement in the lives of farmworkers. It is important to remember that after 1994, the functions of Agriculture and Land Reform were in one ministry: it was only in 2009 that the Department of Land Reform and Rural Development was created. Thus the issues of land reform and agricultural development were practically very closely aligned in 1994. Food security was also an important part of this ANC policy, with the assumption being that if more people had access to land and appropriate support to farm it productively, they would be in a position to feed themselves, as they had been before the promulgation of the 1913 Natives Land Act. Money saved by dismantling the support system for white farmers would help to pay for these programmes.

The ANC was thus enthusiastic about the recommendations of the Kassier Committee and eager to dismantle what they saw as a system that had unfairly advantaged one group of farmers over another. White farmers in general were not a group for which the ANC felt any affection, and they did not buy into the apartheid government's view that they were central to national food security. They were viewed as mostly conservative, often racist, and having benefited extensively from the apartheid theft of land from black communities. It is little surprise that the ANC was keen to dismantle what they saw as 'their' support system, and they wholeheartedly endorsed the recommendations of the Kassier Committee.

But these recommendations did not come into effect immediately after the 1994 elections, which saw the ANC win a large majority of the votes. South Africa was operating under an Interim Constitution at the time, with negotiations around a final document still in process. It had been agreed that, no matter the outcome of the 1994 elections, the country would be run by a Government of National Unity (GNU) in which all the main political parties would be represented, including in the allocation of Cabinet posts. Agriculture was allocated to the National Party and Kraai van Niekerk (who had served under PW Botha and FW de Klerk as Deputy Minister of Agriculture and Minister of Agriculture, respectively) was appointed as the minister. It was clear that Van Niekerk was not as keen to dismantle all the marketing protection for farmers as were the members of the Kassier Committee. Instead he appointed his own Commission of Enquiry and produced a *White Paper on Agriculture* (in 1995), which recommended a less radical approach. Although, to be honest, it is not entirely clear what was planned since the *White Paper* recommended that 'trade in and the marketing of agricultural products should reflect market tendencies',[10] which has to represent a triumph for vagueness. In any event, we never got to find out exactly what a new marketing dispensation under Van Niekerk would have looked like: in July 1996, the National Party pulled out of the GNU (the Constitution was now finalised) and he was replaced by Derek Hanekom from the ANC.

With considerable haste – implying that it was already almost fully formulated by the ANC prior to Hanekom's appointment – the Marketing of Agricultural Products Act (47 of 1996) came before parliament. This is still the most important piece of legislation governing agricultural markets in South Africa, and its central theme represented a huge departure from previous policy. In a nutshell, the Act made it almost impossible for government to intervene in agricultural markets, displaying a quite extraordinary level of faith in the ability of 'free' markets to address South Africa's twin problems of rural poverty and food insecurity. A policy paper issued by the National Department of Agriculture in 1998 illustrates this faith very well:

> One of the main reasons for promoting greater flexibility and diversity in the marketing system is that it will become better able to provide the types of market services needed by new entrants into agriculture. The Government is confident over time this will prove to be the case.[11]

That is, government was convinced that a free market would provide the kinds of markets and market-access services (such as transportation) that emerging black farmers would require, for no apparently better reason than that they *were* required.

At much the same time as the promulgation of the 1996 Act, almost all of the import protection for South African agriculture was dismantled, making it the second least protected agricultural sector in the world. In contrast to many other ANC policies at the time, which focused on the need for government to *take* action to address inherited injustices, the Act is clearly based on the assumption that *reducing* the role of government in agricultural markets is highly desirable, and that the market would provide for all. As the same 1998 policy paper put it:

> Input and Output prices are now, and will continue to be, determined by market forces, and the Government will not intervene directly to influence them. Producers, processors and consumers are expected to take their own measures to manage price risk.[12]

This approach is a little curious. There is a point of view that the

ANC government was under considerable pressure in its early years in power from organisations like the World Bank to adopt free-market policies in return for access to funds and support. The World Bank was a strong supporter of the idea that market deregulation always generated economic benefits and reduced poverty, and the deregulation of agriculture was one of the bank's very favourite policies. That World Bank push view is likely, but it does not explain why the government went so far in 'liberating' the agricultural sector, way beyond what would have been required by the Bank, or why it was done so quickly. (The Marketing Act came into force on 1 January 1997, and stipulated that all the control boards had to be gone within a 12-month period.) There is little doubt in my mind that the ANC was more than happy to pull the financial rug from under white farmers, and to use those funds for other pressing development needs such as housing. It is also clear that there was considerable appeal in a discourse that suggested that the only thing preventing black farmers from achieving commercial success was equity when competing with white farmers. In other words, they did not 'need' such byzantine market regulation to succeed – just an equal opportunity.

But it should be noted that there was little or no opposition from the white, commercial-farming sector to the promulgation of the Act, although they would be losers in this withdrawal of state support. Certainly this reflected, in part, the unpopularity of some of the marketing schemes. However, it has been suggested that perhaps a regulatory environment that kept government out of agricultural markets was what many white farmers wanted, given their suspicions (well-founded) about the antipathy with which the ANC government viewed them, as well as lingering notions of the ANC as some kind of 'communist' organisation, which might nationalise the farms into giant Soviet collectives. A law that made it almost impossible for government to intervene in agricultural markets might mean losing benefits now, but it would also prevent government from introducing future measures that were biased *against* white farmers.

Whatever the reasons for it, the 1996 Act made it clear that government intervention in agricultural markets would become almost impossible. Section 2 of the Act states that it has the following four (and only four) objectives:

(a) the increasing of market access for all market participants;
(b) the promotion of the efficiency of the marketing of agricultural products;

(c) the optimisation of export earnings from agricultural products; and

(d) the enhancement of the viability of the agricultural sector.

(You may be surprised to note the absence of objectives such as food security, rural development or equity, but at the time the assumption was that all these 'secondary' objectives would be delivered by the magic of the market, through its 'efficiency'.)

More importantly, the 1996 Act made it quite clear that 'statutory measures' (that is, one of a limited group of regulatory tools such as a tariff or a levy) could be introduced only if it could be shown that they would 'directly and substantially advance one or more of the (above) objectives … without being substantially detrimental to one or more of such objectives.'[13] Where food security was mentioned in the Act, it was to stipulate that government could not introduce a statutory measure that would undermine food security. There was no possibility, however, of introducing a measure specifically designed to *improve* food security, since this was not one of the four objectives of the Act. Issues such as 'unfairness' or rural poverty do not even feature.

This single piece of apparently innocuous – and largely unknown – legislation has had enormous consequences for both the producers and the consumers of food, since it is through agricultural *markets* that farmers earn a living, and it is in agricultural *markets* that consumers must purchase food. The following 20 years would show exactly how misguided policy-makers were about market magic.

The law of unintended consequences

Who, exactly, has been made free or liberated by agricultural policy since 1994? As we shall see in Chapter 2, it certainly is not consumers. But what about the producers of food – the farmers and the people who work on the farms? Well, you would be hard pressed to find much good news there and, paradoxically, it is black farmers, small farmers and farmworkers – exactly the people that the new agricultural dispensation was intended to support – that have the least to celebrate.

For the first few years after the deregulation of the agricultural sector, the passing of the 1996 Act and the opening of local markets to international competition, there was a fairly widely held view that the policy had been a success – that it was making farmers more productive, creating opportunities for new black farmers and benefitting consumers through lower food prices. This optimism was reflected in the 1998 National Department of Agriculture policy paper referred to above, but it was also found in other places. One of the most enthusiastic reviews was a 2000 monograph commissioned by the Free Market Foundation (FMF).[14] The FMF's position on free markets is quite clear (even if you didn't think the organisation's name a bit of a giveaway) from the foreword to this document, written by Duncan Reekie, then Professor of Economics at the University of the Witwatersrand: 'deregulation has benefited both farmers, farm workers and the overall economy … food price inflation has decreased, and investment in agriculture has increased'. He concludes with the conviction that 'market control, not state control, unambiguously best serves farmers, consumers, and the economy at large'. Certainly not an unbiased point of view, but also one that would prove to be remarkably wrong given that it was made by a professor in a field of study in which practitioners pride themselves on making forecasts for a living.

Certainly the authors of the document painted a glowing picture of the triumph of the market: one of the things that they pointed out was that food-price inflation had declined from 1994 to 2000. Although they acknowledged that the overall rate of inflation had also declined (largely in response to tighter monetary policy as part of the Reserve Bank's new inflation targeting policy), they felt justified in saying that it was 'fair to argue that the decline in food price inflation can partly be attributed to the process of market deregulation'[15] without offering much in the way of concrete proof. There was more 'good' news: although they acknowledged that the agricultural sector was shedding jobs (not exactly in line with Reekie's belief that deregulation was great news for farmworkers), they suggested that the jobs that remained would become better paying at some future point, since they would require more skills, and this would somehow compensate workers for jobs lost. This is wishful thinking at its best.

Other – more empirically detailed and less biased – investigations into the effects of deregulation started to paint a very different picture, of outcomes that had not been predicted by most of the advocates of drastic market deregulation and the 1996 Act. The National Agricultural Marketing Council (NAMC) was established in terms of that Act. Its main function is to advise the Minister of Agriculture on marketing policy (including the recommendation of statutory measures where these are deemed necessary) and on the progress made in implementing policy. The NAMC is also mandated to undertake investigations into agricultural marketing. One of the NAMC's first tasks was to oversee the process of deregulation, but thereafter the organisation turned its attention to investigating how that deregulation was actually playing out in agricultural markets. Section 7 of the 1996 Act allowed the NAMC to appoint a special committee to investigate the impact of deregulation on various agricultural sectors and, if necessary, to propose actions that should be taken by the Minister of Agriculture to address marketing 'problems'.

A number of Section 7 reports to investigate the impact of deregulation were commissioned by the NAMC, between 1998 and 2009,[16] as indicated in the following Table 1.

Table 1: Section 7 investigations undertaken by the NAMC, 1998–2009

Year	Reports
1998	*Fresh Produce*
	Joburg Fresh Produce Market
1999	*Impact of Deregulation on the Wheat-to-Bread Value Chain*
2000	*Fresh Produce Study*
2001	*Impact of Deregulation on the Dairy Industry*
	Effect of Deregulation on the Red Meat Industry
2002	*Investigation into Fresh Produce Marketing*
2003	*Impact of Deregulation on the Red Meat Industry*
	Effect of Deregulation on the SA Ostrich Industry
2005	*Global Trends in Fresh Produce Markets*
2006	*National Fresh Produce Markets Investigation Final Report*
	Growth and Development in SA Wildlife Ranching
2007	*National Fresh Produce Markets*
	South African Sorghum Industry
	Statutory Measures on Pork
2009	*Wheat-to-Bread Value Chain*

Source: www.namc.co.za

Apart from an apparent obsession with fresh-produce markets (unexplained) the Section 7 reports have covered three basic food sectors – bread, dairy products and red meat. Perhaps surprisingly, there has never been a Section 7 investigation into either the maize meal or the poultry sectors, despite the fact that these are key food groups for lower-income families. Poultry could be excused on the basis that it was never regulated to the same extent as other agricultural products (and thus perhaps could not be justified for investigation into the impact of deregulation), but the exclusion of maize meal seems odd. The last Section 7 investigation was undertaken in 2009, and it is not clear why no others have been commissioned since. Perhaps the NAMC believes that so much time has elapsed since deregulation that it is no longer worth investigating its impact. However, after you have read the next few pages, you might come to the same conclusion that I have: they got tired of writing reports to which no one seemed to pay the least amount of attention.

These initial, post-deregulation investigations of the NAMC – particularly dairy, red meat and bread – showed that many of the actual impacts of deregulation had not been anticipated, and that in fact there was quite a lot of bad news for quite a lot of people to report. These documents are worthy of our attention: not only do they represent almost all official efforts to critically investigate the workings of our agri-food system, but they were also usually based on rigorous and comprehensive data collection undertaken by teams of well-respected academics.

Let us start by taking a look at the 2001 investigations into dairy products[17] and red meat.[18] It had been almost four years since the dismantling of the control boards and direct marketing schemes. What had been the impact on farmers (had they benefited by having better market access options), farmworkers (had their working conditions and wages improved) and consumers (were they able to purchase cheaper food)?

Dairy first: the 2001 report makes it clear that there were many losers from deregulation and not many winners. The main findings of the NAMC can be summarised as follows:

- Imports of many dairy products (such as butter and milk powder) had increased rapidly, undermining local producers, but most of the benefits of these cheaper products had not reached consumers.
- As a direct result of deregulation, producer prices had come under significant pressure and many dairy farmers had gone out of business.
- With respect to farmworkers, the Milk Producers' Organisation reported to the committee that 17 000 jobs had been lost in the

dairy sector over the previous five years, as dairy farms closed down.
- The declining profitability of dairy farming had made it very difficult for smaller and emerging (that is, black) farmers to enter the sector, and thus almost none had done so.
- The committee was clear that the retail sector (that is, supermarkets) had been a big winner from market deregulation. Under the old Dairy Board the retail margin on milk had varied between 1 per cent and 5 per cent. By 2001, this margin had increased to between 15 per cent and 30 per cent. The margin had increased through a combination of downward pressure on prices paid to milk suppliers and increased retail prices. Since more than 50 per cent of milk sales went through supermarkets, they had considerable market power, which they appeared to be using to good effect to benefit their shareholders. (The NAMC had invited representatives from the retail sector to participate in the investigation but they had declined. This was the pattern for most of the Section 7 investigations.)
- Consumers had also been adversely affected (in addition to higher prices) by the withdrawal of state milk-inspection services that had been part of the old dairy industry regulation. The NAMC noted that there had been a considerable decline in the health and safety standards around milk, as well as around quality control (such as the fat content of milk).
- Bigger processors and distributors had benefited, through a combination of access to cheap imports and the ability to drive down prices paid to dairy farmers.

So a final tally of benefits would be:

Consumers = 0
Existing dairy farmers = less than 0
New black dairy farmers = less than 0
Farmworkers = quite a lot less than 0
Some processors = a bit more than 0
Retailers = quite a lot more than 0

Clearly the magic of the market did not work in quite the same way for everyone.

What about the red meat sector? This 2001 NAMC investigation came to similar conclusions as those of the dairy investigation: prices received by farmers had declined, but consumers had not benefited from these lower prices as much as might have been expected. Instead, the gap between producer and consumer prices had increased, with most of the benefits from lower producer prices accruing to higher retail margins, rather than to more affordable food for consumers. Much the same had happened with imports: the reduction in import protection had resulted in increasing imports of red meat at relatively low prices. These imports had put pressure on local producers to accept lower prices, but little of these price benefits had been passed on to consumers.

In terms of whether or not emerging farmers had benefited, the report stated the belief that they must have benefited somehow because the market was now more 'open', but it did not offer much in the way of empirical evidence to support this. Perhaps the thinking was that if you had not previously had access to a particular market, you would now consider it a plus to have access to that market, even though you received a very low price?

Farmworkers (as usual) had been the biggest losers: the committee reported that all parts of agriculture had reduced employment, but that the largest numbers had been lost in livestock production.

And now on to the third basic food that the NAMC investigated – bread. The first report into the wheat-to-bread value chain was undertaken in 1999,[19] the first commodity to be investigated by the NAMC in terms of the impact of deregulation. Pressure for the investigation had been sparked by media reports alleging that retailers were taking an 'unfair' share of the total value of a loaf of bread. Bread was a particularly sensitive topic for consumers, not just because it was seen as a basic foodstuff, but also because of the long history of government subsidies, which had kept bread prices below international levels. As a result, the investigating committee decided that it would focus on 'the shift in share of each role-player in the final retail price of bread' (that is, who along the value chain from wheat in the field to bread on the shelf was taking what share of the price paid by consumers). Once again, all the retailers were invited to participate, but only one (Pick n Pay) actually did so. The findings of the committee were as follows:

• Wheat farmers' share of the retail price of white bread had fallen from 33 per cent in 1991 to 18 per cent in 1998, and their share of the retail price of brown bread had fallen from 32 per cent to 17 per cent over the same period.

- The milling sector's share of the retail price of a loaf of bread had also fallen – from 17 per cent to 10 per cent and from 21 per cent to 13 per cent, respectively, for white and brown bread.
- The bread bakers had increased their share – from 40 per cent to 44 per cent, and 36 per cent to 46 per cent, respectively, for white and brown bread.
- Retailers were the big winners: their share of white bread had grown from 3 per cent to 12 per cent, and from 4 per cent to a whopping 20 per cent for brown bread. The report concluded that this increase in retailer share was due in large part to 'the retailer's relative bargaining power'. The committee also stated that much of the increase in the retail margin on brown bread was because they (the retailers) were taking advantage of the fact that brown bread was zero-rated for value-added tax (VAT), while VAT was payable on white bread. Effectively, this meant that brown bread should have been significantly cheaper than white (by *at least* the VAT margin – brown bread is cheaper to produce than white), but it was not. Instead, retailers were pricing the brown bread at much the same price as the white, banking on consumer ignorance of what the price of brown bread 'should' be and pocketing the difference.
- Consumers were generally paying higher prices for their bread than they had before deregulation, particularly in rural areas. In addition, the removal of government inspection services (exactly as had happened in the dairy industry) had resulted in widespread 'underscaling' of bread – that is, consumers were being sold loaves that weighed less than they should have. The committee did state its belief that consumers had benefited from a better product range and bread that now came in plastic packets, but it is difficult for me to understand how a bit of plastic would have cheered up consumers who were paying a lot more for a lot less.

Ten years later – in 2009 – the NAMC undertook another Section 7 investigation into the wheat-to-bread value chain, in response to concerns about the rising price – and thus unaffordability for poorer consumers – of bread.[20] The report makes for depressing reading, mostly because almost nothing had changed in the intervening 10 years. For example, the investigation found that brown bread was more expensive than it should have been, most likely because retailers were taking advantage of the zero-VAT rating to increase their margins. This was a practice that had been evident 10 years prior, and yet government had taken no action whatsoever to prevent it, most likely because there was no legislation that gave them the power to do so. Wheat farmers' share of the retail price of bread was still under pressure, while their production costs had increased. This had reduced the profitability of wheat farmers and created further barriers to entry for new (black) farmers.

The deregulation of the markets had not only reduced opportunities for new black farmers, but it had also put the few, black wheat farmers, who had existed under apartheid, out of business. Genadendal* is a rural community located about 130 kilometres east of Cape Town. The original mission station was established in 1738 by German Moravian missionaries and it is the oldest in Africa. Most of the current inhabitants (about 1 300 households) are descended of Khoikhoi people who had found refuge there when they were pushed off their land by white settlers or slaves freed in the 1830s (South Africa abolished slavery in 1834). The Moravians had selected the site for their mission with care and had chosen well: Genadendal is made up of about 4 000 hectares of mostly high-value agricultural land. It is situated in a good rainfall-catchment area and is on the banks of the Riviersonderend** – a perennial river offering excellent irrigation potential.

Apartheid legislation made it illegal for coloured people (which is how the inhabitants of Genadendal were classified) to own land, and the community of Genadendal would have been a prime target for forced removals, given the high agricultural value of their land. But the apartheid government had reached agreements under the Mission Act with a small number of mission stations (many of them Moravian) that protected them from forced removals. Genadendal was one of these areas. Up until the early 1990s, there had been 8–10 wheat farmers in Genadendal, farming fairly successfully on a medium scale. Today there are none. Although these farmers would not have benefited to the same extent as white farmers under apartheid regulation, they did benefit indirectly, through the guaranteed producer price for their wheat. The main reasons why they went out of business were that this protection disappeared, while at the same time the 'support' (such as access to capital and infrastructure services), which the ANC was so convinced would be provided by the 'free' market, failed to materialise. They could no longer afford to stay in business growing wheat and now they have to pay significantly more for their bread in the local store.

---

*   Meaning 'dale of mercy' in Dutch.

**   Literally – the river that never ends.

It is important to pause a moment and consider these outcomes: there is always some kind of trade-off in the welfare of different groups in an agri-food system. For example, we might believe that lower prices for farmers are a good thing if this means that most consumers have access to affordable food. However, we generally would not think it is a good thing (certainly not in the South African context) if prices for farmers are so low that they all go out of business, since this has negative implications for rural poverty and employment in the sector, as well as the ability of emerging farmers to succeed and create a more equitable economy. So there are always a number of possible scenarios balancing the interests of the producers of food against those of the consumers of food. But what the NAMC reports illustrated clearly was that, while producers and farmworkers (and thus entire rural communities) were being negatively affected by deregulation, this was not being balanced by a benefit accruing to consumers, as had generally been anticipated. In addition, market conditions had become so hostile for agricultural producers that 'equality of opportunity' for the new class of black farmers meant, in reality, an equal opportunity to go out of business rather than to succeed.

The one common thread present in all these reports, but which most of them did not articulate clearly, was *power* – clearly some market participants had it (supermarkets, the bigger processors and the biggest farmers) and some did not (essentially everyone else). This is the problem with neo-liberal theories of economics, which assume that opening up markets will be to everyone's benefit. Unlike these benign, 'everyone wins', abstract models of reality, actual reality in the real world of business is very different. For the corporate entities in the food sector, the overriding number one priority is not economic benefits for everybody; it is the maximisation of shareholder wealth (and the management bonus pool). And the best way to maximise shareholder profits is through market power – the ability to extract value from both suppliers and customers. Market power is correlated with size – the bigger you are, the greater your ability to squeeze more value from the chain (just ask any billionaire). Unfortunately for South Africa's farmers, farmworkers and consumers, the actual market conditions in 1996 were conducive to an unequal power outcome. The problem was that no one really noticed (or else they did not want to see.)

The Kassier Committee had made a brief reference to market concentration in some agricultural sectors, which had been facilitated by regulation. For example, the process of compulsory registration for millers and bread-bakers by the Wheat Board meant that there were only a few companies in each sector. After deregulation, anyone was free to enter the market, but obviously the companies that had been there the longest were in the best position to squeeze out their competitors by virtue of their existing market share and infrastructure. This is exactly what happened. Immediately after deregulation, reports noted a significant rise in the number of new, smaller bakers entering the bread market. By 2009 most of them had disappeared. Unfortunately, the concerns about the possibilities for market concentration went unnoticed and never made it into the 1996 Act.

Despite all the evidence presented in the Section 7 reports that deregulation had failed to deliver most of what it had promised, there was no meaningful response from government. It is not even clear that those who could have done something about the situation closely read any of these reports. Or perhaps they realised too late that actually there was nothing that could be done because the 1996 Act had effectively painted them into a regulatory corner. Nothing could be done because the ability to do anything had effectively been legislated away.

Do not get me wrong: I am not advocating that the cumbersome and expensive system of subsidies and marketing controls should have been kept intact. For one thing, we definitely could not have afforded it, and it was a system that focused largely on supporting agricultural producers, rather than a wider group that included consumers and farmworkers. But its wholesale dismantling and replacement with essentially nothing has not been in our (society's) best interests. The Kassier Commission's vision of individuals having the right 'to follow his/her own will within the limits set by society, rather than a situation where the individual is considered to be part of society' is exactly where the vacuum created by thoughtless deregulation has brought us: to a place where the most powerful effectively have almost all the rights, and the less powerful have very few.

In any event, no more Section 7 investigations have been undertaken since 2009. Instead the NAMC now busies itself with 'market research' and produces, on a regular basis, a series of reports showing quite clearly that the trends highlighted in those Section 7 investigations have not gone away; instead, they have deepened and intensified. No one seems to be reading these reports either.

The implications of these trends for farmers are very clear: declining farm profitability has meant that it is only the biggest and the best-capitalised farms that are thriving, since they can produce sufficient volumes to compensate for lower prices. Smaller farms – as well as new market entrants that do not have access to the necessary capital – find themselves in a very different situation. Ironically, the result has been that South Africa's commercial agricultural sector looks much the same as it did 30 years ago – dominated by large-scale, white-owned farms.

Use it or lose it: Separate development makes a comeback

You might be forgiven for thinking that – in dismantling the farmer-support systems and abdicating responsibility for governance of the market – there was little more that government could do to undermine the viability of farmers, particularly the smallholders and the black farmers that had been a central policy focus in 1994. Sadly, you would be wrong. It turned out that there was plenty more that they could do.

Initial (pre- and around 1994) ANC land and agricultural policy had focused on how to redress the injustices of apartheid with respect to land and how to address rural poverty through the creation of a class of prosperous black farmers. There was a particular focus on smallholder and family farming in these documents, and a sense of optimism that rural poverty would be addressed through the creation of a large number of successful smallholder farmers. Land restitution and redistribution got underway, and a number of programmes designed to provide support to new farmers were initiated. Most of these shared one outstanding (and ultimately suicidal) feature: they focused almost entirely on production. That is, they included financial support for buying land and equipment, and they had a strong focus on farmer education and training on almost every aspect of agronomy and farm management. They were clearly focused on creating farmers with the same production skills and capital assets as their white counterparts. What they did not include was market access: that is, how exactly, to whom and at what price would the produce of these farms be sold? Astonishing as it may seem, many of the 'feasibility' studies for emerging farmer projects did not include detailed farm profitability projects, and many did not even include a marketing plan. Instead they focused almost entirely on how much output could be produced. There seemed to be an overwhelming point of view that the sole criterion for success as a farmer was to *produce* something, rather than to *sell* it for a price at which you could make a decent living. This glaring gap in support has undermined the best efforts of many emerging farmers.

You might think that I am making this up – I am not. I have reviewed project reports for substantial, government-sponsored, developing small-farmer programmes that have gone bust because – well after the initial investment has been made and farming activity commences – it is 'discovered' that the price that the main buyer will pay for the produce is insufficient to cover the cost of production. During my own PhD research, I spent much time with community garden projects that had received extensive technical production support from government extension officers, but no input or support whatsoever on how they were expected to sell their produce. Many of these project 'beneficiaries' had to watch piles of their produce (for which they had worked extremely hard) rotting in the sun because they had no means of transporting it to a market where it could be sold. Their 'support' officials had never thought about this problem.

Nazeer Sonday – a farmer and activist in Cape Town's Philippi Horticultural Area (PHA) – tells of receiving government support to set himself up as a farmer, only to lose everything because no supermarket would pay him a price at which he could make a profit. He – quite correctly – feels betrayed by a government who professed to be liberating him, but instead merely set him up for failure. The ANC's first Minister of Agriculture – Derek Hanekom – had a strong focus on smallholder farming, seeing it (correctly in my assessment) as a key component in any successful and sustainable rural poverty alleviation programme. The problem, of course, is that smaller farmers need to receive reasonable prices for their output to compensate for their smaller volumes. Exactly the opposite was happening as a result of deregulation, but no one in government seemed to be registering this as a problem.

Hanekom's successor as minister – Thoko Didiza – had a very different view of what a 'proper' commercial agricultural sector should look like, and it was not one dominated by small-scale farmers. Instead, her preference was for the large-scale monoculture farms of apartheid agriculture, and this bias continues today. Support for smallholders and projects that directly prioritised poverty alleviation was cut back, and resources focused on large-scale, commercial projects. Didiza's appointment coincided with the government's implementation of the Growth, Employment and Redistribution (GEAR) policies – a set of economic growth plans that incorporated clear neo-liberal ideas. The focus was now on large-scale agriculture that could contribute to GDP growth and export targets, rather than smaller-scale, family farming initiatives.

Despite (or possibly because of) this change in focus, land reform has not been a success. Leaving aside the slow pace at which land has been transferred to black South Africans, a significant number of land-reform projects have been commercial failures. My assessment is that one of the key reasons for this high failure rate (although not the only one – patchy and inefficient government 'support' certainly contributes) is the market system into which these new farmers are inserted – one that is extremely hostile to producers. If farming enterprises that have been in business for generations are closing down because they are no longer profitable, what chance of success is there for the newcomers? Rather astonishingly, this reasoning never features in official reports on why land-reform projects fail (or how they might succeed).

The problem that government faces, of course, is that it has created an entire agricultural policy based on blind faith in a free-market system. This means that when things go wrong – such as when land-reform projects fail – they never look for the reasons for this failure in the system itself, but rather find it in the farmers. This 'blame the victim' approach has become deeply entrenched over the past 20 years.

Lulu Xingwana – Minister of Agriculture and Land Affairs from 2006 to 2009 – was the first to take a hard line against emerging black farmers who were not achieving the levels of success that were 'expected' of them. In March 2009, she was reported to have instructed senior officials in the department to implement – with immediate effect – a policy of 'use it or lose it', meaning that those who did not farm the land they had received* under the land-reform programme 'properly' would be summarily evicted and replaced with more dedicated persons. Land-reform legislation requires that beneficiaries use the land 'productively', which should allow for a range of activities, from household food provision all the way through to commercial production for export. This is not what Minister Xingwana had in mind. Under the new 'use it or lose it' rule, the department quickly set about repossessing a number of land-reform farms in 2009 – summarily evicting the tenants. In one instance, on a farm in Guateng, Xingwana was present at the eviction, and reportedly told the tenant who was occupying the house on the farm:** 'Do you know who I am? I am the minister of land affairs and

---

* Most land-reform 'beneficiaries' did not receive the titles to the land under the new regulations – that was held by government. Instead they received the right to farm it, which could be taken away.

** The land-reform beneficiary had allowed a third party to stay in the house on the farm for free, in return for assisting with the farm work. She (the beneficiary) was nervous about staying on the farm with her daughter after two robberies. This tenancy arrangement was cited by the department as 'proof' that the beneficiary was not committed to farming.

this is my house. Pack your bags and get out of my house right now.'

If Minister Xingwana's statement that 'Those who are not committed to farming must be removed from the allocated farm and be replaced by those who have a passion for farming'[21] seems familiar in the sentiments that it expresses, you would be correct: it is not too far from the exasperation voiced by apartheid officials at the apparent inability and reluctance of homeland farmers to farm 'properly', thus making them responsible for their own poverty. The idea that land reform is primarily about addressing the injustices of the past – captured in the ANC's 1994 Land and Agricultural Policy – has effectively been erased.

The most insidious aspect of this 'blame the victim' approach to land 'reform' is that many of the victims are buying into their government's view of them as fundamentally incompetent. In casual conversation with a community gardener a few years ago, I enquired about the history of the people who lived in the informal settlement in which he resided. He provided a couple of brief histories of how various groups of people had arrived there, and then told me that 'the people who live on that side, they are from Portion Four'. I asked what Portion Four was and he said that it was a failed land-reform project. 'Those people were given a lot of stuff,' he told me, 'land, tractors, but still the project was not a success. I think, Tracy, it will be a long time before us black people know how to farm as well as white people.'

Liberation indeed.

Farmworkers

Initial ANC policy documents highlighted the plight of farmworkers as something that required serious attention. In its original form, land reform was not just about redressing the dispossession of land under apartheid; it was also about ensuring that farmworkers had security of tenure (that is, the right to live on the farms on which many of them had been born). In 1994, the new government was also determined to improve the working conditions and incomes of farm labourers.

Farm employment (both permanent and temporary) peaked at just over 1.6 million in 1970, and is currently around 600 000 – although the full effect of the recent drought, which has put a number of farmers out of business, and thus most likely also their employees, will probably mean that the number will decline in coming months.

From 1993, labour legislation was extended to farmworkers, who had previously been excluded. This meant they now fell under a sectoral minimum-wage dispensation, as well as the Basic Conditions of Employment Act and the Unemployment Insurance Act. The Agricultural Labour Act of 1993 further regulated the relationship between farmers and their workers. As we have seen, however, in the unfolding of the 2012 farmworkers' strike, all this regulation has not made much difference in the lives of many farmworkers, who, in practice, often find it extremely difficult to exert their rights under this legislation.

Farmworkers earn the lowest wages of all formally employed persons in South Africa, and generally live in poverty and experience high levels of food insecurity. A number of studies have found that farmers routinely violate farmworkers' rights and, clearly, do not anticipate any official censure. Many workers live in appalling conditions and are often exposed to highly toxic pesticides and herbicides, without being provided with adequate protection by their employees. None of these, however, is the worst things that can happen to a farmworker: this is being evicted from the farm on which he or she works and lives.

In the early 1990s, most farmworkers lived on the farms on which they worked. Many of them had been born on these farms and, in many cases, even their parents had known no other home. Despite this, they had no legal protection to remain on a farm and could be summarily evicted, usually if their employment was terminated. Most evicted farmworkers ended up in informal settlements, with no work and no income.

In recognition of this problem, the Extension of Security and Tenure Act was promulgated in 1997. This law does not prevent a farmer from evicting an employee, but it does prevent them from doing so without following due legal process. The Act also specifies a group of farmworkers who may be evicted only under a very particular set of circumstances. These 'long-term occupiers' are persons who have lived on the farm for more than 10 years and who are older than 60 years or unable to work because of disability or injury. These people can be evicted only if they have engaged in some kind of unlawful behaviour. While it seems morally correct that this kind of security of tenure should be extended to the old and the poor, who have no other home, this Act has been something of a double-edged sword.

Research suggests that more than 1 million people (farmworkers and their families) were evicted from farms between 1994 and 2004, and that three-quarters of these were women and children.* The vast majority of these evictions involved no legal process. (The only large

---

*   Women and children are often evicted when their husbands or fathers die, or are fired, or in some way incur the displeasure of the farm owner. Many of these children were born on these farms.

survey of evictions was done in 2004/05[22] and so it is not clear what has happened since then, but anecdotal evidence suggests that illegal evictions continue, albeit not at the same rate.) It appears that many farmers evicted workers in *anticipation* of the 1997 legislation, fearing that they might not be able to do so very easily after it had come into effect. Workers approaching the age of 60 years may also be summarily evicted to prevent them becoming 'long-term occupiers'. Combined with the reduction in employment in the sector as farms have either been consolidated or closed down in the deregulated market environment (such as the tens of thousands who have lost their jobs on dairy farms), farm evictions have created a staggering rural poverty problem.

You can see this for yourself if you take a drive through any of the small towns in the Free State. These usually have an established (historically white) little town – often picturesque – on the one side of a main road and an extensive township (historically and currently black) on the other. If you drive into this township you will initially find yourself in an obviously older part, often made up of small brick houses with modest gardens. Go any further and you will see evidence of many recent arrivals – little RDP houses (if the inhabitants of this particular place are lucky) or hundreds, even thousands, of shacks (more likely). Vast numbers of people live in these settlements, often outnumbering the inhabitants of the small town across the road by a factor of many hundreds. You might wonder where all these people came from, and what they are doing here, stuck in the middle of nowhere. Mostly, they came from the farms, a great percentage of them in the last 20 years. And what are they doing? Very little – there are no job opportunities, few public services and not much food.

Perhaps someone from the Free Market Foundation might look at all these ex-farmworkers and see evidence of increased farm productivity, through a reduction in wage costs. I think most of us would see only despair. This is not what our countryside was supposed to look like.

Chapter 2

A space at the table: Who gets to eat and who does not

Hunger in the Rainbow Nation

Drive through the suburbs of any of South Africa's big cities – Cape Town, Johannesburg or Durban – and you would be forgiven for thinking that there is no significant food problem in South Africa. Big, well-stocked supermarkets are around almost every corner. Food markets and 'artisan' food stores have become very popular over the past few years, and are frequented by hundreds of enthusiastic shoppers. Catering to rather different tastes, fast food and takeaway outlets are even more ubiquitous than the supermarkets.

Take a road trip from Johannesburg to Cape Town and you will drive through hundreds of thousands of hectares of productive farmlands – grains, livestock, fruit and vegetables. South Africa is an exporter of a wide range of agricultural products such as citrus, stone fruit and wine. In most years the country produces a surplus of food. This only really changes in times of extreme drought – as is being experienced at the time of writing this book, after a poor rainy season in the summer of 2015/16. So there is no real problem in terms of the *availability* of food – South Africa has plenty of it, certainly enough in most years for everyone who lives here. The question of who actually gets to *eat* that food and who does not is a very different matter.

Many South Africans are aware of the fact that there is some kind of 'problem' with malnutrition in the country; that not everyone gets to eat well; that many households live on a limited diet of not very nutritious basic food stuffs; and that some vulnerable groups – like orphans and child-headed households* – may sometimes go hungry. Many people regularly contribute to food charity drives in recognition of this – dropping a couple of cans of food into a bin in the supermarket; adding a few rand to the price of their takeaway meal to 'feed a hungry child'; and packing food parcels as part of their community service on Mandela Day.** What most of them are not aware of is the extent of the hunger, and the debilitating misery associated with it in families across the country. This is not (in most cases) the result of callousness or cold indifference: despite the abolition of apartheid legislation like the Group Areas Act (which prohibited different race groups from living in the same areas) more than 30 years ago, South Africa is still a very spatially divided country – rich and poor, white and black inhabit very different realities. In 2016 the vast majority of poor people are still black and almost all of them live out of daily sight of the privileged – either in the sprawling townships on the urban edges or in remote rural areas. Despite the odd policy document and speech, food security does not appear to be a priority for the government, and is almost never one of the key issues in political debate, even during elections.

The media runs the occasional story about the high cost of food, but hunger is clearly not a focus area. In 2011, South Africans were shocked to read how four children – aged between two and nine years – died of hunger and dehydration in a field in the rural part of North West province after setting out in search of their mother and a meal. Autopsy results showed that the children had almost no food in their stomachs when they died. According to their mother, there had been little to eat in their house for weeks before their deaths, and the family had survived on food borrowed from their neighbours. She had set out on an 18-kilometere walk that morning to try and get food from her mother's boyfriend, who worked on a local farm, and received a food parcel as part of his wages. The children followed her a few hours later, apparently to try and reach the farm and something to eat (they had not had any breakfast). The outcry sparked by this story did not, however, last more than a few days. The incident was also treated in large part as some kind of one-

---

* South Africa's HIV-AIDS pandemic is the main reason for the relatively high number of orphaned children and households headed by under-18s.

** Each year, on 18 July, South Africans are encouraged to do 67 minutes of community service in commemoration of our first democratically elected president.

off tragedy, not the result of a wider social problem. To compound this assessment, the local police announced that the mother of the children might be criminally charged with child abuse for leaving them unattended, thereby 'allowing' them to die for want of food. The fact of this family's *hunger* and its existence and cause in a country as wealthy as South Africa just slipped away, as quietly and unnoticed as the children themselves in that field.

Nowhere in the popular media or around middle-class dinner tables or in the supermarket aisles will you find any indication that hunger is real, that it is everywhere and that it threatens the hopes that we have for our society. It is as if there is a great battle underway, but none of us can see or hear it. You may believe that this is because it does not really exist, but let me assure you that it is there – you just have to know where to look.

One of the difficulties of assessing the scope of the problem is how exactly one goes about defining 'hunger'. The general perception is that hunger is the same as, or at least on very close terms with, starvation. And we all know what that looks like on a 24-hour news channel. There is, however, very little death *directly* from starvation in South Africa (the 2011 incident is, thankfully, not often repeated). This leads most of us to the conclusion that there is not really any hunger problem. But just because thousands of people are not dying of starvation – and not being broadcast doing so on national television – does not mean that hunger in South Africa is not real, or that it is not damaging individuals and families in ways that we will all have to deal with.

'Hunger' has many definitions, some of them objective and scientific measures, and some subjective and personal. What feels like hunger to one person may not feel the same to another. Should a family whose main daily diet is watered-down maize meal not be considered 'hungry' because they mostly have a sense of a full belly, even though their diet is woefully nutritionally inadequate? How should a child who misses meals only during the school holidays because their main meal is obtained through a school-feeding scheme be classified – 'hungry' or 'not hungry'? Many families move in and out of hunger during the progression of a month – money to buy food tends to run out in the last few days before payday and parents will then often skip a daily meal so that their children have food. How should we classify them?

The difficulties of determining just who is 'hungry' means that most analysts and experts in this field prefer to talk about 'food security'. Basically, being 'food secure' means having access to sufficient nutritious food at all times. Households and individuals that do not have that permanent access are defined as 'food insecure'. The lines between food secure and food insecure, and between food insecure and hungry are fluid and not always easy to measure. There are also degrees of food insecurity, as well as the risk that you might become food insecure to consider. Some families are only at risk of hunger if some external shock is experienced, such as the main breadwinner losing their job; while others do not know from week to week exactly how they will put food on the table. These complexities are compounded by the fact that there is no official (government-mandated) comprehensive definition or measure of food security in South Africa: that is, there is no official indicator which says 'if you eat less than this amount of this kind of food every day you are considered to be hungry'. This is just another example of the official lack of interest in the subject.

There are thus no straightforward answers to the question – how many hungry people are there in South Africa and what is the extent of their hunger? Different surveys use different methods, different samples and ask different questions. What is clear, though, is that the problem is much greater than most people realise (and why that should be the case is something that also requires our attention).

So what do the existing data tell us? There are a number of national surveys and focused research projects that have attempted to determine how many South Africans are hungry, the extent (that is, how hungry are they and how often) and the impact of that hunger.

Statistics South Africa (StatsSA)[23] publishes an annual General Household Survey (GHS), which aims to measure the progress of socio-economic development indicators – education, health and social development, housing, household access to services and facilities, food security and agriculture. It is a sample survey, meaning that data are collected from a representative sample of households across the country – 21 601 in total. Although the survey methodology and sample periods have changed somewhat since the survey was introduced in 2002, it does provide useful information in terms of *trends* around hunger and access to food.

Between 2002 and 2008, the GHS asked only one kind of hunger question: if and how often adults and children in a household went hungry because there was not enough food. Although this measure is an indication of the degree of food stress that a family is under, it does not give us any idea of the *nutritional* status of the family – how much are they actually eating at each meal (the number of calories) and what is in that meal (the nutritional content). In 2009 an additional set of questions was included in the GHS, asking households about modifications that they had made to their eating patterns or diet (such as substituting maize meal for meat or eating smaller portions). This latter set of questions is considered to be a more sensitive indicator of household access to food. In 2015, the GHS suggested that just over a quarter of all South Africans could be considered as having limited access to food, and just over 13 per cent experienced hunger. This equates to some 14 million and 7 million people, respectively. Think about those numbers: *14 million* people – many of them children – regularly change their eating habits because they do not have enough food in their homes; this in a country in which the gross domestic product *per person* in the same year was just over R72 000 (about US$5 600 or US$15.60 a day – well above the global poverty-line indicator set at about US$3 per day).

Although it may seem counter-intuitive, the GHS shows that the highest percentage of households experiencing hunger is found in the rural areas, although in terms of absolute numbers, there are more hungry people in urban areas (reflecting South Africa's high rates of urbanisation over the past 20 years). This is because rural South Africans are more likely to be very poor than their urban counterparts, and – as we shall see – it is money and not proximity to agricultural output that largely determines who eats and who does not eat. Farmworkers and their families are among the hungriest people in South Africa, despite working (and often living) in the midst of agricultural plenty.

The 2016 Community Survey (undertaken by StatsSA every 10 years as a 'mid-census' population survey and which in 2016 covered 1.3 million households around the country) included some basic questions about food security, and came to similar conclusions as the GHS: 20 per cent of respondents indicated that they had run out of money to buy food at least once in the 12 months prior (the survey did not ask how *often* this had happened, merely whether or not it had happened).

One of the largest and most comprehensive recent surveys of health and nutrition in South Africa is the 2013 *South African National Health and Nutrition Examination Survey* (SANHANES-1). The survey is designed to collect a relatively wide range of data about the health and nutritional status of South Africans, as well as people's knowledge, attitude and behaviour around their health. The rationale for the survey is expressed as 'health and nutritional status, particularly that of young children, serves as an important indicator of development, social upliftment and access to resources within communities at large'.[24] Just over 25 000 individuals in 8 168 households across the country participated in this survey.

One of the categories of information collected by SANHANES-1 is around food security – nutritional intake and nutritional status. Data were collected through a combination of questionnaires administered in interviews and clinical examinations. Children aged 14 years and under were a particular focus of this survey. In determining levels of hunger, SANHANES-1 made use of a far more sensitive and calibrated measure than the GHS survey. The Community Childhood Hunger Identification Project (CCHIP) index is an internationally validated standard used in many food-security surveys. It is based on eight questions that represent a scale of increasing severity of hunger. The questions are based on events in the 30 days prior to the survey, and ask about how often the household had run out of money to buy food; how often and to what extent they had had to make changes to their diet or skip meals to accommodate a shortage of food; and the extent to which children in the household were required to skip meals, eat less than they would have liked or had their dietary choices restricted because of a lack of food. Points are allocated for each positive response to the eight questions. A score of zero indicates that the household is entirely food secure. A score between 1 and 4 indicates that people are at risk of hunger (that is, not food secure), while a score of five or more indicates hunger.

SANHANES-1 thus differentiated between being completely food secure, at risk of hunger and actually experiencing hunger on a fairly regular basis. The results showed that *less than half* of the respondents were food secure, about a quarter were at risk of hunger and a quarter qualified as hungry, regularly missing meals because there was no food in their homes. These are notably higher percentages than the number of people identified as hungry by the GHS, suggesting that there are in fact nearly *30 million* South Africans who cannot be considered food secure, or are at regular risk of going hungry.

In confirmation of the GHS findings, SANHANES-1 also found that those in rural areas were most likely to experience hunger. In addition to hunger, the survey measured dietary diversity – that is, how well the diets of survey participants reflected the necessary spread of nutrients. This is an important indicator, both for the individuals in question and the broader society. As more food groups are consumed (that is, dietary diversity is higher), the likelihood of meeting the body's nutritional requirements is increased. Low dietary diversity (such as a diet composed largely of maize meal) is positively correlated with poor nutrient intake, which in turn contributes to malnutrition and long-term health implications. These health implications translate into a significant burden of nutrition-related, non-communicable diseases (NCDs) such as heart disease and diabetes. And treating these is the responsibility of the public-health system. It is estimated that diet-related NCDs make up *more than a quarter of the burden of disease* in South Africa.[25] This represents a significant drain on our already stressed national health system and the R38 billion annual budget of the Department of Health.[26]

SANHANES-1 indicated that the mean Dietary Diversity Score (DDS) at a national level was 4.2. This is very close to the level (4.0) below which a person's dietary diversity is considered to be completely inadequate. Once again, it is people in rural areas that recorded the lowest DDS outcomes. These findings confirmed other studies, which suggested that about half of all South African households had a diet comprising mainly maize meal, bread and sugar. These foodstuffs may fill you up but they contribute little to your nutritional well-being.

On a (very slightly) positive note, almost all longer-term surveys do show that the level of self-reported household hunger has declined over the past 20 years, although it still remains unacceptably high. There has not been much detailed investigation into why this is the case (another example of the official lack of interest in the subject), but my best guess would be that it reflects the widening of the social-grant system in South Africa, particularly the child-care grant. This grant is paid to the primary caregiver for each child under the age of 18 years in their care. Claimants are subject to a means test – with current thresholds of R42 000 per annum for single parents and a combined R84 000 per annum for a married couple.[27] The grant has been progressively extended since it was introduced, by increasing the age of the children for which it could be claimed (to the current 18 years of age). A total of around 320 000 child-care grants were paid in 2000: this figure has now risen to 11.9 million.[28] Child-care grants now make up 70 per cent of all social grants in South Africa. The grant is a very modest R350 (just over US$25) a month, but in a household with three children, the extra money makes an enormous difference to the resources available to purchase food. My assessment would be that it is the money paid out as child-care grants (about *R50 billion* a year) that is responsible for the decline in absolute hunger rates. In fact, it is this money that is the most likely reason why we have not seen real starvation in this country.

The idea that it is the social-grant system that stands between moderate hunger and outright starvation was underscored by Ishtar Lakhani in her research in Tembisa township (more details about this study later). She reported on the importance of the disability grant, for which people who have HIV/AIDS are eligible *if* their CD4 count* is below 50 or if they are suffering from a major infection as a result of their HIV status. The disability grant has a monthly value of up to R1 500, and so is a relatively valuable grant. The aim of the universal state-funded HIV-treatment programme is to provide patients with treatment to raise their CD4 count. But if your count goes above 50, you no longer qualify for this grant (although this is a temporary rather than a permanent disability grant, you can receive it for longer than 12 months if you requalify under medical examination). The result is that some people – knowing that they will face an enormous struggle to feed their families without the grant – purposefully skip their medication in order to stay ill. The pastor of a church that runs an HIV-support group in Tembisa eloquently described to Lakhani the daily choices that these people face: 'If you are healthy, there is no guarantee of a job. If you [are] sick, you have your grant every month. It takes a long time to die from AIDS, it takes a short time to die from hunger.'

Are you still sceptical that we are engaged in a battle – possibly to the death – around hunger?

SANHANES-1 makes for depressing, and sometimes heart-breaking reading about the reality of many South African children's lives in the midst of this hunger. Although the vast majority of the children who participated in the survey (almost 90 per cent) indicated to interviewers that they believed breakfast was an important meal because it helped them to concentrate at school and gave them the energy they required for the day (and many children have no choice but to walk long distances to school), only 68 per cent actually ate anything in the morning before they left for school. Reasons given by the children for not having breakfast included not having food in the house (34 per cent of children), not getting up early enough (19 per cent – many of these children get up very early to start the walk to school, especially in rural areas), or being too little to be able to make their own breakfast, with no one at home to do it for them (15 per cent).

Fewer than 40 per cent of the children interviewed during SANHANES-1 took a lunch box to school. Why? Although about a third of the children responded that they did not need a lunch box because they got enough food at school (via the national feeding scheme), a significant number responded that the reason was because

---

*   The measure used to calculate the strength of the human immune system.

there was 'nothing at home to put in the lunch box'. The majority of these children were also in rural areas.

There are, of course, some problems with the kinds of questions used by the GHS (and to a lesser extent SANHANES-1) to determine levels of hunger: families who are already consuming relatively small amounts of low-nutrition food may not cut back on meals when money is limited, simply because to do so would push them over into starvation. Instead they cut back on other expenditure, such as walking instead of using a mini-bus taxi, or they defer their electricity or rental payment. Or they borrow a little money from somewhere. And if people have become accustomed to having too little food – if this has become 'normal' – they may not self-report to questionnaires that they are experiencing hunger.

An alternate – and perhaps more accurate – way of determining how many people are consuming less food (and less good food) than they should be is to compare the cost of a basic basket of food with the actual amount of money that they are spending on food. A big difference between the two – that is, if families are spending much less on buying food than they should be (jn terms of their calorie and nutritional requirements) – can really have only one of two explanations: the first is that the family is supplementing their purchased food with what they are producing themselves in their backyards. This is clearly not the case for most households, even in rural areas. The 2016 GHS showed that only 13 per cent of South African households were engaged in growing additional food for themselves, and a number of other studies have shown that even where households are undertaking this activity, the impact on their overall nutritional status is generally limited[29]. So a second explanation becomes much more likely if people are spending less on food than they should: they are eating less than they should, and less of what they should be eating.

The latest available comprehensive survey of household expenditure is the 2010/11 Income and Expenditure Survey (IES), which is compiled by StatsSA every five years (and only released more than a year later, which is why the 2015/16 survey was not available at the time of writing). The IES estimates household expenditure on a wide range of items, by expenditure decile. This means that the total population of households is divided into 10 equal groups – deciles – based on their total level of expenditure. Each decile corresponds to 10 per cent of the total number of households. Decile 1 spends the least amount of money and Decile 10 spends the most. The survey requires participants to report what they recall spending on various items over a 12-month period (from September to August). Although there are some possibilities of inaccuracies in this recall method (very few people can remember to the cent exactly what they spent money on), it is the most comprehensive survey of its kind.

The 2010/11 IES indicated that households spent between R3 313 and R24 821 in a year on food across the 10 deciles. The percentage of total household expenditure that this translated into varied considerably: 35 per cent for the poorest households, but less than 6 per cent for the richest. The amount spent on food by poor households may seem to be 'too' low, but there are many other urgent claims on the income of these families. The poorest households spend more than a quarter of their money on housing and almost 10 per cent on transport. It is generally very difficult for them to cut back on these main expenditure items in order to allocate more funds to food. These competing claims on the income of the poor have been well documented in a number of studies in other places, such as that conducted in 13 countries by Abhijit Banerjee and Esther Duflo from the Massachusetts Institute of Technology in 2006. Their monograph – *The Economic Lives of the Poor* – described the consumption patterns of poor and extremely poor people (deemed to be those living on US$2 and US$1 a day, respectively). Bannerjee and Duflo started their research with the assumption that the priority for poor households was food – after all, they reasoned, the most basic definition of 'poor' almost always includes the idea of not having enough to eat. They thus expected to find that the majority of available resources in most households would be directed towards food. This, they soon discovered, was not the reality of the poor, who face a number of competing ends for their limited cash resources.

The poor in South Africa have to make many hard choices about how to allocate their very limited cash resources. People need a place to live, ideally within travelling distance of job opportunities. Transport – to school, to work, to a hospital and to buy food – is becoming increasingly expensive, and the spatial realities of South Africa mean that most people are critically dependent on some form of motorised transport. All this means that even the very poorest households simply cannot afford to allocate the bulk of their income to food, no matter how pressing the need.

In order to adjust those 2010/11 IES food expenditure numbers into 2016 figures – to work out how much is being spent on food now – I applied an 8 per cent annual increase to the data. This is a generous estimate, since it is unlikely that most households would be able to increase their spending by that much each year: the annual increase in the value of social grants has been much lower than that, as have most wage increases. I have kept the share of food expenditure of total expenditure at the same level it was in 2010/11, even though food-price inflation has outstripped overall inflation since then. This is to reflect the difficulties that households face in cutting back on other expenditure items, such as housing and transport.

On this basis we could estimate that in 2016 the annual, total household expenditure on food by expenditure decile was as follows:

Table 2: Estimated household spend on food

Expenditure decile	Annual food spend (2016)
Lowest	R4 868
2nd	R8 550
3rd	R11 148
4th	R13 603
5th	R15 917
6th	R18 489
7th	R20 828
8th	R22 929
9th	R26 457
Upper	R36 470

Source: Own calculations based on 2010/2011 IES data

The next step was to calculate the cost of a basket of sufficient and nutritious food for an average household, and compare this to what people were actually spending. This is a good way to calculate whether or not there is a *food-spend deficit* and the extent to which families are not able to afford to eat properly. This exercise is not without its challenges: not all households eat the same thing; poorer households in South Africa tend to have diets composed mainly of maize meal, bread, dried beans, sugar and small amounts of eggs, meat, fruit and vegetables. Wealthier households eat proportionally more meat, fruit and vegetables. There are also differences in household composition and size across communities, which impact on what food – and how much of it – is required. For the purposes of the discussion that follows, I have used the average South

African household size of 3.3 persons and, where the information allows me to, have assumed that this mythical household is made up of 2 children and 1.3 adults, in an attempt to represent population demographics.

Surprisingly (or unsurprisingly if you are starting to get into the swing of the story), information regarding various nutritionally complete baskets of food is not collected systematically by either StatsSA or the National Agricultural Marketing Council (NAMC) – the two organisations officially mandated to collect information about food prices. Both of these organisations do collect information about the price of a basket of food determined to represent the items most commonly consumed by poor households, but this is not the same thing at all as calculating how much it costs to eat sufficient calories and nutrition. If poor households are choosing foods based on how cheap they are – as opposed to how nutritious they are – then tracking the cost of that basket of food simply tells us how affordable or unaffordable their bad food choices are.

The NAMC publishes a *Food Basket Price Monthly*[30] in which the cost of a basic basket of food – determined to represent the foods most commonly consumed by lower- to middle-income consumers – is calculated. The basket looks like this (presumably for one person, although the NAMC reports do not state this very clearly):

Table 3: NAMC food basket components

Item	Amount	Item	Amount
Baked beans	1 tin – 410 g	Chicken portions – fresh	1 kg
Peanut butter	400 g	Chicken portions – frozen	1 kg
Instant coffee	750 g	Fish – tinned	425 g
Tea	62.5 g	Brown bread	700 g
Full-cream milk	1 l	White bread	700 g
Eggs	18	Super maize meal	5 kg
Margarine	500 g	Rice	2 kg
Sunflower oil	750 ml	Cabbage	1 kg
Apples	1 kg	Onions	1 kg
Bananas	1 kg	Potatoes	1 kg
Beef chuck	1 kg	Tomatoes	1 kg

Source: National Agricultural Marketing Council

The purpose of collecting these prices is not entirely clear to me: the basket contains a limited number of items in quantities that appear to have been based on the ease of collecting price data for the amounts in question (like a 500-gram brick of margarine), rather than reflecting how much food is actually consumed (for example, how much margarine a person eats every month). It also differs significantly (mostly in terms of what it *excludes* from the food purchases of poor households) from more detailed interview-based food surveys, such as those published by the Pietermaritzburg Agency for Community Social Action (PACSA)[31] (discussed later). The PACSA basket includes 36 basic food items, compared to the NAMC's 22 items. Most importantly, the NAMC basket does not make any attempt to represent the *nutritional* requirements of different households or different household members. For example, small children have different nutritional requirements from adults, and adults engaged in hard labour (the most common option available to the poor) have greater nutritional requirements than those who are not. In summary, the publishing of this monthly NAMC report seems more like a random data-collection exercise than a serious attempt to understand the challenges facing poor families, who are trying to feed themselves in a nutritionally adequate way.

For what it is worth, the cost of this NAMC basket of food was R602.45 in May 2016. If we do a rough calculation and multiply this by 3.3 people in our imaginary household[32] and then by 12 months, we derive a very rough estimate of annual household food expenditure of R23 857, which would imply that about 80 per cent of South African households are not spending enough on food to purchase even the NAMC basket. Needless to say, there is no mention or discussion of this fact in the *Food Basket Price Monthly*. (Earlier NAMC reports – published around 2008 – did include a section on the affordability of food, but this analysis has been discontinued.)

There are other data sources that we can consult to try and answer this question: you may recall that during the 2012 farmworkers strike BFAP had calculated the cost of various baskets of nutritious food, for a family of two children and two working (farm labour) adults. They worked out that a modest, but calorie- and nutrition-sufficient plate of food would cost that family R7 074 per month. A reasonably nutritionally diverse basket of food, which contained only about two-thirds of the calorie requirements, was determined to cost R2 308 per month. If we apply the increase in general food-price inflation[33] – from December 2012 to mid-2016 – to these numbers, we arrive at a monthly expenditure of R8 970 to purchase the best basket and R2 926 to purchase the nutritionally diverse but low-calorie basket. We can further adjust these numbers by using the South African average household size of 3.3 people, and turning our monthly numbers into annual figures, which gives us a corresponding number of *at least* R28 967 as a proxy for the amount of money that households 'should' be spending on food in a year. Referring back to the IES food expenditure data, it appears that more than 90 per cent of households are not spending enough on food to purchase this basket, which does not even meet the basic calorie standard. Even if we do a little statistical massaging, and adjust for the fact that people interviewed for the IES might not have been able to accurately recall all their food expenditure, and adjust the figures upwards by 30 per cent, we still have to conclude that close to 80 per cent of South African families are not spending enough on food to feed themselves properly.

There is other research that looks at the cost of a nutritious basket of food: the PACSA describes itself as 'a faith-based social justice and development NGO'.[34] The organisation has been in operation for nearly 40 years, and operates in a rural area of KwaZulu-Natal. A focus of PACSA's work is food prices, given the difficulties that poor households face in feeding their families, and the organisation publishes monthly food price data,[35] reflecting what foods are actually purchased by families in the communities in which they operate. The basket was compiled on the basis of conversations with women in the focus communities, who are purchasing food for households comprising an average of seven members. The basket contains many more items than the 'official' NAMC basket set out earlier, and is probably a much better description of actual food purchases. In May 2016 this basket cost just under R1 900.

This information is a useful counterfoil to the official price statistics published by StatsSA and the NAMC, but as PACSA themselves point out, this basket is a reflection of reality and does not represent a nutritionally adequate food intake. PACSA reviews this food basket every three years to keep it as relevant as possible. What they noted in recent years was that the nutritional quality of the basket was declining, as the women in the survey were forced – through a combination of rising food prices and substantial increases in other demands on the household budget, such as electricity and transport – to reduce the amounts of certain foods purchased, or to stop buying them altogether. Quality protein and vegetables were the biggest victims of the cutbacks, being substituted with higher volumes of starch (such as maize meal), sugar and oil, to try and make up the volumes of food and some of the calories.

In response to this, and in recognition of the fact that it is important to keep track of what adequate nutrition costs (rather than just 'food'), in 2014 PACSA put together a 'minimum nutritional food basket'. This is a basic (cheaper cuts of meat, no luxury items at all), but nutritionally complete basket of food, and has been calculated for various household members (children, women and men), as well different activity levels for members of a household. Prices are collected for this basket each month and this information can be used to gain insights into the food-deficit gap. If we use the cost of this minimum nutrition basket (as at May 2016 – the most recent report available at the time of writing), and make a few adjustments for our average household of 3.3 people, we can estimate a monthly required food spend of R1 948, which translates into R23 372 a year. Going back to the actual food expenditure suggested by the IES, it is clear that even this very modest basket of food is out of reach of *80 per cent* of South African families. These conclusions support research done in 2009 by the Human Sciences Research Council (HSRC),[36] which found that only about 20 per cent of South African families were spending enough on food to buy a basic, nutritionally adequate diet. Since that report, increases in the price of food have routinely outstripped overall inflation, and so it should be expected that the food-deficit gap has risen. One important point to make here is that, contrary to popular discourse, hunger is not something that affects only the poorest households or the unemployed. Instead, there are clearly very many South African families that do not live in informal settlements, whose main breadwinners are not unemployed, and who would probably not be considered 'poor' by most people, who still cannot afford to eat well.

Right now, the drought of the 2015/16 summer season is pushing food prices even higher, without any corresponding increase in the incomes of poor households. Against this background, we can expect that adequate nutrition is going to slip even further away from the average South African family.

Coping strategies

Apart from social-grant income (and the measures to which people will go in order to keep receiving it), why we do not see more starvation in South Africa is because of the efforts of the hungry themselves. Food-insecure families have to manage their very limited cash resources carefully into a number of competing ends. They also use a number of non-monetary strategies to get access to food, such as borrowing food from friends and relatives, or attending social events where food is part of the occasion. Rather than being the passive (that is, 'lazy') recipients of taxpayers' funds, as they are so often depicted in popular discourse and around the middle-class dinner table, families with precarious food sources work very hard to make sure that they and their children are fed.

In fact, far from being helpless victims, food-insecure South Africans (and particularly women, who often carry the main responsibility for feeding the children in a home) exercise considerable ingenuity to fill the gaps in their family's food supply. Ishtar Lakhani did her research for her Master's degree in Anthropology in this area;[37] she spent time in 2012 and 2013 with a group of women in Tembisa – a sprawling township to the east of Johannesburg, home to about 350 000 people – documenting their food-coping strategies. Her research provides many insights into the reality of food insecurity in urban South Africa, and the complex strategies that people devise to put food on the table.

A common coping strategy that she witnessed regularly mirrored the information captured in the GHS and SANHANES-1 – consuming fewer meals and reducing the content of those meals. In the families with whom Lakhani spent time, the most common breakfast was a cup of tea with plenty of sugar and some bread. That was usually all that was eaten until dinner. When they had to choose, women prioritised making sure that their children ate something before they went to school (where they would often get a midday meal), and something before they went to bed. If money in the household was tight, mothers skipped meals for themselves. Meals at night sometimes consisted of nothing but cooked maize meal, but the women in question said that at least the children would not be too hungry to sleep. The importance of this food item as the main filler of every meal – and sometimes its only ingredient – was reflected in the fact that the priority purchase, when cash was available, was almost always a bag of maize meal.

Many families are also trading down in the composition of their meals: older women told Lakhani that they had witnessed a steady decline in the quality of what they ate – more and more maize meal and beans, and less and less protein such as meat and milk. The little meat that is eaten is often the very cheapest parts of the animal – chicken heads, feet and intestines have been substituted for other parts because this is all that can be afforded. These are far from voluntary 'choices'.

Oxfam's 2014 report, *Hidden Hunger in South Africa*,[38] captured very well how people feel about this forced change of diet through this quote from a young women, Elzetta: 'We have to buy the cheapest of the cheapest. We are rated as the cheapest of the cheapest.'

One of the challenges that the women who participated in Lakhani's research faced in achieving the goal of feeding their families on a regular basis was something that many of us take for granted: the ability to store and refrigerate (or freeze) our food purchases. Many households in Tembisa do not have access to a fridge (or the electricity to run one) or much storage space in the tiny spaces they call home. Rats are also a common problem in these areas, making the storage of food even more difficult. This usually means that only enough food is bought for the next (or at most the next few) meals. This day-to-day food requirement is usually bought from informal food traders, selling both ready-made food and basic grocery items.

Local food traders (who often go around on bicycles with a basket of vegetables or set up store on the side of the road) and spaza shops* in townships like Tembisa may sell items at a higher price than the same items purchased in bulk at a discount supermarket, but they often sell on credit to people they know, and also sell very small portions of food, smaller than can be purchased in those supermarkets. Customers can buy a single tomato or onion or a quarter of a bunch of spinach or a few hundred grams of maize meal. Although this purchasing strategy usually means that poor households end up paying more for their food than they could in theory, this does not reflect any ignorance on their part. Lakhani reported that all the women she spoke to knew exactly which stores had 'specials' on which items, and the exact price of every item on the 'special' list. Instead of any ignorance of frugal housekeeping, the reality of these women's lives does not permit anything different.

Most of the families with whom Lakhani interacted told her that they usually did only one bulk monthly shop (usually from a supermarket and based on a detailed price comparison exercise), but this was limited in its diversity and amount by several factors: the storage problems referred to earlier; a shortage of cash with which to actually purchase these items; and the cost of transporting the goods – there is only so much shopping that a person can put on their lap in a minibus taxi, and each journey represents a drain on the family's limited cash reserves. This means that it is usually only maize meal, tea,

---

* A tiny general trading store, often operated from someone's house.

sugar, cooking oil and soap that are purchased this way. The majority of poor families are not sure of exactly how much cash they will have from one week to the next (save for the monthly social-grant payment, which is used for the monthly bulk shopping), and so they tend to buy small amounts of whatever food they can afford on that particular day.

Many families will also buy cheap ready-made food on a fairly regular basis, much of it sold by informal traders in the township, because it often costs less than cooking the equivalent meal, when all the peripheral costs – such as paraffin for a stove, transport to buy the raw ingredients, the necessity of buying a certain minimum size portion at a supermarket, refrigerated storage – are taken into account. Lakhani reported that a frequent meal chosen in this way was a portion of fried potato chips, a loaf of bread and a litre of cheap, fizzy soft drink. This cost (at the time) about R40, but it could be shared among four or five people. It is certainly not a nutritious meal, but it makes your stomach feel full and the sugar and carbohydrates provide a chunk of the day's energy requirements.

There are limited ways in which poor people can earn money to buy food: Lakhani described the workings of a food stokvel,* to which she belonged, with about 15 members. The aim of the stokvel was to raise money through selling food. Every Monday, one of the members would cook a meal (usually maize meal, some meat and some vegetables), with a maximum budget of R100 (borrowed from the stokvel, to which each woman makes a small contribution). This would then be sold from her home for R30 a plate. Each stokvel member was each obliged to buy one plate of the food, but the rest was sold to other people, with the stokvel members engaged in marketing. In this way, each woman gets the opportunity to use the pooled savings of the others to earn money, through a venture that she would otherwise not have the capital for.

Social networks – who you know and your ability to rely on these people in times of need – are thus absolutely critical, not only for the opportunity to join groups like a stokvel, but also when you are not sure from week to week how you will feed yourself or your family. The ability to get credit from the local food trader or spaza shop is one good example, since they will usually extend this only to people they know and from whom they believe they can collect. Borrowing (and lending) food is a fairly common coping strategy. Dr Jane Battersby's 2011 investigation into food insecurity in Cape Town[39] provided insights into

---

*   An informal savings and/or credit club, often (but not exclusively) with women members.

how social networks are preventing many families from suffering from serious hunger. Her study covered just over 1 000 households in three poor areas – Ocean View, Philippi and Khayelitsha. Food insecurity was particularly high in these areas, affecting around 80 per cent of all households and almost 90 per cent in the part of Khayelitsha where the study took place. Dietary diversity scores were also uniformly low. More than 40 per cent of the surveyed households indicated that they shared meals with their neighbours or other households, the majority doing this at least once a week. Almost 30 per cent of the households reported that they had borrowed food, from relatives or community members, and about half of these said that they did so at least once a week. These social networks are clearly providing a critical safety net between many families and starvation.

Another way in which people access food from their community is through attending events such as weddings and funerals, where catering for a large number of guests is common. Although people may be going to a funeral primarily for the food, and the family providing the food may not be wealthy, it does not seem that this is begrudged, either by the hosts or by the wider community. Lakhani reported in her study that sometimes people even bring a container to the event so that they can take food home. Their friends and neighbours see this as an acceptable way to deal with the pressure to provide food – after all, few are completely immune from this worry.

Swapping sex for food (or the money to buy food) is a strategy that many women engage in when there are no other options. This is generally not viewed as prostitution, but rather as something inevitable under certain circumstances. That this should be so – that it is so inevitable that a poor woman would have to resort to selling herself to obtain food for her family that it has become, if not socially acceptable, at least not socially objectionable – should make each of us who do not have to make this 'choice' deeply ashamed.

Should we imagine that the drastic measures taken by many South Africans to feed their families are what the policy-makers had in mind in 1998 when they wrote the following with respect to the 1996 Marketing of Agricultural Products Act? 'Producers, processors and consumers are expected to take their own measures to manage price risk.'

Perhaps not.

The impact of hunger

Despite the social-grant system and the best efforts of hungry families themselves, the impact of all those skipped meals and poor-quality diets is significant, and growing. This is the real food battlefield, and there is little doubt here that we are losing, and doing so on a massive scale. The most damning – and troubling – studies are those that show the impact of this low-level hunger, particularly on children. There is no good news to be found here.

SANHANES-1 identified a range of health implications of the poor nutrition of South Africans: 17.5 per cent of all study participants over the age of 15 years were found to be anaemic, with women twice as likely as men to be so. Just over 13 per cent of all women of reproductive age were Vitamin A deficient. Iron deficiency was also relatively common.

The term 'malnutrition' refers to both under- *and* over-nutrition, since each can have serious consequences for a person's health. We should not confuse over-nutrition with some kind of luxury, gourmet indulgence, or with the intake of too much nutritious food (the use of one word – 'nutrition' – to refer to both good and bad food intake is confusing I know, but it is the standard term in this field of study). It is quite possible for low-income families to have relatively high intakes of fat and sugar (and thus consume too many calories – that is, 'over-nutrition') while still having a poor diet in terms of their nutrient requirements, simply because these foods are usually much cheaper sources of calories than quality food.

As we have seen, according to official statistics (such as they exist), the prevalence of hunger has declined over the past 20 years. But this is on a fairly radical definition of what constitutes 'hunger', and there is plenty of good evidence (such as the fact that most households cannot afford to eat well) to suggest that the problem of malnutrition has probably not declined over the same period, and may even be on the increase. But how concerned should we be? One way to answer this question is to consider the various impacts of malnutrition. If these are on the increase, we would have good reason to be sceptical of the official position which says that the scale of the problem is declining. The impact of malnutrition – particularly in children – can be measured in various ways, looking at a range of health indicators.

A common and universally used method of calculating the impact of poor nutrition on children is the collection of *anthropometric* data. This refers to measuring the height and weight of children and then comparing this information to the average for their age group. The term *wasting* refers to significant underweight compared to the height of a child (the physical attributes that we would link with our picture of starvation) and is associated with acute undernutrition. Wasting is considered to be a strong predictor of death in children.

Stunting refers to a low-height-for-age result and is associated with chronic (that is, long-term) under-nutrition (as well as other environmental factors that adversely affect children's health). It is a less severe effect of poor nutrition than wasting, the significantly low weight of children that we generally associate with starvation. Researchers also differentiate children as *underweight,* which refers to how they compare with how much they should weigh at a particular age. Data from 2008 indicated that 4.8 per cent of South African children were wasted, 24.6 per cent were stunted and 8.8 per cent were underweight. That is, *almost 40 per cent of South African children were suffering measurable side effects as a result of poor nutrition.* These numbers – although still shockingly high – represented an improvement from 1993. This should be expected: the period from 1993 to 2008 coincided with two factors likely to be positive for household food security. Firstly, the economy started to grow in the early 2000s and job creation was positive. Secondly, the social-grant system was introduced and expanded.

A 2015 study by a group of South African medical researchers[40] looked at the question of whether the prevalence of stunting in South African children under the age of six years had changed in a 40-year period, based on a review of academic papers published between 1970 and 2013. The study came to a couple of important conclusions: firstly (and not really surprising if we consider the general level of official apathy towards the subject), the study found that malnutrition needed to be better monitored by public-health authorities. The gaps in long-term malnutrition knowledge tend to be concentrated in rural areas – precisely the places where food insecurity rates are highest. Secondly, the study concluded that, overall, the prevalence of stunting in South African children had declined slightly, although it remained significant and way above the country's Millennium Development Goals targets.

It appears that currently around *one in four* South African children can be considered 'stunted', almost entirely the result of chronic poor nutrition. Worryingly, although the study indicated that stunting rates had declined slightly over their review period, the most recent research that they consulted (which was undertaken in 2013) showed that the stunting rates of children aged 0–3 years was *higher* (at around 26 per cent) than that of children aged 4–6 years. If younger children are showing more signs of stunting than older children, this suggests that the problem is getting *worse,* not better. Intuitively, this is what we should expect: a combination of the general economic slowdown since 2009 (which has reduced employment opportunities) and the fact that food-price inflation has outstripped overall inflation since then would suggest that families are under increasing pressure to feed themselves nutritiously. South Africa's stunting rates are also much higher than its gross domestic product (GDP) or national income per capita should suggest. Columbia has a similar GDP per capita to South Africa (that is, it is ranked alongside South Africa as a 'middle-income' country), but less than 5 per cent of Columbian children are considered 'undernourished'. Serbia also has similar GDP per capita outcomes, but malnutrition is estimated to affect around 6 per cent of children. That is, South Africa's child malnutrition rates are *four to five times higher* than other countries with similar size economies. The implication is that our hunger outcomes are the exception rather than the rule.

A high incidence of stunting should be considered as a serious public-health issue, but it also carries life-long implications for the children who are the victims: stunting is positively associated with slow cognitive development (that is, difficulty in learning), and higher risks of illness and early death. Contrary to what most us imagine, being stunted as a child *increases* the likelihood of becoming obese later in life, with all of the negative health implications associated with significant overweight (such as diabetes and heart disease).

Research indicates that obesity in South Africa is on the increase: SANHANES-1 reported that almost a quarter of women and a fifth of men can be considered obese. The response of some people is to cast a disapproving eye over the obviously overweight and to come to the conclusion that 'she obviously isn't hungry – just look at the size of her'. Nothing could be further from the truth. Obesity in South Africa (and in many other countries) is as much the result of poor nutrition as stunting is (in addition to the fact that stunted children are more likely to be obese adults). The sad truth is that it is often only the wealthy that can afford to be a healthy weight. The cheapest food options are usually those that contain the most fats, sugars and salts: as meat and dairy products become more unaffordable for people, so they have to resort to cheaper sources of calories, such as sugar or oil. Many of the people that I talked to during my research into South Africa's food system consumed a great deal of sugar – either in tea or in cheap, fizzy soft drinks. 'Sugar gives you go' was the phrase often quoted to me and it was well understood that consuming large amounts of sugar is necessary to have the energy to get through a day. Fat is another important source of calories in a poor diet: a homemade vetkoek,* deep fried in oil, provides a calorie kick at the start of a day, which often involves a long-walk to a taxi rank and low-paid manual labour.

This means that it is entirely possible to be both food insecure and obese. One study undertaken in the rural areas of Limpopo province[41] found that nearly one in five children was both stunted *and* overweight. These children face a bleak personal health future, and we should expect their numbers to increase as families are forced into consuming more and more bad meals.

Why it matters

Why should we be concerned – very concerned – about all of this? We all know that South Africa has high poverty rates and that many families live on very small incomes. This is the direct result of our high unemployment rate, which has greatly reduced the opportunities for earning additional income. After all, as I have pointed out, death from starvation is something that happens very seldom in this country. Maybe a little childhood malnutrition is simply the price of our economic reality. It seems to me that this is the argument that is going on in many people's heads, and that is what concerns me a great deal.

The deprivation and low-level suffering associated with not knowing where your next meal is coming from seem to be *normal* in South Africa, in that it is accepted as *normal*. This is why it does not get much media attention or government response. And the telling point here is not that this has *become* normal, but rather that it has simply remained so, continuing an unbroken line from the early 20th-century grand plans of apartheid, through 'liberation', to the present day. It has long been acceptable for poor, black people to live on the edge of hunger in this country, and it seems to me that not much has changed. The fact that there have never been any food riots in South Africa – or even regular mass marches to protest the unaffordability of food, is also telling. South Africans are not shy to vent their anger at not receiving government services or public housing, but we never see this aimed directly at food or hunger. It seems that even the hungry have accepted

---

*   A type of doughnut.

that their situation is somehow inevitable – 'just the way it is' – and that they cannot expect it to change.

Diana Wylie's book, *Starving on a Full Stomach*, is a history of the politics of hunger in South Africa under apartheid. It provides a keen insight into the linkages between cultural racism and the way in which the white government understood and reacted to the hunger and malnutrition experienced by black South Africans. But the most chilling result of reading Wylie's book is the realisation of how little has changed, both in terms of who the victims of hunger are, and the indifference with which their suffering is viewed by the government and the wider public. I think that it is not too dramatic to use the word 'indifference': after all, how else could we interpret the general lack of interest in the subject or the absence of meaningful action to change things?

Almost 100 years ago – 1938 to be precise – death by starvation in South Africa was relatively uncommon. Instead, as Wylie puts it, widespread malnutrition and hunger meant 'the survival of the poor in a compromised or diminished state'. She also documents the ongoing debate in apartheid South Africa over whether or not hunger actually existed in black communities, or whether malnutrition was simply the 'normal' state in African lives. It is a little difficult for me to see any radical change in either the outcomes or the acceptance thereof in the intervening period.

The real costs of hunger in South Africa are not economic, although these are significant, in terms of the burden on the healthcare system, the reduced ability to work and lower productivity. The real threat is to the fragile fabric of our society: despite 20 years of 'freedom', access to food – who gets to eat and who does not – is entrenching our inherited patterns of inequality and discrimination. The prevalence of stunting is strongly associated with poverty. The inability to access sufficient quantities of nutritious food is the best guarantee that the most marginalised children in this country – those who are poor and who are black – will graduate into a bleak future: struggling to learn in school and thus unlikely to receive a good education, burdened by disease that will make it more difficult to earn a living, and an early death. It is impossible for me to imagine that we can build a long-term future on this foundation of deprivation.

Even more troubling, our collective failure to even recognise and publicly acknowledge the extent of the suffering caused by hunger in this country reinforces the idea that some people are more valuable than others, that some people count while others may as well be invisible, no matter how much 'freedom' they may have on paper. The young woman Elzetta, who remarked that people like her are 'rated as the cheapest of the cheapest', was remarkably accurate in her assessment of her worth in the eyes of her fellow South Africans. Is this the kind of society we have aspired to be?

Chapter 3

The winners

Of course, every story has (at least) two sides, and in the battle for our food system there are not just losers, but also clear winners. These are mostly the entities that stand between farmers and consumers – the food retailers and the food processors and manufacturers. Most consumers do not buy their food directly from a farmer, and much of what passes as 'food' in our daily lives bears little resemblance to what left the farm. It is in this intermediary role (standing between producers and consumers) and as the creators of a wide range of 'food' that a number of companies have been able to turn a basic human requirement into piles of money. Food is a good business everywhere in the world and South Africa is no exception.

Despite the fact that so many South African families cannot afford to feed themselves very well, they do still spend money on food – they have no option. It has been estimated that the poorest households spend somewhere between a third and half of their income on food. And they spend most of their money with a relatively small group of food retailers (including fast-food outlets) and food processors and manufacturers. The demand for food is what economists refer to as 'relatively inelastic'. This means that, despite adopting the kinds of coping strategies to manage rising food bills described in Chapter 2, there is a limit to how much a person can cut back (reduce) their demand for food. It is not like shoes: if you really cannot afford to buy a pair this month, you wait until next month or the month after. If you do not eat, you die.

This makes food consumers guaranteed customers for South Africa's big food corporations. And the social-grant system – which currently pays out around R140 billion a year to just under 17 million recipients – has been a significant bonus for these companies, since the greatest single part of it is probably allocated to food. This means that South African taxpayers are also good 'customers' of corporate food.

South Africa's food industry is worth about R600 billion, and growing each year. Most of the benefits of this big business, however, accrue to only a relatively small group of companies, and over the past 20 years this group has got smaller, and mostly richer. The story of how this happened – how a small group of corporates effectively got to decide who eats what and who can make a living from farming and who cannot – is a combination of poorly conceived government policy, and a local corporate sector doing exactly what business is supposed to do – make as much money as possible. It is also a story of consumer apathy and effective collaboration – after all, it is our money that has put these companies where they are today.

Minding the gap: Big business and the governance of our food system

In Chapter 1 we saw how the hasty exit of government from the agricultural marketing sector had facilitated a situation in which a relatively small number of firms (such as bread bakers) were effectively given a strategic advantage over industry newcomers. This allowed them to consolidate their market position and eventually grow to a dominant size where they could dictate market terms to other participants, such as wheat farmers and the buyers of bread. But government's wholesale dismantling of the single-channel marketing schemes left many more gaps in the local food market than just the regulation of bread baking. There was also a range of supporting services that government either provided or regulated around food under these schemes. These included a lot of health and safety regulations, such as setting hygiene standards for the storage and transportation of milk, and regularly inspecting milk outlets to make sure that they complied. Government set and enforced rules for how much a standard loaf of bread had to weigh and how it had to be manufactured. Companies that did not comply would be punished through a set of fines, or could even lose their registrations or be closed down. And so the *governance* of the local food system was controlled largely by the state.

We can think of a 'governance structure' as the rules of the game – who is allowed or not allowed to do what in a particular system. This means that power and the allocation of power is both central to *and* a key outcome of a particular governance structure: those who have power can take control of governance, and a particular governance structure determines who gets (or does not get) power. A change in governance structure thus almost always implies a change in the relative power relationships among the various participants in a particular system. And, of course, this will impact the outcomes of that system – who benefits and who loses. Those who have governance power can effectively set the rules of the game, and thereby have a big influence on who wins and who loses. There are obvious benefits to being both referee and player in terms of governance: if you are a system participant who also gets to make the rules, you are in a very good position to makes rules that benefit you, rather than others.

It is important to point out that the governance structure that impacts a particular agri-food system (and thus influences who wins and who loses) is much wider than just legislation or regulation *directly* related to food. There are all sorts of other arrangements that impact the structure of a agri-food system, such as the location of and access to retail space; the transportation system; and who has access to what kinds of land. We will get back to these peripheral governance issues a little later on; for now let us take a look at what happened in the aftermath of government's decision to pull out of *directly* regulating agricultural markets.

Under the pre-1997 regulated agricultural marketing system, there was a lot of power for the state to dictate terms of business to private food companies. Consumers also had some power, since many of the rules of the game had been devised with their interests in mind – such as a guarantee that an 800-gram loaf of bread would actually weigh 800 grams, or that their milk came from a certified disease-free herd of dairy cows. From the early 1980s the state slowly began to withdraw from the direct governance of agricultural markets, with a very sudden and almost complete withdrawal in 1997 (if you recall, the 1996 Marketing of Agricultural Products Act came into force in January of that year, and set a target of dismantling all the marketing schemes and control boards within the following 12 months.) Of course there was still state involvement in the governance of certain parts of the food system (such as the legislation around food labelling, which falls under the Department of Trade and Industry, or international trade regulations), but for the most part the withdrawal was complete.

This was not a particularly unique South African phenomenon: all around the world – under the influence of neo-liberal economic thinking about the desirability of reducing state involvement in the economy, optimism around the ability of the 'free' market to ensure the most efficient allocation of resources and the growing globalisation of business – other governments had been doing much the same thing. This is one of the reasons why the South African food system – and the business practices of its biggest players – so closely resembles that of other countries, such as the United States and the United Kingdom. It also means that there is not much room for anyone to argue that the outcomes of market deregulation in South Africa could never have been anticipated, or are some kind of one-off fluke.

There are, however, two key differences between us and other countries that do make the South African example unique: the first is that, while policy-makers in most of these other countries have begun to realise that handing over responsibility for their food to those whose primary focus is profit was probably a bad idea, and are now starting to think about ways to address this, the South African government (and, to be fair, most South Africans) does not seem to give this the slightest thought. Secondly, the negative impact of this corporate control of the governance of our food system is greatly amplified in South Africa because of our history and our demographics. It is a cautionary tale of what happens when unbridled corporate power is set loose on the poor.

But surely, you might respond, the government did not 'hand over' responsibility for the food system to a few private-sector companies? It may not look like they did (certainly there was no handing-over ceremony) and most government officials would strenuously deny that they did anything of the sort. In fact, they would assert that they did not hand over responsibility to anyone. Well – that is the problem: sometimes doing nothing is the same as doing something because it leaves room for someone else to do something; and usually that someone who gets to do something is the richest and most powerful someone around. And this is exactly what happened.

The way in which the Free Market Foundation (FMF) (in their glowing 2000 monograph about market deregulation) saw things was that the large-scale withdrawal of the state from market governance '[had] serve[d] to minimise the risk of decisions aimed at favouring the few and disempowering the majority'. Actually, the opposite happened and deregulation, in fact, served to *maximise* the likelihood of a market that favoured the few and disempowered almost everyone else.

The gap left by the state in the governance of our food system was not filled by either the producers of food or by the consumers. Instead it was effectively taken over by the manufacturers and retailers of food, who dictate who eats and who does not, what we eat, and the state of our farming sector. Rather than the magical 'free' market imagined by the FMF and the Minister of Agriculture, where all companies would now be able to compete with each other on a level playing field, the food system in South Africa in 1997 was characterised by an existing unequal distribution of power. I have already referred to some of these, such as the bread bakers. And bread baking and flour and maize milling would become the foundation on which today's biggest and most successful food processors and manufacturers (such as Tiger Brands and Premier Foods) would be built. However, there was another group that had considerable power, but who, for some reason, did not feature in the discussions around what kind of agricultural marketing system would be 'best' for South Africa. This omission seems to me to reflect a peculiarity about the way in which public officials and many South Africans understand (or, rather, misunderstand) how our food system operates.

Supermarkets: The real power in the food system

Almost every one of us (whether we are the Minister of Agriculture or a person living in an informal settlement) gets our food in a similar way: we go to a shop and hand over some cash. Mostly, we go to a supermarket and buy it. Many of us have never set foot on a farm and would not dream of driving to one and packing part of a recently slaughtered cow into our car as a substitute for the regular drive to the local supermarket and a vacuum-pack of mince. And yet when we read policy documents or articles in the media, or discuss the state of our food system with our friends, we act as if the main players in the food system are farmers and consumers, as if it is these two groups that determine what is produced, what it costs, where it is available for sale and to whom it is available. Even when we grumble about the rising cost of food, we ascribe it to things like the drought or international wheat prices, or the fact that we don't get paid enough. It is time to wake up.

The fact of the matter is that – in a corporate agri-food system such as ours, where the direct relationship between farmer and consumer has been broken – the most powerful entities are those that control access to the market (and the 'market' would be you and me). That is, as the distance between food producer and consumer increases, it is supermarkets that are the most important 'gatekeepers' controlling access to the consumer. This means that as the dominance of the supermarkets increases (that is, as they increasingly become the only source from which to buy food), they also become the only market to which the producers of food can sell their produce. As you can imagine, this would put the supermarket in a pretty good place with respect to both the producer and the consumer.

A value chain (or supply chain) can be defined as all the activities and participants involved in getting a product from its raw material state to the customer. For example, a simple bread value chain involves a wheat farmer, a flour miller, a bread baker and a bread retailer. All along this chain, 'value' (or margin) is created: so the 'value' of the loaf of bread at the retailer (its price) is higher than the value of the amount of wheat in it, since each participant in the chain gets the opportunity to charge for their input and, hopefully, to turn a profit. There is thus a total amount of value created over the entire chain, which is shared among its participants. It would be extremely naïve of us to believe that everybody who participates in a value chain is determined to be as fair and as equitable to each other as possible (although you would be surprised – or not – to find out that most of our agricultural policy is based on this charming, but deeply inaccurate, perception of the real world). Instead of genteel cooperation, most corporate value chains are characterised by cut-throat competition to capture the greatest share of available value. After all, this is what shareholders demand – a continuous increase in profits.

Gary Gereffi is a leading theorist in the area of governance in value chains, and he coined the phrase 'lead firm' to refer to those companies that had sufficient power to govern everyone else in the chain, and therefore to extract more value than anyone else. In a corporate agri-food system, the lead firms are almost always the big supermarkets. And it is the push to be big that is the defining feature of supermarket growth in South Africa. Each of the country's Big Four (Shoprite, Pick n Pay, Spar and Woolworths)[42] has increased their market share of retail food sales over the past decade, pushing out independent retailers and informal traders as they do so. Even in relatively remote rural areas, most households source the bulk of their foods from supermarkets, sometimes travelling in round trips of more than 100 kilometres to do so.

It is not entirely straightforward to work out exactly what the food retail market share of each of the Big Four is, since only one of them (Woolworths) reports food sales separately from the sales of all other items. It is also not that easy to work out exactly what the size of the overall retail food sector is, given the split between formal and informal trade, and the growing share of takeaway food. The best guess[43] is that about two-thirds of all retail food sales and *97 per cent of formal retail food sales* go through the Big Four, with the following estimated formal, retail food market shares for each:

Shoprite   38%
Pick n Pay   31%
Spar   20%
Woolworths 8%

The overwhelming business objective in supermarket food retailing is to maximise profits, and the best way to do this is to maximise your share of the value of a particular product and to sell it to as many people as possible. And in order to be able to do *that*, you need power, combined with a governance structure that allows you to exercise that power. As the size and market share of each of the Big Four has increased, so, too, has their power over other participants (particularly farmers) in the agri-food system. In 1999 the United Kingdom's Competition Commission initiated an enquiry into the procurement practices of supermarkets in that country. The report (published in 2000) found that a supermarket needed only an 8 per cent market share to have enough power to be able to implement what it termed 'abusive' procurement practices in respect of farmers. This implies that each of our Big Four have market power (some of them to a very considerable degree) relative to other market participants.

And they have been able to use this power to excellent effect, not just to extract value from producers, but also from the consumers of food. The initial series of Section 7 reports undertaken by the NAMC showed clearly that deregulation had been associated with producers receiving a decreasing share of the retail price of food. It also showed an increasing margin for retailers (and the biggest processors), meaning that the 'gap' over the producer price paid by you and I for our food had also increased. This is how good profits are made in food retailing – by paying suppliers less and getting consumers to pay more. And South African retailers are showing themselves to be very good at exactly this.

One of the ways in which this value extraction skill is clearly illustrated is in the growing gap between the price that farmers receive and that consumers pay for food, in other words, the margin that accrues to whoever has bought something from a farmer and then sold it on to us. If we were discussing processed food, such as a ready-made meal, we would expect to see that the share of the farmer in the final product (such as that of a beef farmer in a pack of ready-made beef lasagne) is relatively low, and we could explain that with the idea that whoever manufactured, packaged and branded the ready-made meal had in all likelihood 'earned' the greatest share of the value in that product. We might also believe it was 'fair' that we paid a relatively high price for this product (that is, quite a lot more than the cost of the ingredients), since someone else went to the trouble and effort of making it.

However, when we are talking about food that has seen little or no processing, or even packaging by the retailer, we would not expect to see the same thing. Instead, for items such as milk, or fruit and vegetables, or unprocessed meat, we would expect the farmer (the person who did all the work and incurred the greatest share of production expenses) to receive the greatest share. (We would be even more inclined to think this if we remembered that the cost of packaging and some of the cost of transportation is often also for the farmer's account, which is discussed later). This is most definitely not the case.

In the absence of state-mandated producer prices, regulated retail margins and retail prices (or any real resistance from consumers), the food companies have simply taken this food-pricing authority for themselves; and they have used this power to extremely good effect to benefit themselves. The NAMC regularly (every three months) collects and publishes information about the retail price of food, focusing on basic food items.[44] If we compare the retail-price information contained in these *Food Price Monitor* reports with data on producer prices (some of which are included in the *Food Price Monitor*, but otherwise collected from other sources such as the fresh-produce markets and other market-analysis reports), we can see quite clearly the considerable and growing gap between the price that farmers receive for food and what you and I pay for it.

Table 4 sets out this information, using for the source of retail prices the most recent NAMC report that I consulted, which contains prices for April 2016. This is an overview of general trends in the market: individual retailers may be paying more for certain items and/or charging more for them. It provides, however, a very good indication of the general structure of our food market, and – most importantly – where power lies and how it has developed. The 'margin' is simply the difference between the retail and producer price of an item. The 'farmer share' column refers to the share of the producer's price in the final retail price, and it is an indication of the farmers' share in the price that you and I pay for our basic food items.

Table 4: The gap between the producer and retail price of food and the farmers' share

Item	Producer price	Retail price	Margin	Farmer share
Milk (per litre)	R4.50	R12.71	R8.21	35.4%
Beef (brisket) per kg	R38.00	R69.94	R31.94	54.3%
Chicken (whole) per kg	R23.10	R41.81	R18.71	55.2%
Apples (per kg)	R6.60	R17.56	R10.96	37.6%
Potatoes (per kg)	R4.80	R16.03	R11.23	29.9%
Tomatoes (per kg)	R6.10	R20.73	R14.63	29.4%
Onions (per kg)	R5.57	R13.74	R8.17	40.5%
Pumpkin (per kg)	R1.90	R11.87	R9.97	16.0%

Sources: NAMC April 2016, and fresh-produce markets

For many products, the farmer's share of the retail price is less than half. It is also important to note that while this percentage has decreased a little over the past decade or so, the rand value of the farm gate–retail price gap has risen very significantly. The gap for milk was R2.98 in 2005 – it is now more than R8. In 2008 the price spread for apples was about R4, now it is nearly R11. In 2010, the gap for chicken was around R10, now it is close to R19. The rising gap means that the same volume of food sales is associated with a much larger margin for intermediaries. The increasing farm gate–retail price gap is a clear indication of who has power in the food system (the retailers) and who does not (the producers and consumers).

To most people, the size of this gap comes as an unwelcome surprise, but this is part of the problem. Although much of this information is relatively easy to find online (if you know what you are looking for) it is not consolidated into one user-friendly report by the NAMC, which, I would argue, should be doing just that. (Over the past five years, the NMAC reports contain – to my mind anyway – less and less comprehensive and detailed information that is useful for consumers.) As a result, the farm gate–retail price gap is not the hot topic of popular discussion it deserves to be. Much the same seems to apply to our politicians and policy-makers: the idea that the rising difference between the farm gate and the retail price of food should at least make it into the public debate around food security and land reform seems never to have occurred to anyone who could do anything about it.

It is not hard to work out that if the margin between the producer and consumer prices of food were reduced, food would become a lot more affordable for a lot of people. *This is the real tragedy of our food problem – we already produce enough food in South Africa to feed everyone and farmers are selling it at a price at which most people could afford to eat it.* At the same time, consumers are paying a price high enough that – if it were the price they actually received – many more small and family-run farms could be successful and farmworkers could earn a decent wage.

Make no mistake: the ever-widening gap between what farmers receive and what people pay for food is one of the key factors that is perpetuating rural poverty. A few years ago I spent some time with a community that had had their farm – which had been illegally taken by the apartheid government – returned to them soon after the change of dispensation in 1994. They were farming maize and working hard at doing so. They did not make much profit from it, given that their farm was not very large and their limited access to finance meant that they needed to rent capital equipment. They were starting to think that they were wasting their time. Why? Because the money that they earned from farming and selling maize was not enough to pay for the community's annual maize-meal consumption. (The margins between maize and milled maize meal – and thus the price that farmers receive for maize and the retail price of maize meal – have also increased steadily over the past 20 years.)

The poor returns from farming (whether you are a smallholder or an emerging farmer or a farmworker) are a critical factor driving rural poverty. In many rural areas, farming is the only major economic activity available, but under the existing set of circumstances it will never contribute to real change. The current dominant market structure is effectively extracting value from rural areas and redistributing it to the shareholders and senior management of a handful of companies.

This logic of the market – buy low, sell high – also applies to the biggest food manufacturers and processors, such as Tiger Brands or Clover, or Premier Foods. They might have less overall market power than retailers (after all, they also need a place to sell their products), but they do have a lot of power over farmers. Those who own popular branded products are in a stronger bargaining position with retailers than those who do not. Food processors are also in a good position to increase their margins by reducing the 'food' (nutritional) component of the food that they sell, and substituting cheaper ingredients, such as water, salt and flavourants (more on this later). Clearly this business practice might be good for their shareholders, but it is not so good for their suppliers or their customers. The extent to which food manufacturers are permitted to engage in these business practices is also a good indication of how much governance power they have in the food system.

In the absence of a state that prioritises access to food and rural development, and consumers who seem happy to go along with whatever they are offered, big food corporates have simply assumed the power to govern our agri-food system. Although there has been no official formal 'food companies are in charge of the agri-food system' announcement, one way in which we can see quite clearly who *effectively* runs the system is by looking at who is accumulating the greatest benefits from it. And it should be quite clear by now that this is neither the producers of food, nor the consumers of food: both groups are under increasing pressure, to make a living from farming or to feed their families. In contrast, we have a small group of companies that are most certainly not under any financial pressure and regularly report not just profits, but growing profits. These profits – when contrasted against the losses of both farmers and consumers – serve as a *proxy* for the power of big corporates in the governance of our agri-food system. They are winners in large part because they have the ability to set the rules of the game, because they took for themselves the governance space created by deregulation.

Squeezing the lemon till the pips squeak

It is not only through their ability to increase the margin between the farm gate and the retail price of food that a small number of corporates are exercising their self-allocated power in our agri-food system. There are all sorts of other ways in which they are able to squeeze value from both producers and consumers. Some of these are borderline illegal, some are completely illegal and some would just be considered immoral by most of us. The great thing, though, about being both referee and player is that you seldom have to worry about recriminations.

The bigger you are (that is, the bigger your market share and the more customers you have), the more you are able to dictate to other firms in the chain (that is, your suppliers) terms and conditions that are to your benefit and/or that shift your costs to their account. And this is where it becomes particularly handy if the state has left the governance table. In many countries, including South Africa, private standards – rather than standards set by the state, such as how much a loaf of bread should weigh – are what comprise agri-food-system governance. Via these private standards, supermarkets (and certain processors) determine to a very great extent what varieties of food are grown, what the acceptable aesthetic standards for food are, how processed food should be manufactured, how food is packaged, how it is delivered, and – very often – what it says on the label. They also get to decide who is a supplier, what suppliers get paid and what consumers pay for food. Although you may not think there is anything wrong with a range of private standards – after all you are probably quite appreciative of how nicely packaged and fresh your food looks in the supermarket – it is important to know that the imposition of many private standards is not actually in your best interests, or in fact in anyone's best interests, except for those of the company that imposed them.

The kinds of private standards that are imposed by supermarkets on suppliers generally increase their (the supplier's) costs while reducing the supermarket's costs. For example, strict aesthetic standards are often imposed – green beans have to be perfectly straight and a certain length; peaches and plums must be blemish free and fall within a narrow range of sizes; and so on. You might be happy with your straight and equilength beans, but achieving this goal routinely means that farmers must overplant by a significant amount in order to discard what does not meet these requirements. Clearly this increases the costs and the risks for farmers. Most supermarkets also require that the producer packages the item to their specification, labels it and delivers it to a central warehouse. This also increases costs for the farmer and means that they need access to capital to fund the infrastructure required to meet these standards, such as packaging equipment and delivery vehicles.

It is not only about packaging and delivery though; there are all sorts of other (less benign) ways in which supermarkets (and processors) extract value from their suppliers. In 2009 Professor Johan Kirsten undertook an investigation for the NAMC on the effect of supermarket power in the local dairy industry.[45] The report was written in response to concerns that had been raised by milk producers about the growing power of supermarkets, and was intended to inform the Minister of Agriculture about the worrying state of affairs in the dairy sector. His report also covered milk processors (that is, those who bottle milk under their own brand and manufacture dairy products, such as yoghurt or cheese) since they had become an important market access point for dairy farmers (and are even more so since the report was written).

Kirsten's report documented the declining profitability of dairy farmers (increasingly struggling to meet their production costs) and the rising retail margin on milk, but also reported a number of 'non-price' ways in which milk processors and supermarkets go about protecting their margins and market share. A good example of these kinds of practices is to prohibit a dairy farmer from selling any milk at all to anyone else, under threat of the termination of their contract. These kinds of threats are illegal in terms of the Competition Act, but Kirsten was clear that this had taken place, and I have been told exactly the same thing by dairy farmers. My personal belief is thus that this is a relatively common practice. This practice means that a farmer who supplies, say, 10 000 litres of milk a day to a dairy processor or supermarket will not be allowed to sell 200 litres off the farm to the local community from a roadside stall. Given that the farmer in question would probably be more than happy to sell that 200 litres at somewhere around R8 or R9 a litre – about double what the processor or supermarket would pay, but at a substantial discount to what his customers would pay in the local supermarket – this practice is effectively preventing rural communities from accessing a more affordable foodstuff. I buy a lot of milk from a local dairy farmer who sells all his milk this way (he has access to a big enough direct sales market not to have to rely on a processor or supermarket contract at all). You bring your own bottle and pay R8.50 a litre. Many of his customers are people from nearby Tembisa, pleased at the opportunity to be able to buy a quality product at a substantial discount from what is on offer in the local retailers. More consumers (and farmers) should have this opportunity to participate in a (genuinely) free market. You might believe that a milk processor or supermarket has the right to defend their market share by preventing their suppliers from competing with them, but (leaving aside the fact this practice is probably illegal) how many of us really believe that this 'right' should effectively be elevated over the rights of the poor to access basic foodstuffs? Unfortunately, our opinion does not count – we are not the ones who run the food system.

Another issue raised by Professor Kirsten in his report was payment: he reported that many milk suppliers had to wait up to 60 days to get paid. In the interim, their cows had to be fed and their employees had to be paid. Those who protest too much may find themselves without a contract. Supermarkets often also make suppliers responsible for breakages or spoilage of products that happen as a result of the supermarket's actions – such as dropping a crate of milk or leaving it out in the sun.

Kirsten's report concluded that procurement practices in the local dairy industry posed a significant threat to dairy farmers, particularly smaller farmers. Although this was a much more comprehensive investigation than the Section 7 one undertaken by the NAMC in 2001, it came to very similar conclusions about the effect of the state's exit from the governance of our food system, and its replacement with the private sector. Needless to say, no official action was forthcoming. Dairy farmers have continued to go out of business, with a corresponding loss of jobs, and only the biggest have survived. Between 1998 and 2014 more than 5 000 dairy farmers went out of business,[46] resulting in an estimated loss of 50 000 jobs. The majority of these have been smaller farmers. Dairy herd size has increased steadily over the past 20 years, and the milk market is now dominated by herds of more than 300 cows. This market structure has created a very effective barrier to market entry for smaller producers, and thus job creation in rural areas. Things are very different in places like India, where millions of smallholder farmers meet (relatively efficiently) the country's milk demand. It does not seem coincidental to me that Indian legislation has prevented the kind of supermarket concentration we see in South Africa. If we consider that around 50 000 jobs (predominantly in rural areas) have been lost in dairy farming over the past 20 years, we can start to understand the impact of 'market efficiency' on our rural communities.

The poor are good business

It is not only supermarkets that have accumulated enough power to push their suppliers around. Clover holds almost 32 per cent of the fresh-milk market and almost 40 per cent of the butter market;[47] four companies – Premier Foods, Pioneer Foods, Tiger Brands and Foodcorp – control around 70 per cent of the local bread market;[48] and Tiger Brands holds around 75 per cent of the local tomato-processing sector. These companies are not shy about using their market power to their advantage. We have already seen evidence of how the milk processors have put many dairy farmers out of business, while growing their own profits. Clover increased its revenue by just over 50 per cent from 2010 to 2015,[49] while the number of dairy farmers declined by around 40 per cent over the same period, representing the loss of tens of thousands of jobs.

But it is the bread bakers that have provided one of the very best examples of why it is a bad idea to hand over our food system to those whose main motivation is profit. In December 2006, a Western Cape bread distributor reported to the Competition Commission that he suspected there was price fixing taking place in the bread market. He had come to this conclusion after receiving letters from all three major bread bakers to signal a coming price increase, at exactly the same time. Not long after that, another bread distributor reported that he had seen officials from 'rival' companies meeting. The Competition Commission decided to investigate and came to the same conclusion: that a price-fixing cartel was in operation and included some of the biggest companies in the food sector – Tiger Brands, Premier Foods and Pioneer Foods. The commission found that these companies had colluded over an eight-year period to set the price of bread. They had also colluded to fix the price of maize meal and flour (the biggest bakers also own the milling companies, which puts them in a good position to charge smaller bakers a higher price for flour, and thus push them out of the market).

Tiger Brands was fined just under R100 million by the commission in 2007. Pioneer Foods (who had fought the commission's decision) was eventually fined R195 million in 2010. Premier Foods had been quick to admit liability and opted to cooperate with the commission. As a result, they were granted immunity. These fines do not seem to match the crime: stealing from the poorest of the poor. In 2011, the combined profits of the baking divisions of the three major companies accused of bread-price fixing was just under *R2.5 billion*,[50] and their control of the market seems just as secure as it was before the Competition Commission investigation.

In a 2013 edition of *Food Ethics,* the magazine published by the UK

Food Ethics Council, the editor, Dan Crossley, wrote:

> I hope that we never live to see the day when the right to profit
> is pitted against the right to eat – although some might argue we
> are pretty close to that now. But if it ever comes, surely even the
> most hardened capitalist would agree that the latter must take
> precedent over the former.

If Mr Crossley would like to see exactly what happens when the
right to profit is not only pitted against the right to food, but wins, he
needs only to make an 11-hour flight south. Clearly our capitalists, and
the government that supports them, are a lot more hardened than he
could imagine.

Chicken brining is another way of making a whole lot of money
at the expense (and health) of the poorest consumers. If you do not
know what 'chicken brining' is, here is a short introduction: if you
stroll around the frozen-food section of your local supermarket you will
see plastic bags of frozen chicken portions. This is called 'individually
quick frozen' (IQF) chicken and it is big business, making up about
60 per cent of all retail chicken sales. IQF chicken is manufactured
by injecting a mixture of water, sugar, salt and other flavourants (the
brine) into the chicken meat and then freezing it. The packages (mostly
2 kilogram bags) are weighed on the basis of the chicken *and* the brine,
so someone who buys it is buying both chicken and water, but most of
the water comes out when the chicken is cooked. Since it is made up of
a significant portion of water, IQF chicken (per kilogram) is generally
cheaper than unbrined chicken, which makes it attractive to the
poorest consumers. It also makes it pretty attractive to the people who
manufacture it – after all, it is not every day you get to sell flavoured
water at R30 per kilogram. Of course that is not quite how they see it
– instead, they suggest that the brine is in fact 'preferred' by consumers
since it makes the chicken more 'tasty' (as well as adding considerably
to their intake of sugar and salt).

In 2010, *City Press* exposed the practices of certain chicken
processors, who were not only selling chicken portions that were made
up of almost 50 per cent brine (that is, selling poor people a lot of
flavoured water), but also routinely 'reworking' chicken as part of the
brining process. Their story implicated Supreme Poultry, which they
alleged was thawing expired frozen chicken, washing it in chlorine, and
then injecting it with high levels of brine before packing it and selling

it as IQF chicken. (In this case you might understand why brine would be necessary to make the chicken 'tasty'.) Supreme did not deny the allegations – instead, it said that the process of 'reworking' chicken in this way was not illegal (which is true).

You may be surprised (or not) to discover that, until 2012, the manufacturers of IQF chicken were not obliged to disclose what percentage of the weight of the product was made up of brine. You would think that this would be very useful information for poor people who really need to spend their limited food budget on chicken rather than flavoured water. But, in a telling indication of exactly who is in charge of our agri-food system, government had decided that the interests of corporates were more important than those of the poor.

After 2012 (in terms of new food-labelling legislation) manufacturers had to disclose on the packet what the percentage of brining was – most products were around 30 per cent. But they were not obliged to disclose what the price of the *chicken* in the package was, as opposed to the price for both chicken and water. This lack of disclosure obviously worked against those consumers who simply compared the price per kilogram of IQF and fresh chicken. I did a couple of calculations myself in the frozen-food aisles, and when you discounted the flavoured water, many of the IQF chicken offerings were, in fact, more expensive than fresh chickens. And that is leaving aside the health implications of what exactly is in the pack of IQF chicken.

After 2012, government started a protracted process of setting maximum brining limits. It took until 2016 to actually finalise and publish these limits, and chicken processors fought the legislation hard. It is telling that it was mostly these processors that were involved in negotiations with government around the proposed new limits, rather than consumer-rights or food-security advocates. Once again, this gives us insight into who has the top seats at the food governance table – who gets to have the most say on what the rules of the game are.

Despite their best efforts, the new brining regulations were announced in April 2016 and processors were given six months from that date to comply. Brining of chicken pieces has been set at a maximum of 15 per cent – a limit that has generally been greeted with howls of outrage by the industry, understandably miffed at the fact that their ability to sell flavoured water has been curtailed. My favourite quotes come from the CEO of the South African Poultry Association, Kevin Lovell: 'this [that is, the new chicken brining regulation] constitutes an assault on the poor of South Africa who will now find the price of

Individually Quick Frozen [IQF] chicken unaffordable.'[51] The fact that the higher price will be paid for more chicken, as opposed to water, and that *this* might be in the best interests of the poor does not seem to have crossed Mr Lovell's mind. Or perhaps a more accurate, 'the new chicken-brining regulations will reduce our ability to make a profit out of selling flavoured water to poor people' did not have quite the same ring to it.

In respect of complaints that the high salt and sugar content of the brine is bad for the health of the poor, Mr Lovell was clear that, 'this practice actually improves the national diet by reducing the cost of South Africa's favourite protein product'. And then again, perhaps not.

Giving the haves even more

It is not just by walking away from food system governance, and thus creating a gap to be filled by a relatively small group of companies, that government is tipping the power scales in favour of this small group. There are also many other ways in which the state is (mostly inadvertently we have to hope) putting in place policies and programmes that are benefiting big business in the food sector, to the significant detriment of the rest of us. The problem is that, without a big picture of what is going on, the linkages among these various policies is not immediately apparent.

A good example of what is going on is the way in which spatial development and land use (particularly in urban areas) is managed. These powers fall mostly under local government, and there is a strong convergence of views across municipalities about what constitutes desirable 'development'. For all the talk of shared growth and equitable development, if you take a walk around any of South Africa's big cities it will become clear that the real priority is modern, shiny spaces – the development of the 'world-class city'. This means that preference in the development of retail space is given to the kinds of places that have big supermarkets as their tenants. This preferential development strategy contributes significantly to the increased market dominance of the Big Four supermarkets. There is no similar (or at best very little) investment in retail space that supports small businesses, such as greengrocers, or that could provide a place for farmers to sell their produce directly to consumers. Where these farmers' markets do exist, they are inevitably located in wealthy areas and are clearly focused on wealthy clients. They are also the result of private initiative, rather than local government. In contrast, what we see from government is a concerted effort to drive small traders – particularly hawkers – out of the cities. The few opportunities that are available to poor people to earn a living from food are being slowly eroded, in favour of even greater market domination by the Big Four.

The decisions of local government on land use can also have an enormous impact on the ability of small farmers to make a living, and of nearby communities to access affordable, quality food. The current battle between the City of Cape Town and activists* over the future of the Philippi Horticultural Area (PHA) is a case in point. The PHA covers about 2 400 hectares and is an area of high-value agricultural land and abundant water: in many places the water table (the massive Cape Flats aquifer) is only 1 metre below the surface. Most importantly, the PHA is located less than 20 kilometres from downtown Cape Town. The area currently produces the majority of Cape Town's vegetables.

On this basis (and given that there are high food-insecurity rates in many parts of Cape Town, including in areas adjacent to the PHA), we might think that the city would be focused not just on protecting this valuable resource, but leveraging it as a key tool to transform the local agri-food system. Sibongile Fityedi is the Chairperson of the Vukuzenzele** Urban Farmers Association (VUFA) and a member of a group that farms a small plot in Gugulethu (more about that farm later). In his role with VUFA his priority is to try and find a place for the 70 or so members who would like to have access to more land. You might think that the PHA would be the perfect spot for such a land-reform project: committed and experienced farmers, high-value resources and an enormous market on their doorstep.

You might think so, but you will not find anyone in the City of Cape Town administration that does. Instead they have decided that this high-value urban agricultural area should be the site of a large, mixed development – something between 26 000 and 40 000 houses, private schools and (of course) shopping centres, anchored by a couple of big supermarkets. The proposed development is planned for one of the highest-value farmland areas of the PHA and would also pave over a key catchment area for the Cape Flats aquifer.

On the day that I first travelled to the PHA to meet with activists

---

*   The PHA Food and Farming Campaign and the Schaapkraal Civic and Environmental Association. They have little funding and run almost entirely on the goodwill of volunteers and pro bono legal services.

**   Literally 'get up and do it yourself'

Nazeer Sonday* and Susanna Coleman,** Susanna took me on a drive through the PHA. It is breathtaking in its scope and agricultural productivity, but also disheartening. Nazeer and Susanna both maintain that the City of Cape Town is on a conscious mission to degrade the area, to ruin it so that they can turn around and justify their decision not to protect it. I must admit that I thought they were exaggerating a little, until I took a tour. Illegal dumping is everywhere and the city refuses to do anything about it, despite repeated objections and the filing of complaints. There is pollution seeping into the water in the northern part of the aquifer – no one in the city seems too concerned about doing something about this. In all the years that the local community has been fighting the proposed development, their government has made it quite clear that they are not interested in the views of the people who live and work in the area (some 4 000 of the latter) or in considering any alternative kind of vision for the PHA. In this way, land that could be vital in reducing poverty – through the creation of land-based livelihoods and increased access to affordable food – is prioritised for profit-maximising, private, corporate development.

Transport infrastructure is yet another way in which government policy – and tax revenues – is effectively supporting one kind of system over another. Transport is a critical factor in the workings of a modern food system, given the distance between food producer and food consumer. Farmers need to transport their produce to buyers, and consumers need to travel to buy food. It is not hard to work out that the way in which public or subsidised transport is organised can have an enormous impact on who wins in a system and who loses. And once again, it is important to make the point that if government does *nothing* in a particular part of the transport sector (that is, does not subsidise it or provide a public alternative), this is not neutral. Instead, what it means is that it is those who have access to money to pay for their own transport (that is, the already wealthy and powerful) who will benefit from the absence of the state. This point is about to become clearer.

Consider some examples of different policy approaches to transport: when government subsidises the public transport of *people* around a city (such as in rapid bus systems or trains or taxi ranks) it makes it easier and cheaper for those people to access the retail nodes that are dominated by supermarkets. There is nothing wrong with this because the cost of transporting food is important in poor households. But

---

* Farmer and part-time activist

** Optometrist and part-time activist.

these public-transport nodes tend to skip out alternative markets that the poor could access, because they are often centred or focused on *formal* (that is, supermarket-dominated) shopping destinations. So, for example, it is relatively easy for someone who lives in Johannesburg to access a supermarket using public transport, but a lot more difficult for them to get to the Joburg Fresh Produce market, where fresh fruit and vegetables, which are much cheaper than in a supermarket, are available. Public-transport systems are thus effectively making food choices for people, and making choices that entrench the power of the few at the expense of the many. Public transport also does not allow people to transport large amounts of shopping. It makes sense for poor households to get together and buy in bulk, but how do they transport this home? Certainly not on the bus.

Even more importantly, there is no public, subsidised transport for small farmers to enable them to access customers. The lack of affordable transport options is a key reason for the failure of many small farmers, rather than the lack of farming knowledge or technical skills. One small farmer – who is producing very high-quality organic produce and selling it at an affordable price – told me that if you do not have a car you cannot make money from farming because you cannot sell your produce. He had to make huge sacrifices and scrimp and save to buy a 'skorra skorra'* – his business could not survive without it. This car often broke down at the side of the road, leaving him and his vegetables stranded, but it worked often enough to allow him to start building his business. He has since been able to buy a bigger and more reliable vehicle, and it is critical to his business.

Small pig farmers in the Free State told me that they spent most of what they earned on hiring a bakkie to transport the pigs to the nearest abattoir. I have heard similar stories from many small farmers, most of whom would probably never be able to put together the resources to buy their own vehicle. But transport is seldom considered in any of the farmer 'support' programmes, and there is no public-transport system in cities like Johannesburg or Cape Town that facilitates the transport of food from nearby farms to the millions of consumers who would like to purchase it directly from the producer. And this absence of the state means that those who are able to pay for their own transport networks (such as the big supermarkets and processors) are able to exert even more power in the system, and entrench their positions.

---

*   Colloquial term for an old, cheap car.

You may recall the enormous number of social-grant payments made in South Africa – R140 billion a year and going up. Social grants have traditionally been paid in cash on certain days of the month in thousands of centres around the country. And not all grants are paid on the same day of the month, so there would be a number of 'social-grant' days in a particular area. Social-grant days have provided a great opportunity for small farmers and traders to set up shop – usually an informal affair in any available space – and sell to those who have just received their grant pay out. I once accompanied a group of small farmers to one of these, and watched how they had a very good day, selling all their quality and affordable vegetables. I thought that this was a great thing – some of the billions of rand that was going into social grants was having a 'double' pro-poor effect by supporting small farmers, and thus putting them in a better position to feed their own families. I did, however, think that government could be doing more to support this virtuous market circle, perhaps by providing small traders with better facilities in close proximity to the pay-out points.

Government's thinking on this, however, was completely different. When they looked at these informal markets, they did not see the possibilities for rural poverty alleviation or a virtuous market circle, or the ability of grant recipients to access affordable food. Instead they saw a problem – something that needed the cure of 'progress'. In 2012, the South African Social Security Agency (SASSA – the people in charge of managing the social-grant system) announced a new 'smart card' for grant recipients. This new system allows the grant to be automatically uploaded to the recipient's card, and thus removes the requirement for grant recipients to congregate in one place each month. This very effectively removes the reason for a market on a particular day. These smart cards can also be used as debit cards within supermarkets, and cash withdrawals in these supermarkets are free. There is thus a considerable incentive to use the cards within a supermarket.

According to the Minister of Social Development[52] (Bathabile Dlamini) 'the previous antiquated system indicated that beneficiaries were able to receive their grants only on specific dates and at specific pay-points'. That this 'antiquated system' (which has now been replaced with a 'smart' system – the language is very clear) supplied income-generation opportunities for many of South Africa's small farmers, and provided support to the rural economy does not seem to have been considered at all. I am not saying that it is not easier for grant recipients to make use of a smart card – it means that they do not have to travel to the pay-out points (although most still do since they are usually in the same place as the shops), and they are much less likely to be robbed if they do not have all that cash in their pockets. However, there must be a better, a more equitable solution – one that benefits both grant-recipients and small farmers (who are often able to provide food cheaper than the supermarkets). If only a fraction of that R140 billion went to support small farmers (and this happens in many countries under government-sponsored programmes), it would make a significant impact on rural poverty and, thus, food security. The real problem, of course, is that no one in SASSA believes there is a problem.

Sometimes it seems to me as if the entire effort of government is directed towards benefiting the few that have at the great expense of the great many that have not. How long can this continue?

Us versus them: Why it matters

It should be clear by now that the state's exit from the governance of our food system has not created a 'level' playing field and neither has it been neutral in its impact. Instead, it has facilitated an environment in which the most powerful companies effectively run the system, and do so for their own benefit. Privately imposed standards – which allow a supermarket to offer a wide range of attractively packaged and fresh items – greatly increase the risks and costs of farming. Only the biggest farmers with access to capital are able to meet these requirements. This means that private standards are often operating to exclude smaller and emerging farmers – exactly the kind of farmers that need to be supported in order to make a start in addressing our very high rural poverty levels. Corporate profit is being traded off against rural poverty, and it is winning.

But there is more to be concerned about. As Professor Kirsten pointed out in his 2009 investigation of the impact of supermarket power on the dairy industry, putting farmers out of business is bad for food security. If we wipe out our local dairy industry (something that does not seem that unlikely given current trends), where will our milk supply come from? There is growing international competition for agricultural resources, and imported food will become even more expensive when the rand takes one of its periodic downward dives (as is happening while I am writing this book). Milk and dairy products are already underconsumed food groups in South Africa, to the detriment of national nutrition standards. Do we really think that it should become even more unaffordable just so that a handful of companies can make a lot of money? I certainly do not.

And it is not just rural poverty or our food security that is at stake: the relentless expansion of supermarkets and the capture of the markets by the biggest food processors and manufacturers is putting hundreds – if not thousands – of small businesses (many of them black owned) out of business. From bakers to greengrocers to spaza-shop owners, people are losing their businesses, their jobs and their livelihoods, and no one seems to care or notice. Instead, every annual report from a big food corporate showing a gain in business and an increase in profits is greeted with cheers and admiration in the media. But the biggest share of every extra rand is taken from families that cannot afford to eat, farmers that cannot afford to stay on the land, and small businesses who cannot afford to stay in business. So what, exactly, are we so very pleased about?

PART 2

The empty promises and the kindness that cuts

The fact that there is hunger and malnutrition in South Africa has not gone unnoticed by either government or the wider public (even if the extent of the problem is seldom appreciated). In response, there are several government initiatives and thousands of private-sector initiatives that have been designed to try and address this. Government – at all levels, from national to local – is also involved in farmer development and the support of small-scale agriculture. If we add up all the time and money that goes towards attempts to 'fix' these problems, we will come to a fairly substantial total. You would be forgiven then for wondering why so little seems to have been achieved.

I would say that the lack of success is not from lack of effort, but it certainly is from lack of the right kind of effort. In chapters 4 and 5 we are going to take a good look at what has and is being done – by both government and hundreds of thousands of well-meaning private individuals – and compare those 'solutions' against what we understand as 'the problem'. The gap between the two is almost always considerable, and the bad news is that you might be one of the people who, with all the best intentions in the world, are actually making it more difficult for us to address hunger and rural poverty.

Chapter 4

Government policy:
A better life for some

The South African government allocates a lot of time, money and effort towards policies and programmes that aim to reduce hunger, improve nutrition and address rural poverty through the creation of job and livelihood opportunities in agriculture. By most measures – the number of households experiencing food insecurity, malnutrition levels and rural poverty rates – it would not be an exaggeration to say that the majority of these (with the social-grant programme being the exception) have failed to make even a moderate impact. I am certainly not the first commentator to point that out, and there is an extensive debate across academia, civil society and the general public as to what has gone wrong. Some are of the opinion that we have fundamentally sound policies and that what has gone wrong is the implementation of these policies. Others believe that the problem is that we have the wrong policies – we cannot fix our problems with the tools that we are using because we are using the wrong tools. I would place myself firmly in the latter camp, proposing that we are using the wrong tools because we have misunderstood the problem.

But before we get to this discussion – why exactly the tools that we are using are the incorrect ones and how we could change this – we need to work our way through the details of those policies and how they got to be our official response to hunger and poverty. It is a cautionary tale of how making a few incorrect assumptions (held not just by policy-makers, but also by most South Africans) can create a huge bureaucratic system, with thousands of well-meaning people spending billions of rands doing almost exactly the opposite of what is required.

It is also a story of betrayal – of how the poor have somehow come to be 'responsible' for their own hunger and their own poverty, despite the promises of liberation and a better life.

Putting an end to hunger

Since 1994 South Africa's government has constantly portrayed itself as 'pro-poor', stating that its overarching priority is to address the injustices of the past and to create a better life for all South Africans. We are lucky enough to have one of the most progressive constitutions in the world. Chapter 2 of this Constitution contains the Bill of Rights, and Section 27 within this Bill of Rights ensures the rights to water, food, healthcare and social assistance. (This makes South Africa one of only 22 countries in the world to have a constitutionally guaranteed right to food.) The state is obliged to give effect to these Section 27 rights, although the Constitutional Court has ruled that the extent to which it does so needs to be limited by the resources at its disposal. This is a pragmatic approach: the state has certain obligations, but we need to be realistic about what can be done with what is available. It is in the interpretation of 'what can be done', however, that we will find the most cause for questioning what has actually been done.

An important part of the promised 'better life' is improving standards of living (income as well as access to basic services such as housing, healthcare and education) and reducing inequality. South Africa is ranked as the most unequal country in the world in terms of the distribution of income: a few people have a lot, and a lot of people have very little. Clearly this is not a sustainable or a desirable situation. We could probably all (or at least the majority of us) agree that it is in all of our best long-term interests to build a society in which most people have a reasonable amount, and as few people as possible suffer real deprivation. And most of us would agree that one of the most serious aspects of deprivation is hunger. Because of this, post-1994 South Africa has always had some kind of official policy that aspires to reduce hunger and malnutrition. This is a good thing (obviously). What are not such good things are how this policy has been conceived, how it has been put together and how it has been implemented.

There is a critically important issue at stake here: the way in which we understand a problem determines to a great extent how we think we should go about trying to fix it. That is, if we understand that the cause of something is X, we will (or should) devise and develop policies that are focused on fixing or changing X. But if the problem is actually Y, all our efforts to fix X are not actually going to change anything. This confusion of X with Y is at the heart of the much less than successful attempts by the state to address food insecurity and malnutrition.

Missing the big picture

The very first problem is that there is no single government department or agency that has responsibility for our agri-food system. As is hopefully clear by now, the reasons why people are hungry or malnourished is the result of the interaction of a number of factors, not all of them immediately apparent. Most importantly, hunger and malnutrition are *system* outcomes – they do not occur in isolation. Instead they are the outcomes of the ways in which a particular agri-food system is constructed and how it is governed – the rules of the game that determine who has power and who does not. It is the *system* that determines winners and losers, who is hungry and who is not, rather than individual components of that system.

In recognition of the challenges presented by the cross-cutting complexities of food system governance, many countries have established either national or local departments of food. Their overarching responsibility is to ensure that the entire agri-food system is structured in such a way that it generates the kinds of outcomes that are wanted. One good example of this was the Ministry of Food, set up (or rather re-established – it had been active in the First World War) in the Second World War in the United Kingdom. This is a fascinating story, showing quite clearly how a sharp focus created by great necessity can completely restructure an entire agri-food system (and one in which food supply is limited) to serve the greater good, rather than the interests of the few, in a very short space of time.

The British government knew that ensuring that everyone (those at home as well as those fighting) had access to sufficient food at an affordable price was going to be a critical factor in winning the war. If families started to run out of food – either because not enough was being produced or because it was priced beyond their means – there would almost certainly be civil unrest and an undermining of the war effort. The United Kingdom was particularly vulnerable to shortages of food because much of its supply was imported, and the blockade by the German Navy meant that only limited amounts of food would actually reach its destination. In addition, shipping needed to prioritise the movement of soldiers and army supplies, not food.

The Ministry of Food took responsibility for the governance of the entire agri-food system, and implemented a multifaceted policy. This included increasing the domestic production of food, both by maximising output on farms (using the Women's Land Army to replace men who had gone to fight) and in private gardens and public spaces. The 'Dig for Victory' campaign saw domestic gardens, public parks and sports fields turned into Victory Gardens. Even the gardens at Buckingham Palace and the moat at the Tower of London were planted with fruit and vegetables. More than one million tons of fruit and vegetables were being produced in these Victory Gardens by 1943. People were also encouraged to keep small livestock, such as chickens, goats and pigs, which a great many families did.

But the Ministry of Food understood that ensuring that everyone had access to sufficient and affordable food required much more than just producing more agricultural produce. They thus took effective control of the agri-food system by law, becoming the sole wholesale buyer and distributor of food (including imports). A system of guaranteed producer prices made sure that farmers stayed in business. The ministry also managed the distribution of most (although not all) food via the rationing system. This gave everybody equal rights to most food items (with allowances for different religious and dietary requirements) through the distribution of ration coupons. The government supplied the food in question via existing food retailers. The coupons then determined whether or not you could access a particular item, such as butter, and how much of it you could access: once you had used up your weekly allocation of coupons, that was it – no more butter, no matter how much money you had.

Ration coupons did not, however, mean that you got the item in question for free; you still had to pay for it. But the prices of items were set at a rate deemed to be affordable for most people, and because the state managed the entire system, it was run on a cost-recovery, not a profit-making, basis. Every part of the system structure was designed to reduce costs. For example, grocery stores were obliged to get their stock from the nearest supplier in order to reduce transportation costs. There was no point in spending a lot of money to advertise either specific foodstuffs or a particular store, since the choice of food was extremely limited and people were restricted to shopping at the stores at which they had registered. Some people qualified for different or extra rations, such as children and those engaged in hard labour. Everybody in the United Kingdom fell under this system – even the royal family were issued with ration books and registered at the closest grocery store where their coupons could be redeemed.

Profiteering from food was a criminal activity, and waste in the agri-food system was avoided as much as possible. This policy approach – managing the entire system to ensure the best outcome for the greater good – was considered a great success. Drastic food-price increases were averted, and the egalitarian distribution of food meant that much of the population ended the war with a better nutritional and health status than they had started it. This was particularly true of children from the poorest households, who, under the rationing system, got access to a greatly improved diet.

If, however, you do not have one single authority – like a Ministry of Food – that is responsible for managing the outcomes of the entire agri-food system, it is very likely that the big picture – that is, the workings of the entire *system* – will go entirely unnoticed. Instead, individual departments of government will look only at their part of that big picture, from their point of view, and on that basis make a decision about what the problem is, and thus what the solution should be. It does not take much imagination to work out that this is probably not a good way to come to the correct conclusions. Sadly, this is the story of food security, nutrition and rural poverty-alleviation policy in South Africa.

There is no Ministry of Food in South Africa. Most food security and nutrition issues fall under four national government departments: food security is located within the Department of Agriculture, Forestry and Fisheries (DAFF), in the Food Security Directorate. Some nutrition-related activities fall under the Department of Health, while others – and most 'emergency' hunger-alleviation efforts – fall under the Department of Social Development. But the Department of Rural Development and Land Reform (DRDLR) also runs many food-security programmes under its 'rural poverty' mandate. It is by no means clear exactly where one department's responsibility ends and another begins, or who exactly is responsible for what.

Nor is the situation much clearer with respect to the production of food: post-1994, land-reform programmes fell under the Department of Agriculture and Land Affairs, which meant that there was some alignment between agricultural policy and land reform – in other words, that agricultural policy would support the goals of land reform. But in 2004, land reform (and thus most of what goes on with respect to the allocation of land and the settlement of new farmers) was moved from that department (which was renamed the Department of Agriculture Forestry and Fisheries – DAFF) to the newly established Department of Rural Development and Land Reform (DRDLR). To add a bit more complexity to an already unclear national situation, the DRDLR is responsible for 'rural development', which clearly would include agriculture, as well as 'settlement support' to land-reform beneficiaries. In reality, the DRDLR appears to have oversight over small-scale and subsistence agriculture and activities on land-reform farms, while DAFF busies itself with 'big' farming. But DAFF is also responsible for overall agricultural policy-setting and the management of most of the agricultural-support programmes, including those accessed by land-reform beneficiaries. The NAMC (whom you have already met) falls under DAFF and is responsible for producing information on agricultural markets that will instruct policy development (in DAFF, rather than in any other department involved in food or farming).

As if that was not confusing enough, there are also provincial departments, which have significant responsibility in terms of food security, nutrition, agriculture and rural development in their particular areas. Very often these departments are structured to reflect provincial priorities and resources rather than the national structure. So provinces have single departments of Agriculture and Rural Development, rather than two separate entities, and these take responsibility for a wide range of projects, including food security and small-farmer development. Finally, many local municipalities (particularly those in rural areas) design and implement small-scale agricultural and food-security projects as part of their integrated development plans (IDPs). The end result is that there are a large number of public servants running around developing and implementing all sorts of food and agriculture initiatives, but none of them is doing so on the basis of a big picture of the entire system, and clear goals in this respect.

And to make matters worse, and despite all these busy people, a big chunk of the agri-food system is not really under any government department at any level. There are thousands of pages of policy around agriculture and farming, but very little around food manufacturing, processing and (especially) retailing that would suggest that these are an integral part of this same agri-food universe. They are generally absent from government scrutiny, save for some food-safety and labelling legislation, which mandate sits in other national departments that seldom discuss their policy plans with entities such as the Directorate of Food Security. So for, example, the growth and development of the food-processing sector would clearly have an impact on food security and small farmers. Certain policy decisions could entrench the existing distribution of power in the sector, while others could change it. One would think, therefore, that these kinds of decisions would fall under DAFF, and have critical input from the Directorate of Food Security as well as DRDLR. Instead, they fall largely under the Department of Trade and Industry, since 'agro-processing' is generally considered to be part of industrial development and not an integral part of the agri-food system. The result is that we have duplication of efforts existing at the same time as significant gaps in governance.

That all of this institutional confusion might be a problem does not seem to have been seriously considered. At one time (around 2001/02) there was talk about a Food Security Bill that was in the process of being drafted, and that it would be presented to parliament some time in 2002. Apparently the Bill contained provisions designed to address these institutional complexities by establishing one authority that would have overall responsibility for food security. I say 'apparently' because the Bill was embargoed and I have never seen a copy. It – rather oddly – just disappeared without making it into the statute books. For a year or two (until about 2003) the annual report of the Department of Agriculture included a line about how the Bill was almost ready to be tabled, and then that went away as well. I have never been able to find out why.

Why are people hungry? Identifying the problem

In its 1994 Agricultural Policy Document,[53] the ANC was clear that, 'Most people in urban and rural South Africa are net food purchasers – policies ensuring affordable and stable food prices are therefore crucial.' So far so good, you might think – that seems like a pretty good assessment of the problem. Do not get too excited … just a few lines later come the assumed policy implication:

> [F]ood and agricultural policy will seek to ensure that national
> food requirements are met by the most efficient combination of

domestic production and trade that is consistent with broader targets for economic growth, employment and agricultural restructuring. Household food security will be enhanced by a range of measures to improve the affordability of food. These include VAT exemption on basic foods, as well as measures to raise incomes such as public works programmes, improved welfare provision, and the development of a thriving rural economy.

That is, the solution to *affordable* food was seen not so much as how to actually make food more affordable (which we might think would be the logical conclusion), save for making some food exempt from VAT. Instead, the 'solution' was seen as increasing people's incomes, via employment creation and a social-grant system. Nothing has changed in the intervening period: the 2002 national *Integrated Food Security Strategy* had, as one of its strategic priorities, the need to 'match' (that is, increase) people's income to food prices. A central part of how most public officials and many South Africans understand why people are hungry is linked to the idea that they do not have enough income, mostly because of our high unemployment rates. This is, of course, a perfectly logical way of thinking about the problem, and all around the world it is understood that poverty is strongly correlated with limited access to food.

It is not, however, a particularly helpful conclusion in the South African environment. We have extremely high unemployment rates (somewhere between 25 and 45 per cent, depending on which measure you believe is most accurate) and you would have to be optimistic to the point of requiring medication to believe that this is going to change significantly any time in the near future. The saying 'the poor are always with us' has never been truer than it is in South Africa. So to conclude that while people are poor they cannot afford to buy the food they require might be true, it is completely unhelpful in terms of addressing the problem. People are hungry *now*, not in three or eight years' time when we have addressed our unemployment problem.

This is, however, only *one way* of thinking about affordability – that we must increase people's income so that it can accommodate a certain amount of food spend (and this implies an acceptance of the 'inevitability' of one kind of food system rather than another, which we shall examine critically later). There is, of course, another way to make food more affordable and that is to make it cheaper – to make the cost of food fit a poor family's income, rather than the other way around.

Given our particular challenges, this would seem to be a more sensible approach. But because the ANC government (or, to be fair, most South Africans) has never really thought about *how* or *why* food ended up having one price rather than another, it has never seriously considered the possibility of a different price. That is, because no one is thinking about how the entire food system works (which determines how and where food prices are set), we have never got to the point at which we think that the system is a problem that needs to be addressed. And so we have arrived at the current situation – where even those people who have formal-sector, full-time jobs are struggling to feed their families, and yet we still insist that the reason why people are hungry is because they are unemployed.

But this lack of systems thinking is even more clearly illustrated in the first part of the 1994 policy statement quoted above – that food requirements will be met through the production of food. This idea that food production and food consumption are two sides of the same coin is the defining feature of the way in which our food-security policy conceptualises the relationship between farmers and consumers. Despite the fact that all current policy documents (and you really should read a few) invariably start off by pointing out that national and household food security are not the same thing, there does not seem to be any appreciation of the fact that there is *no direct relationship* (none at all) between how much food is grown in the country and how many people actually get to eat well. Most policies on the subject of food security (whether at a national, provincial or local level) appear to work from the assumption (usually to be found in the first few pages) that food security will be addressed by higher agricultural production.

The implication is that programmes that support farming (and these are the preferred strategies) will automatically result in better food-security outcomes, as if the extra food that is produced will somehow magically find its way onto the tables of the hungry. Every government official (or consultant) that writes this nonsense goes into a supermarket on a regular basis to buy their food – they do not sit at home waiting for it to appear on their tables, spirited in from some farm. And yet they seem to be under the impression that poor people live in some kind of parallel food universe, where this is exactly what happens.

Nowhere is this fanciful (and imaginary) version of the lived reality of the hungry more clearly illustrated than in our official food-security policy – the 2014 *National Policy on Food and Nutrition Security*, a joint collaboration of the Department of Social Development and DAFF (with the latter being the lead department).

This policy document is only 19 pages long, which does not seem to be a particularly serious response to what is clearly a serious problem. According to this document, South Africa's food-security challenges are the following:[54]

- There are inadequate safety nets and food emergency management systems to provide for all those who are unable to meet their immediate food needs or to mitigate the impact of natural and non-natural disasters on food security.
- Citizens have inadequate access to knowledge and resources to make optimum choices for nutritious and safe diets.
- In cases where productive land is available, it is not always optimally utilized for food production.
- There is limited access to processing facilities or markets for small-scale primary producers.
- Climate change and altered patterns of land use pose a threat to domestic production.
- There is not adequate, timely and relevant information on food security.

You may now be thinking that you have been unlucky enough to have bought a copy of this book with a page missing. Surely this cannot be the whole thing? What about how much food costs, or that we already produce enough food for everyone, or the disgusting reworked and brined chicken that the poor are forced to buy, or the fact that farmworkers are starving, or that farmers are going out of business, not because of climate change but precisely *because* they have access to markets, or that we already produce enough food for everyone (it is worth repeating), or any of the other key things that actually determine who eats what and who gets to make a living from farming? None of these things feature in the version of reality that forms the basis of official policy to address food security, malnutrition and rural poverty in this country. Neither does the food retail sector, despite the fact that this is how almost every single South African accesses the bulk of their food. Where the policy talks about 'markets' it is entirely with the aim of integrating more small farmers into the existing market structure, rather than questioning the very foundations of this market structure.

It gets worse: the strategic goal of the policy is listed as, 'to ensure the availability, accessibility and affordability of safe and nutritious food at national and household levels'. There is nothing wrong with this, except that the fact that many people cannot access affordable nutritious food was not listed as one of the country's food-security challenges. You may now think that I am being pedantic – after all, surely it was implied? Well, that is the point. Simply implying that the problem is access to affordable nutritious food, rather than clearly specifying that this is *the* challenge that needs to be addressed, is exactly why we have ended up with a policy that does not directly address the issues of access to affordable quality food. Instead it addresses all the things that are *assumed* to impact on access to affordable food. This means that policy efforts are focused on the *assumed drivers of hunger, not the actual drivers.*

Think about it for a few minutes: if you want to fix a particular problem, you need to do so directly, not indirectly. If our food-security challenge were to be phrased as being '*households cannot access affordable nutritious food*', policy-makers would have to go out and think about *why*, exactly, food is neither affordable nor nutritious, and then make policy recommendations *directly* linked to addressing this problem. Instead, because this thinking has never taken place, we have a policy that focuses on all sorts of other things, like:[55]

- The availability of **improved nutritional safety nets**, including government-run and -supported nutrition and feeding programmes, emergency food relief, as well as private-sector, CBO and NGO interventions.
- Improved **nutrition education**, including district level nutrition services to assist households and communities monitoring nutritional indices, providing consumer literacy and assisting with better food management and improved meal planning.
- The alignment of **investment in agriculture** towards local economic development, particularly in rural areas. This includes the provision or subsidisation of inputs and support services for increased food production, as well as more effective food storage and distribution networks, involving government and private agencies, to eliminate waste and ensure better access to food for all.
- Improved **market participation** of the emerging agricultural sector through public–private partnerships, including off-take and other agreements, a government food purchase programme that supports smallholder farmers, as well as through the implementation of the Agri-BEE Charter, which requires agro-processing industries to

broaden their supply bases to include the emerging agricultural sector.
- Food and Nutrition Security **Risk Management**, including increased investment in research and technology, to respond to the production challenges currently facing the country, such as climate change and bio-energy. It would also include the protection of prime agricultural land.

These five 'pillars' make up the policy – all of it. None of these things has actually got much to do with consistently getting affordable nutritious food on the tables in poor households, but this is what happens when you substitute assumptions for empirical analysis.

This version of reality has not gone uncontested, but the drafters of this policy have not paid much attention to those who would propose a different view (or, indeed, to anyone outside of the two departments who prepared it). The policy was drafted with hardly any consultation with either hungry people or civil-society organisations working in the area of food security or, indeed, the average citizen. We should see this as something more serious than a mere oversight: every single one of us is a participant in our agri-food system and every one of us will feel the impact if things continue as they are. The least we might expect is for someone to ask us our opinion on how they are planning to fix things.

In 2015, the year after the policy was gazetted and thus became 'official', a relatively small number of organisations (mostly NGOs in the field of food security or food rights such as Oxfam and Section 27) were invited to a 'consultation session' on the *National Food and Nutrition Security Policy Draft Implementation Plan*. Almost all of them objected on the basis that they did not want to be invited to consult on the *implementation plan* of the policy, but rather on the contents of the policy itself. They also pointed out that it was insufficient 'consultation' to simply invite a few NGOs to a presentation. What about the hungry themselves? Surely they were entitled to make input into a policy that would have a major impact on their food-security status. A petition to this effect was drafted and submitted to the DAFF, to little effect.

The DAFF was polite, but firm. The contents of the policy itself were not up for discussion, but they would welcome our input at their consultation session on the implementation plan, which was held in September 2015. In preparation for the session, a formal submission was drafted by a number of these civil-society organisations. This submission listed the main concerns about the contents of the policy, as well as the manner in which it had been developed. I am pretty sure no one read it.

I attended that consultation session, and it was a deeply frustrating experience. The officials from the DAFF who presented the implementation plan were all extremely welcoming and clearly believed that their policy was going to make an important contribution towards addressing a serious problem. We watched a number of presentations on all the ways in which the DAFF was going to increase the productivity of farmers (particularly small farmers) – access to the best seeds and fertilisers, tractors and training in farming skills. Food production would increase as a result, and the problem of food security would be solved. Rural poverty would also be addressed because small farmers would be able to sell their produce to food processors and supermarkets.

Members of the audience stood up and spoke about the role of supermarket power in making food unaffordable, and the fact that focusing on own food production as a means of addressing food insecurity is essentially meaningless for the hungry that live in cities. Nazeer Sonday was there (you might remember him as the disillusioned farmer we met in Chapter 1) and he recounted his own unpleasant experiences with having 'market access' to big supermarkets. Others also told stories of market power that had put small farmers out of business, and the growing margin between the farm-gate price of food and the retail price of food, and everyone suggested that the DAFF was looking in the wrong place for answers. The response from government officials was polite, but disbelieving. It was clear that they neither followed the version of reality that we were proposing, nor did they believe it. Despite ongoing efforts from some of the organisations to get amendments to the policy to reflect the real world of hunger in South Africa, no changes have been made. Nor have officials demonstrated the slightest interest in even discussing a different point of view.

It is not entirely clear why this policy – which so many people believe has missed the point – is so strongly held onto by the DAFF, but I have some ideas on the subject. Let me start by saying that almost all the officials in the Directorate of Food Security with whom I have engaged are deeply concerned about the issue of food security, and clearly believe that this is an unacceptable state of affairs in a country as wealthy (and which produces as much food) as South Africa. So their inability to see the big picture is not the result of not caring about the poor, neither is it one of indifference to hunger. Instead, it is the result of how government 'officially' sees the problem, and thus how they have structured the various state institutions mandated to address it. By the very act of allocating the responsibility for food-security policy (or at least most of it) to the Department of *Agriculture*, the underlying assumption is that this is an *agricultural* problem. This is compounded by the fact that many of the people who work in the Food Security Directorate are agronomists – their skills and training are focused on problems of agricultural production (which are exactly the skills that this department wants). And so we should not be surprised that their policies are focused on agricultural production. The DAFF has no authority over food retailers and thus the department operates largely as if these do not exist. Officials from the Food Security Directorate will not produce a food-security policy that centralises (or even problematises) the role of food retailing in household hunger because food retailing is not their job – agricultural production is. I believe there is a good chance that if they put together a food-security policy that did *not* focus on agricultural production, their superiors would reject it.

If this were just a case of poorly conceived policy and some wasted resources, we might be inclined to be a bit cross and complain about a poorly structured government department and inefficient programmes. But there is much more at stake here and it deserves our righteous anger. Somewhere along the road (roughly corresponding to government's increasing affection for neo-liberal economic policies) the line between agricultural production and hunger has become so blurred (distorted) that a new kind of 'logic' started to appear in official food-security policy documents. It goes something like this:

> Hungry people are hungry because they do not have enough food.
> They do not have enough food because they do not have enough money to buy food.
> They could produce their own food in their back yards.
> If they grew their own food, they would not be hungry.
> Hungry people are hungry because they do not grow their own food.

You might think that is a pretty big stretch in an argument, but this thinking – that the hungry are somehow responsible for fixing their own hunger by producing their own food – is now the standard in most food-security policies. It is not just the national policy that prioritises the growing of food – although this is where most of its efforts are located – but it is also the main component of provincial and local policies. Gauteng's 2011 food-security policy (*Gauteng 20 Year Food Security Plan*) takes this thinking about the links between hunger and food production even further. The first line of this document is as follows: 'Food insecurity is caused by inadequate access to enough food (due to inadequate household production, insufficient income and weak purchasing power) to meet individual dietary requirements for an active and healthy life.'[56] In other words, not producing enough food is now not merely *a* factor causing food insecurity, it has become *the* most important factor causing food security.

The idea that the hungry can produce enough to make themselves food secure is also a popular one among many South Africans: I cannot recall how often in a conversation about food security and hunger, someone has said something along the lines of, 'Why don't people have vegetable gardens? If there were more food gardens the problem would be solved.' No, it would not – and here is why:

- It is impossible to meet a family's dietary requirements from what can be grown in a small backyard, which is the most common available option (when there is any land at all available). The gaps in nutrition and household food requirements are also around quality protein – like dairy products – and fruit, not only vegetables, although I do not dispute that all South Africans could benefit from eating more fresh vegetables. On a fairly regular basis, someone (not a hungry person) tells me, 'did you know that you can feed an entire family of four from a vegetable garden on a piece of land the size of a door?' No you cannot – and if you do not believe me, why don't you try it for yourself: dig up a piece of your garden, the size of a door, plant it with vegetables and see how well you do feeding your family from that and only that. I look forward to hearing how it went – feel free to email me.
- There is a limited growing season in many parts of the country: the Free State, where there are tens of thousands of hungry families, experiences long, cold winters during which most things will not grow. What are people supposed to eat during these periods?
- Water is an enormous constraint. Many poor people receive shoddy basic services, including water (despite the state's constitutional obligation to provide this). In some places the water supply is so sporadic that sometimes the only way that people can water their vegetable gardens is to buy the water from traders. Those who

cannot afford to do so must simply watch the plants die. In many informal settlements, people have to access water from a communal tap, often several hundred metres from their home. People who do have regular access to a municipal water supply in their yard must pay for it. In a hot summer, the cost of paying for water for a vegetable garden can be considerable for a very poor household. And it is money that they have to find for several months before they can harvest anything from their gardens.

• Vegetable gardening is hard work, which requires calories. Once again, if you have been a proponent of this kind of strategy, let me encourage you to try it yourself, replicating all the hard work and effort required to do so by a poor family. Do not forget to carry all the water from a tap situated at least 200 metres from your garden. This is not idle sarcasm: I used to be one of those people who thought that homestead and community gardens were a wonderful idea, until I spent six months working in a community garden. Hard labour is not exactly the best option to address an existing shortage of calories.

• Theft is a constant problem for those who engage in homestead gardening. After all, they are surrounded by hundreds of hungry people.

• The greatest number of hungry South Africans live in urban areas, often in high density, informal settlements where there is no opportunity to grow their own food. And urbanisation is increasing, as people move to the cities in search of work. A policy that focuses on own production as the 'cure' for food insecurity thus effectively ignores millions of people. Given the highly urban nature of Gauteng, it is incomprehensible to me how the provincial government could place own food production at the forefront of their analysis of food security. (And they are not alone – this is the standard approach to food security in cities across the country.)

So the best that we could realistically hope for is that homestead gardens might provide a small, supplementary source of vegetables for a limited period each year, for a relatively small group of hungry families. This is hardly an all-encompassing solution to hunger.

Despite all these factors, all official food-security plans are focused primarily on 'encouraging' people to grow their own food, mostly through supporting the establishment of 'homestead' (that is, backyard) gardens and larger community gardens. These involve thousands of families each year and tens of millions of rand. Government officials that work in food security are set ambitious targets for the establishment of these gardens, which means that they spend a lot of time going around getting people to start food gardens, and handing out free, basic gardening equipment and packets of seeds. Most people start off enthusiastically, but in about 90 per cent of cases, gardening ceases after the first crops are harvested and the free equipment is sold off. (Which is not really seen as a problem because targets are around setting up the gardens, not about how long they stay operational.) Officials to whom I have spoken are at a loss to explain this, apart from general comments such as 'people don't want to work' or, rather less generously, 'they are lazy'. As a general rule, they never ask the people who have abandoned their gardens why they have done so – no one is really interested in their point of view.

This is not to say that people should not receive encouragement and support to grow their own food where they genuinely want to do so – but the 'support' needs to cover a lot more items than a spade and a packet of seeds. (It needs to include things likes guaranteed access to water and storage facilities, so that harvests can be stored, as well as access to suitable markets to earn extra income.) This is what NGOs like Abalimi Bezekhaya[57] and Project Khulisa[58] in Cape Town, and Siyavuna[59] in Durban are doing, but they are doing it in a very particular way, providing the kind of long-term, hands-on support that beneficiaries actually need, including guaranteed access to markets that pay a relatively high price. These are the kinds of initiatives that can really make a difference, and do, thanks to teams of dedicated and knowledgeable staff who are focusing on working *with* people. But this is a very different matter from what has become the official policy: that people have to produce their own food to address their own hunger.

The real problem with this kind of thinking is that when we start to think that hungry people are *responsible* for fixing their own problem (and, of course, that it is 'their' problem to start off with), it is not a very big jump to start *blaming* them for their own predicament. When government officials say that poor families are 'too lazy' to produce their own food, they are also saying that these families' hunger is their own problem to solve, and that they have 'chosen' not to do so. When they indulge in this kind of 'blame-the-victim' thinking, they absolve those who are actually responsible for where we have ended up; and this is how the magic trick is done.

Nutrition policy: The poor are not as ignorant as you think

Policy-makers are well aware of the problems of malnutrition in South Africa. They are mostly well versed in the statistics regarding stunting and poor nutrition outcomes in children, and well aware of the high burden of non-communicable diseases (NCDs) and the implications for the public-health sector as well as individual families. But – as is hopefully becoming clear by now – you need to have an accurate understanding of the actual problem and what is causing it before you have any chance of designing an effective solution. And in nutrition policy, we find as much misdiagnosis as we do around the access to food. Because the *agri-food system* is not considered to be a problem, policy-makers find the reasons for poor nutrition in hungry families and in individual behaviour. After all, there is no other place to look.

So we have another version of the 'blame-the-victim' approach that characterises all of South Africa's food and nutrition policy: the reason why South Africans eat badly, (why they consume too much cheap starch and sugar; why they do not eat a nutritionally balanced diet containing enough dietary diversity; and – most importantly – why they do not make sure that their children eat well) is because they are ignorant about nutrition. They make these choices because they do not know any better. We can see these sentiments reflected in the *National Policy for Food and Nutrition Security*. One of the challenges to achieving food security is listed as: 'Citizens have inadequate access to knowledge and resources to make optimum choices for nutritious and safe diets.' Based on this assessment of the problem, one of the five pillars of this policy is: 'Improved **nutrition education**, including District level nutrition services to assist households and communities monitoring nutritional indices, providing consumer literacy and assisting with better food management and improved meal planning.'

This point of view is shared by many South Africans – I cannot recall how many times someone has said to me (usually in a condescending tone), 'well, it's all about education isn't it? People don't like to eat healthy food; we have to teach them that it is good for them.' These statements always come from the well-fed; people who have never had to decide which meal their children will skip, or whether they should stop their HIV medication so that they can feed their families for another month, or whether they have to beg food from their neighbours. Instead, they see labourers in their local supermarket buying white bread and two-litre bottles of fizzy, high-sugar soft drink for their lunch, and they shake their heads at all this nutritional ignorance.

Of course, the idea that poverty is strongly correlated with ignorance (that the poor are not as bright as the rest of us) is not a South African invention, although you might argue that – combined with the ingrained racism that is part of our history, part of our cultural DNA – we have probably perfected it. Certainly the idea that bad nutritional choices are the result of ignorance has a long and unbroken history in South Africa: Diana Wylie repeatedly quotes official sources from the early part of the 20th century stating that the lack of 'education' among black South Africans was a key factor contributing to their 'own' hunger and malnutrition. It is now time to start examining these assumptions.

The 2013 SANHANES-1 study, which covered 25 000 individuals in 8 168 households, included as part of its survey an assessment of nutritional knowledge. They did this by asking nine questions: four of these dealt with the fibre content of food and three with its fat content; one was about sugar and the last was about fruit. A total score out of nine was allocated: getting 0–3 points classified you as having a low level of nutritional knowledge; 4–6 as medium knowledge and 7–9 as high knowledge. The adults in the survey achieved an average score of 5.26, putting them in the upper level of the medium knowledge score. Only 14.5 per cent of respondents received a 'low knowledge' score.

So why are so many people eating so badly, if most of them have a reasonable knowledge of good nutrition? The simple answer is that they cannot afford to do anything else. The nutritional-knowledge survey indicates that there is not much difference between the nutritional knowledge of poor people and not-so-poor people – less than 1.0 point separates the groups that got the highest scores from those that got the lowest scores, with one exception.[60] But the food intake data from the same survey clearly shows that the poorer you are, the more likely you are to eat a poor diet. You do not need an advanced degree in statistics to be able to work out that the variable in this instance is income, not ignorance. Poor people are not 'choosing' to eat badly, they are being forced to. As the SANHANES-1 survey points out,[61] poor people are usually forced to buy the least expensive foods, and these often tend to be the least healthy. It is impossible to make the 'optimum nutrition choices' that the *National Policy for Food and Nutrition Security* wants you to make if all those choices lie outside of what you can afford.

Let us look at what women (those most likely to do the regular food purchasing in a household) reported to SANHANES-1 as the main factors that influenced their food purchases: 64.5 per cent of them cited the price of the food item as the most important factor. Health considerations, the nutrient content of the food and how long the item can be kept, all scored more or less equally and much lower than price. Given what we know about the gap between how much money households have available to buy food, and the cost of food, this really should not be a surprise. Remember the children who participated in the SANHANES-1 survey? Most of them understand very well the importance of eating breakfast, but this knowledge is not very helpful if there is no food in your house.

It is not out of 'choice' that the poor are buying expired frozen chicken that has been washed with chlorine and injected with a high salt and sugar brine, or because they are too stupid to know that better food is available. They have no other real options if they want to put some kind of protein on the table. Much the same applies to those labourers with their loaves of bread and sugary soft drink, instead of a nice healthy salad and grilled chicken. They need plenty of calories to do their hard job, and the bread and the soft drink represent the best value way of getting these on a small amount of money. Far from ignorance, it is necessity, and careful calculation of very limited options, that has resulted in that purchase.

Put yourself in the position of one of the women in Tembisa that participated in Ishtar Lakhani's research: you use all your ingenuity and social capital to put food on the table and to ensure that your children do not go hungry. You are sometimes forced to go to extreme lengths to do so. You are aware of the fact that you are not making the best nutritional choices, but you are doing the very best that you can under extremely difficult circumstances. Now imagine how you would feel if your and your children's poor nutritional status was ascribed entirely to your 'ignorance' and government officials were focused on teaching you how to remedy your ways, instead of actually helping you. Perhaps you might be forgiven for thinking that not much has changed in the past 50 years.

It is not about the food

So let us get back to the idea that I proposed at the beginning of the chapter: that the way in which you understand the problem determines how you frame the solution. If you have misunderstood the problem, it is highly unlikely that you will produce a good solution. That is, if we understand that the cause of something is X, we will devise and develop policies that are focused on fixing or changing X. But if the problem is actually Y, then all our efforts to fix X are not actually going to change anything. And this is where our National Policy on Food and Nutrition Security and the Gauteng Food Security Policy, and everyone who thinks that the poor can grow their way out of hunger, have gone wrong: the problem is *not* that people do not have sufficient nutritious food.

Let me repeat this: the problem is not that people do not have food; or that they do not have enough food or nutritious food. The food is not the *problem* – it is the *outcome*, the result, the symptom of the problem. The real problem is the system and everything that supports it. The real problem is that we have an agri-food system *specifically designed and managed* to benefit the few at the expense of the many. Marshalling the poor to grow a few vegetables in their back gardens is not going to make any difference to the operation of the system. Berating mothers to feed their children better food, which they cannot afford, is not going to make any difference to the system. Lecturing those with diet-related diseases, such as diabetes, about the importance of eating well is not going to make any difference to the system. It just gives public officials something to do, and comforts the well-fed with the idea that hunger and malnutrition are self-inflicted.

Chapter 5

Charity: Cutting with kindness

Hunger – especially among children – tends to bring out the best in us, to create an urge to 'do something'. And that 'something' encompasses a wide range of charitable activities including thousands of organisations and tens of thousands of South Africans. If you do a quick search on the internet you will be overwhelmed by the number of groups – from the big and high-profile ones like the Nelson Mandela Children's Fund, to the tiny and informal two or three women who are moved to take some action in their own communities – who are doing something in the area of hunger alleviation. And then there are the efforts of government in 'emergency' food relief, such as soup kitchens and food parcels; and the many corporate-supported food initiatives, or FoodBank South Africa.

Most South Africans have made some kind of contribution to some or other hunger-relief programme at least once in their lives, even if it is just to drop a can of food into the collection bin at the local shopping centre. In fact, for many of us, it is through charity – either donating to one, or actively participating in operating one – that we understand the 'problem' of hunger in South Africa, and thus what needs to be done to address it. But what impact is all this good work having? Is it actually making a difference? Do we have reason to believe that more charity and more charitable efforts hold the key to addressing hunger and malnutrition in South Africa? These are important questions, not least because many believe that the answer to this question is 'yes' – that if more of us got together to donate food to those less fortunate than ourselves, we could make a real difference to the lives of tens of thousands of people. It is the reason why I, too, have contributed to 'anti-hunger' charitable programmes.

But I have started to wonder if all this good work – in the form of *charity* (that is, giving gifts, either gifts of food or gifts of support in assisting people to set up food gardens) – is actually doing any good. And after reading Janet Poppendieck's book, *Sweet Charity*[62] (which investigates emergency food aid in the United States), I had more reason to wonder. Poppendieck proposes that emergency food-relief efforts by the private sector (which is what you and I would understand as food charity – soup kitchens, donations of food to hungry households, and food banking, which is very big in the United States) may in fact be making the problem of hunger in that country *worse*, not better. She puts forward a number of reasons for this, including that it gives people the illusion that something is being done, which removes our attention from the real problem and the pressure to *actually* do something; and since it prevents people from starving, government is able to avoid its obligations. The United States and South Africa are two very different places, of course, and the profile and causes of hunger are also very different, as are the charitable responses. But it got me thinking: is food charity a potential cure that we should scale up or could it actually be making things worse?

And it also got me thinking about something else: why are there so many charities focused on addressing hunger (an acknowledgement that we have a problem) but so little anger or activism targeted at the same issue? Where is the angry resistance we might expect, given the food circumstances in which so many families live?

Let us start with the charity. There are literally thousands of private-sector initiatives focused on addressing hunger in South Africa; all of these aim to help those who appear to be most vulnerable. People volunteer at or set up soup kitchens. They donate food in response to calls from community organisations or radio stations. Often these are spur-of-the-moment responses: I spoke to someone in Cape Town who, together with a few others, had set up a soup kitchen for the inhabitants of a nearby informal settlement. He said that their rationale for doing so was because they felt that they could no longer just drive past the settlement every day, see evidence of real hardship and not do anything about it. They collect money from members of their group and prepare a daily meal for about 50 people, and it goes to whoever wants it. His story is far from unique.

On the evening I met him, I had done a presentation at the Philippi Horticultural Area (PHA) Food and Farming Campaign, and I had touched on the issue of food charity, presenting some of Janet Poppendieck's ideas that it might be doing more harm than good. I suggested that food charity by private organisations and individuals might be providing government with a 'get out of jail free' card: if enough private citizens in Cape Town set up soup kitchens and donated food to the poor, the city's management might not have to think too hard about what was, after all, in large part their problem to address. In addition, I said that all this private charity might convince people that the problem was being solved, and thus remove the incentive to fix the underlying reasons why people were hungry.

After the talk, the soup kitchen man came to speak to me and he was visibly worried about what I had said; that there was a possibility that he might be making a problem (about which he cared passionately) worse with his soup kitchen efforts. Should he shut the soup kitchen down? Maybe it was not a good idea if that was the kind of impact it was having.

I realised right away that I had been way too quick with my assessments – of course I did not think that he should close the soup kitchen down; he was the difference between hungry and not hungry for a small group of extremely vulnerable people, about whom no one else seemed to care. And I have exactly the same thoughts about the thousands of people who go out and provide food to those who would otherwise not have it – I certainly do not want them to stop because if they do, some people really will starve. If those children who died in the field in 2011 had had a charitable someone living nearby, that tragedy would probably have been averted.

But at the same time, I still thought – based on what I had seen and experienced, and the people I had spoken to – that not all food charity was 'good'. In addition, I had also come to believe that the vast majority of those engaged in food charity did not have a good understanding of what it was like to stand on the other side of the donation. This forced me to rethink my ideas and to have a critical conversation with myself on the issue. And I believe it is a conversation that we should all be having.

Rights and gifts: The crucial difference

The debate around food charity hinges critically on the conceptualisation of what we *believe* the hungry are entitled to and what they are *actually* entitled to. This is an important distinction, and one that features centrally in Janet Poppendieck's book. This is about the crucial difference between *rights* and *gifts*, the difference between what the hungry are legally entitled to demand and what they receive at the discretion, goodwill and whim of others. I believe that this distinction is vitally important in understanding the impact of food charity in South Africa, because we have arrived so recently at a place where every one of us is entitled to the same rights.

When we begin to substitute people's rights with gifts – or when government starts to act as if their delivery of people's rights are *actually* gifts, which is the same as substitution – we start to create a situation where the recipients begin to believe that they are no longer entitled to insist on their rights. And sometimes the givers of charity might also come to believe that some people are less entitled to demand their rights than others; that they should be *grateful* to accept gifts as substitutes for their rights. When a person who depends on the charity of others tells me matter-of-factly that she knows that 'we don't count', she is reflecting an all-too-common reality. When this sense of who does not count starts to include thousands of hungry families, it does not take much imagination to work out that this represents a huge threat to our ability to build a socially inclusive democracy.

We need to remind ourselves again that there is a *constitutional* right to food in this country: every hungry person is entitled to expect that the government will take whatever steps are necessary (within resource constraints) to fulfil that right. It is vitally important that we (all of us – the hungry and the well-fed) do not lose sight of this. Food charity needs to be seen as an *interim* measure, something that we do while we are actively working to realise the right to food. We cannot let people go hungry in the here and now while we can do something about it, but there is something more important that we should be doing *at the same time*. And this is working to change the system that has created the problem of hunger in the first place.

Unfortunately, this simultaneous pursuit of goals is generally not what happens: people focus on providing the food and forget about (or never think about) the problem – why these people need food charity in the first place. They believe that food is the problem, when it is not the real problem. It is the symptom that we need to address to keep people alive, but it is not the problem. And this is the first thing that is wrong (or can be wrong) with food charity, particularly the kind that focuses on the direct distribution of food. It contributes to the idea that the problem is the food, and that when we supply food we have solved the problem. So people volunteer in a soup kitchen and convince themselves that they are solving the problem. And of course, *this* merely perpetuates the problem.

When the charity in question is supporting people to grow their own food, the line between contributing to the problem and addressing the problem becomes even more difficult to draw. There are a large number of charities that focus on getting people to start food gardens as a way of addressing their hunger. Where these are a response to a genuine community-driven initiative, they can be a very useful intervention (like Khulisa Streetscape's garden for the homeless in Cape Town). Community garden projects can contribute to social cohesion, provide a sense of purpose for people who otherwise have no occupation, and provide a supplementary source of food or (even better) a little extra income. But sometimes (much of the time) the initiative is presented as some kind of 'cure' for hunger in a community (which it is not). The language that often accompanies these projects includes phrases like 'helping people to help themselves' or (my personal favourite) 'teach a man to fish instead of giving him a fish'. These kinds of initiatives tend to appeal to people who believe that poor people should not be given 'handouts'. The stumbling block here, of course, is that these kinds of discourses start to steer very close to those that imply that hunger is a problem that the hungry have to solve themselves. There is no talk of rights and entitlements here, simply obligations to solve a problem that is not of your own making. Rights often *come with* obligations, but cannot be *replaced with* obligations.

And when the language of the charitable organisation starts to shift over to the kind of 'blame the victim' discourse, which has become so popular in government policy, we have a clear case of making the problem worse, not better. This is often the case when the food garden intervention fails (usually because it was the donor who really wanted the project, not the recipients), and the disgruntled givers start to complain about 'lazy' and 'ungrateful' recipients who have chosen to go hungry.

This is not – let me emphasise again – to say that we should abandon soup kitchens and similar food programmes; they fill a vital role and many people's nutritional status would be better if we had more of them. But it is important that we do not lose sight of the bigger picture: that it is as important to change our food system tomorrow as it is to put food on the table today. This means that everybody who volunteers in a soup kitchen or helps someone to establish a vegetable garden should be clear that this is a short-term solution (and sometimes not a particularly good one). If you really want to make a difference, you need to be working to change the system.

When the soup kitchen or food garden in question is being run by a government entity – such as the City of Cape Town – the line between good and bad charity becomes a much more serious issue. As we have discussed, one of the key factors supporting the food system that keeps people hungry is government policy: both that which focuses directly on the food system and that which frames broader issues of development, such as land use or food retail development. We have seen how the City of Cape Town is determined to undermine even the *possibility* of community-based food solutions through their plans to turn much of the PHA into a middle-class enclave, and their condonation of the large-scale degradation of the area.

If you live in Johannesburg, you will be familiar with the regular round up of informal traders (including large numbers of food traders) by the Johannesburg Metro Police Department (JMPD). These traders are sometimes assaulted by JMPD officers and often have their goods (which are most of their worldly assets) either officially confiscated or simply stolen by these officers. Mostly, these traders' only offence is that they do not fit into the city's vision of itself as a shiny modern 'world-class' space. These people – deprived of both their *right* to make a living and their *rights* to the public space in which they usually trade – are then sometimes forced to become the recipients of their city's food 'gifts'.

All of these actions – from spatial policy and land-use frameworks to the bullying of street traders – often mean that the government is, in large part, *responsible* for people's hunger. That they now wish to paint themselves as the cure is distasteful at best. When this largesse, such as the food parcels that are often conveniently distributed at election time, is portrayed as evidence of the government's generosity (instead of what it actually is – an extremely dismal response to their constitutional *obligations*), a description stronger than 'distasteful' is called for. We need to be quite clear that government should not be allowed to get away with portraying itself as the good guy, when it is anything but.

And then there is the third group of givers for whom we should reserve a very special place in our differentiation between good and bad charity, and these are the food corporates: the processors, manufacturers and food retailers whose business practices are perpetuating rural poverty and making food unaffordable for most South Africans. All of them have ambitious corporate social investment (CSI) initiatives, and many of these are directly related to food. If you read the websites and annual reports of these corporations, you might be forgiven for thinking how very generous they are towards the hungry and how grateful the hungry should be for their largesse. Until you recall why the hungry are hungry in the first place.

Remember Pioneer Foods? They were one of the companies implicated in the bread price-fixing scandal of 2006. They were eventually fined R195 million by the Competition Commission a few years later. This represented 10 per cent of the 2006 turnover of their bread-baking division, Sasko. In 2015, the revenue of Pioneer Food's baking and milling division was R9.3 *billion*[63] (with bread being a key contributor). Given this background, we might be a little underwhelmed to read the following on their website in terms of their CSI Programme:

> Because food security remains a major concern in South Africa, the Group channels its corporate social investment towards addressing societal underdevelopment that leads to hunger and poverty.

We could say something here about how bread price fixing also leads to hunger, but we will not. And what is the extent of Pioneer Food's 'concern' in this regard? Not much …

> We are involved in a variety of community projects focusing on education, conservation and food security. To date, Pioneer Foods has distributed almost R11 million to beneficiaries. These projects, which focus on vulnerable groups such as women and children, receive 90% of the funds distributed by the Group. The remaining 10% is allocated to feeding schemes.

If mathematics is not your strong point, this would make the contribution to the feeding schemes just over R1 million.

Tiger Brands was the second company implicated in the bread price-fixing scandal, and it is the biggest of the lot, with an annual group turnover of just under R32 billion.[64] Domestic milling and baking made up just over R8 billion of this total, thus contributing about a quarter to group revenue. Their CSI policy is to contribute 1 per cent of net operating profits (after tax) to 'community' development (although in the 2014/15 year, this figure was about 3 per cent of after-tax profits). They also have a strong focus on addressing food insecurity, with most of the efforts in this regard being the distribution of food parcels (made up, possibly, in large part of the Tiger Brands products that these people cannot afford to buy).

The third party to the bread price-fixing shenanigans – Premier Foods – is not a listed company so there is less publicly available information about the company in general, including their CSI programmes. However, I did find the following on their website:

Through our CSI initiatives we are able to distribute food to people in need such as:

• Meals on Wheels which feeds 1200 people every day
• Aerobeng Hospice which feeds 300 people every day
• Backhome Foundation which feeds 190 people every day
• Akani Diepsloot Foundation which feeds 1410 children every day
• Vosloorus old-age home which feeds 289 people every day.

They do not disclose what their contribution to each of these charities is, but even if it is considerable, it does not seem much for a company that, in the latest year, produced 500 million loaves of bread and milled 600 000 tons of maize meal, and thus has a very significant impact on whether or not people can afford basic food items.

Remember Supreme Poultry? The company with the reworked, chlorine-washed, brine-injected chicken destined for poor consumers? Their holding company is Country Bird Holdings: when I looked on their website, the most recent annual report available was for 2013. You would be delighted to know that the company does engage in charitable efforts around community development, and that they describe them (without a trace of irony) as follows: 'The company's CSI activities are carried out under the 'Love Chicken' umbrella.' The same report lists Supreme Poultry as having donated chicken to a number of child-welfare projects … yummy!

The supermarkets tend to have much bigger and more comprehensive CSI programmes focused on food than most of the processors. This may be because they are more generous, or may be because they need to do more of this kind of 'business has a heart' marketing to their customers, with whom they are in direct contact (unlike the food processors). Or it may be that they need to deflect more attention from criticism that they are to 'blame' for the rising unaffordability of food. Certainly, supermarkets seem to feel some kind of pressure to show that they are doing something to address food insecurity, particularly right now, when the pressures of the recent drought are being felt throughout the food sector.

Shoprite is the biggest food retailer in South Africa. Here is what they do:

> As a food retailer, we aim to support in [sic] hunger relief efforts by reaching out to the neediest communities in the country in various ways. We share in FoodBank South Africa's vision – a South Africa without hunger – and actively fight hunger on a daily basis through our fleet of mobile soup kitchens, food garden projects, partnerships with sustainable community projects as well as a focussed [sic] effort to rescue food fit for human consumption before it goes to waste.

They are not the only food retailer to contribute to FoodBank South Africa, which collects food that is either past its sell-by date but not yet at its expiry date, or which for whatever other reason cannot be sold, such as damaged packaging. (A Checkers near to where I lived in Johannesburg also used to distribute past sell-by date food every day after closing to a group of people who would wait in the street behind the store – a kind of 'direct food bank'.) FoodBank then distributes this food to a number of not-for-profit organisations that are involved in direct food support for the hungry. According to their website, they distribute more than three tons of food to 550 organisations annually, and thus provide a little over 11 million meals a year. It is impressive stuff.

Food banks are growing in many countries and appeal to a large number of people because they appear to be addressing two important issues: hunger and food waste. Food waste is an important consideration for many of us, and for good reason. Estimates of waste in our food system vary, but some suggest that we are wasting up to 30 per cent of all the food that is produced, at various points in the supply chain from farms to our kitchens. Most people would agree that the food bank idea is a good one, and it certainly benefits many people. But it is important to remember that donations to FoodBank South Africa are also beneficial to food retailers: if the food did not go there, it would have to be dumped, and this carries a cost. So contributing to a food bank allows a food retailer to get kudos for being a good corporate citizen in a very cost-effective manner.

Once again – don't get me wrong: I do not believe that food corporates should make fewer charitable contributions to the hungry. On the contrary, given how much value they have extracted, they should be giving a great deal more. But I do think that they should be giving it in a way that will actually make a meaningful contribution to addressing the underlying issues, such as a campaign to significantly improve the lives of farmworkers, rather than finding a place to send food they might have dumped anyway. Much of the current corporate charity seems to me to represent a better deal for the company that is giving than for the recipients. And I also think that none of us should lose sight of the comparative value of this 'charity' against what they have gained from the way in which our food system is structured.

Despite all the talk of the 'triple bottom line', and being responsible corporate citizens, and the hundred variations on this theme, the real bottom line is that food corporates will *never* take a significant cut in profits to benefit the hungry. Supermarkets allocate more time and effort to nut allergies (important for their customers) than they do to the plight of farmworkers (not important for their customers). I had a conversation with Justin Smith, Sustainability Manager at Woolworths, about this: he said that Woolworths makes sure that all their suppliers comply with labour legislation, including the minimum wage for farmworkers. When I said that farmworkers could not feed their families on that minimum wage, he said that was this not the fault of Woolworths – they had not set the minimum wage. The vast majority of farmworkers could see a significant improvement in their living conditions and food security if food processors and supermarkets were prepared to take a cut in revenue of around 2 per cent, on a limited number of items that they sold.[65] None of them, of course, would be prepared to do so and, in all honesty, we should not expect them to. The real issue, of course, is that the business of corporates is *not* charity – it is to maximise value for shareholders (and often the senior management team as well). When Justin Smith says that the level of the legislated minimum wage for farmworkers is not the direct fault of Woolworths, we might not like the sentiment being expressed, but he is absolutely correct. We should not, therefore, be naïve enough to expect that these businesses sacrifice profits for the greater good in the normal course of their operations; that is not their job. But it also means that we should not be fooled into thinking otherwise. It is not possible to be both implicated in the problem and part of the solution, and we need to stop believing that it is.

'Charity wounds him who receives'[66]

There is another point about soup kitchens and direct food aid (such as food parcels and donations from a food bank) that we need to talk about, but it will be an uncomfortable subject, since it requires many of us to take a long, hard look at ourselves and how we think about the recipients of our or others' charity. It is also closely linked to the issue of rights versus gifts, and thus to the issue of who we believe is entitled to rights, and who is not.

Anthropology is a discipline that has focused much attention on the theory of the gift, and my own work in community food projects has sharpened my attention to the subject. Gifts are intricately tied up with the idea of *reciprocity* – that there is a set of mutual obligations that underpins the giving and the receiving of gifts among certain kinds of people. Gifts are seldom given or received within these groups without at least some of this reciprocity being implied. You may think that this is not true – that you have always given gifts without any thought that the recipient should or would return the favour. Or have you? Do you not get annoyed with that one relative that always arrives at the family Christmas celebration but never, ever brings a gift for anyone, although they get plenty, and they could afford to make an effort? Or that friend who never gives you a birthday gift even though you *always* get her one? Or the person who always comes to dinner at your house with not so much as a box of chocolates? Your annoyance is not an indication that you are a mean-spirited person, rather it is an acknowledgement of the deeply ingrained sense of reciprocity that we have around gift giving – that we need to both give *and* receive in order to maintain this. Reciprocity is deeply aligned with the relative status of giver and receiver, although this is more often implied than spoken out loud. So, traditionally, kings and chiefs would distribute gifts as a symbol of their power; this publicly demonstrated ability to give more than their subjects were able functioned to symbolise the fact that they *were* more.

When the 'gift' in question is something more than a box of chocolates or soap-on-a-rope, reciprocity becomes even more important. If you have been forced through circumstances to borrow a fairly large sum of money from a friend or a relative, there is a good chance that you may feel awkward about the issue; maybe even a little uncomfortable in their presence. You might be more likely to offer them favours such as babysitting their children. This could even place a strain on your relationship until you are able to pay them back. The discomfort that you feel is your sense of obligation – they have given you a gift, but you have been unable to reciprocate (until you pay the money back of course).

Now imagine how you would feel if it turned out that you could never pay them back: every day you would have to see them and be reminded of the one-way gift system. It would not matter if they were very kind to you about it (in fact, this might make it even worse). You would always have this sense that you 'owe' them and this is the basis of an unequal relationship: you might be unhappy that they drop their children off every second day for you to look after, but you are not really in a position to complain – after all, they gave you the money and you are obligated to them. This is what happens when you get a 'free' gift – you find out that it is not actually free.

It is this unequal relationship that generally characterises food charity: the recipients of the food from the food bank or the bowl of food at the soup kitchen are the recipients of gifts that they can never really repay; they are in a permanent state of obligation. Now you might be a person who is involved in food charity and you might be thinking, 'hang on, that is ridiculous; I do not expect anything back from the people I am helping – I just want to do some good'. Generally this is true: the people who are giving the food usually would not dream of expecting something in return from those who come to the soup kitchen. And this is exactly the problem. You do not expect something back from them (as you might expect something back from your sister if you kept lending her your car) because they are not in a reciprocal relationship with you. By the very fact that you genuinely do not expect anything back from them, you have judged them as being *less* than you; as not being on an equal footing with you. No matter how good your intentions, you are still a little like the king handing out gifts to his subjects as a reminder that he is more powerful than they are. The saying 'it is better to give than to receive' was never more true.

And let us forget about the giver for a second, and turn our attention to those who are waiting in line at the soup kitchen – the receivers – and think about how *they* feel. Being in a position where you are dependent on handouts of food to survive is a deeply humiliating experience. Having to stand in a line at a soup kitchen, or accept food parcels is a public acknowledgement that you have no friends to borrow food from, no one to help you; that you are officially at the bottom of the humanity pile. Lakhani touched on this issue in her research in Tembisa: in the assessment of the people she spoke to, going to a soup kitchen was considered to be much the same as begging, and is 'deeply stigmatised'.[67] It was considered as the very last resort for people who were genuinely in fear of starvation. (To put this in context, please remember that occasionally trading sex for food was generally *not* sitgmatised.) So the people standing in front of you at the soup kitchen are not there for the convenience of a free meal – they are so desperate that they are willing to publicly humiliate themselves.

In one of the community gardens where I worked some years ago, the three gardeners were constantly short of labour to keep up with the work. As they were surrounded by a large number of very poor and unemployed people (an informal settlement ran along two sides of the garden), I was under the impression that they would be able to get people to work in the garden in return for food (they could not really afford to pay wages). Absolutely not: people were prepared to work in the garden for a pittance (about R30 a day at the time), but not for food, even if it was of greater value than the money. Working for a wage – even a low one – carries the dignity of a job; working for food is a public admittance that you are desperate.

The fact that we do not always acknowledge that even the poorest people have this sense of self, this sense of dignity, in exactly the same way that we do, says something not very flattering about how we think about these people: that when you are very poor, you somehow cease to be a complete person; that you give up the right to be the same kind of person as the rest of us. The reality is that when you are extremely poor, sometimes your sense of dignity is all you have left, and you cling to it as hard as you can. Even the best-intentioned giver of food charity often fails to see this.

The deep sense of humiliation that comes with having to accept food charity is often invisible to the well-meaning givers. A recent example was a programme at a South African university to give poor students access to free meals in the campus canteen. This was a response to the realisation that many students could not afford to eat properly. There was no problem with the idea, however the programme required students to 'prove' that they could not afford to eat and then they were given a special card that they could use to get free meals. This meant that every time they went to the canteen, everyone around them could identify them as being so poor that they needed subsidised food. The take up of the benefit was very low, and I am sure that the university administrators could not work out why.

Excluding people from the monetary economy is a way to exclude them from society, to highlight that they are *different* from us. Recipients of social grants generally do not feel that they are receiving charity, and nor should they, given the rights that they have in terms of the Constitution. When they are standing in the queue at the supermarket, there is no way to mark them out as 'poor' – their money looks the same as everyone else's. But if the grant system were replaced with food parcels, I am sure that there would be strong opposition, since this would now be seen as 'charity', clearly marking out grant recipients. Losing access to money means losing access to choice and the ability to participate in the economy on an equal footing with everyone else.

When I raise these issues many people respond with some kind of variation along the lines of 'beggars cannot be choosers' or 'something is better than nothing.' They are sceptical that people would go hungry rather than avoid the public indignity of having to take charity food; that someone's sense of dignity can outweigh 'common sense'. But often people who express these opinions will get themselves into debt, borrow money that they cannot really afford so that their children can go on expensive school trips or have the latest gadget, so that they do not stand out as poorer than their friends. Why do they believe that they have some kind of monopoly on human dignity? The reason, of course, is that we often believe that the very poor – those who are reliant on food charity – are *actually* different from us, that they are in this position because they are not as educated as we are or not as hard working, or just simply not like us.

And then, of course, there are the givers who insist that the recipients of their largesse be suitably 'grateful' – after all, we are doing something 'for them'. This is the group who would have frowned at my jibe at Supreme Poultry's gift of chicken (probably reworked and brined) to a children's home. They genuinely believe that poor people do not have the right to refuse food that is bad for their health or that they themselves would never dream of eating. These are the people who are very reluctant to endorse any intervention that would focus on cash transfers to the poor – which they could then use to shop for food like everyone else and avoid the stigma of the soup kitchen – on the basis that 'one never knows what they will spend it on'. These people tend to be proponents of the 'feed your family on the garden the size of the door' theory.

Very often, they will arrive in a poor community ready to tell the people there exactly what their problem is and how they (the givers) are there to fix it – like a nutrition-education programme to teach mothers how to feed their children. They seldom have an interest in the real lives of the people they are aiming to 'help' or their ideas about what the problem really is. They tend to equate poverty with stupidity.

When the people doing all the talking are white and well-fed, and the people doing all the listening are black and hungry* – as is so often the case – food charity is definitely doing much more harm than good. It entrenches our inequalities, and poor black people are forced into believing that they are somehow fundamentally inferior to their fellow citizens.

When somebody tells me (as someone did in a business school forum) that a person should be grateful to work for a loaf of bread 'because at least it is better than nothing', what they are implying is that the person is actually entitled to nothing – so everything above 'nothing' should be cause for celebration. When the person in question is actually entitled to a range of constitutionally guaranteed socio-economic rights, then what is also being said is that this person is not our equal. And that is the outcome of our food system that should concern us the most – the entrenchment and the normalisation of the idea that some people count less and have fewer rights than others; that they are fundamentally *less*.

Nigel Gibson is an academic who has written persuasively that the real struggle for freedom in South Africa is not about material possessions but about being an *equal person*.[68] We need to remember that the people who are the recipients of food charity are our fellow citizens – they have *rights* to food; they should not have to depend on gifts and the whims of strangers in order to be able to eat every day and to feed their families. If we forget this, we are in serious danger of undermining our very society and all that we should be aiming for – we cannot build a nation like this.

Consumer activism: Why are we not angry?

I have suggested that we need to be as concerned with activism around changing the system as we are with (good) charity. But – in sharp contrast

---

* And, of course, the initial version of this phrase is from Steve Biko.

to the thousands of charitable efforts all around the country – there is hardly any food activism around changing the system. And that brings us to the final question in the 'what are we doing about the problem?' chapter. I recently had a conversation with a PhD student who wants to do his doctorate on resistance to the dominant food system that I have described in this book. But he had a serious problem – he could not find any. Although he could identify a number of NGOs that are active in the field (he was himself a member of one), he felt that he could not find enough examples of citizens organising resistance and building alternatives to the food system to be able to write a thesis on the subject.

What exactly is going on? South Africans are not shy about venting their frustration about perceived injustices – public protest (often on a massive scale) is second nature to many of us. These protests are occasionally violent, involving the burning of public buildings, local government councillors' houses, buses and private property. As the statistics I have quoted repeatedly show, there is a real problem with hunger and malnutrition in this country, and the majority of families cannot afford sufficient nutritious food. Against this is the general knowledge that South Africa is not a poor country, and there is plenty of food in plain sight. All around the world, circumstances like this would have resulted in mass marches, online petitions, and hundreds of communities taking action to bypass the system and create meaningful alternatives for themselves. I am by no means advocating any kind of violent protest, but you have to admit, the silence on the subject is deafening.

And we do have a history of consumer resistance: in the 1980s, consumer boycotts (largely by black consumers of products from white-owned businesses) were used to considerable effect as part of the domestic resistance to apartheid; although it has to be said that the demands of the boycotters were around political issues rather than the price of the goods in the stores. A big part of the international anti-apartheid campaign was a boycott of South African agricultural produce. Many big food retailers in the United Kingdom, for example, stopped stocking South African fruit in response to the demands from their customers. So we know from our own history that consumer action can have an important impact on what happens in food markets, *if* we want things to change.

People are angry about the delivery of the public-housing programmes, about the poor state of the delivery of basic services such as water and electricity. Sometimes they are fed up about bad service in state hospitals, or the long distances that children must walk to school, or the cost of public transport, or even because of the decision of the demarcation board to change the boundaries of their local municipalities.[69] Much of the time they are venting their frustration with their general state of poverty, mostly expressed as demands for jobs (for the unemployed) or higher wages (for the employed). But the protests are never specifically about food prices. Even the farmworkers in the 2012 strike, who were certainly very angry about their poverty and their working conditions, never make the explicit point that there was a problem with the determination of food prices. None of the large labour federations (traditionally the site of food-price opposition) have ever taken up a long-term and concerted campaign around the accessibility of food (as opposed to wage increases to be able to afford food).

In May 2016, there was a fairly substantial march organised by the Food Sovereignty Campaign in Johannesburg to protest the increasing price of bread. Much of the focus of the march was on allegations of price fixing and 'profiteering' in the bread industry, with reference to the case in front of the Competition Commission in 2006. The former COSATU[70] General-Secretary, Zwelinzima Vavi, made a speech in which he talked about how consumers and farmers were being 'squeezed' by market intermediaries. But these events are the exception rather than the norm. Most importantly, we do not see protests organised by the hungry – in their communities – on the scale of other protest action. Even as I am writing this book – during a period of hotly contested local government elections – food is not front-page news. So let us ask again – what is going on?

I cannot propose a definitive answer – after all, I have not spoken to every person who has decided to burn down a government building because she is fed up with the state of basic service delivery in her community and asked her why she does not feel as strongly about her food. But I would like to propose some ideas on the subject.

The first point is that people often organise protests about unemployment and/or wages. There is much discontent about 'poverty'. The official discourse (and one repeated by many South Africans) is that it is low incomes that are the reason for the unaffordability of food, rather than the cost of the food or the food system per se. And so we should not be surprised that the average South African sees things in the same way; that the problem is their income (or lack thereof) rather than the actual price of food.

A similar argument can be applied to the lack of protest around the failure of land reform as a result of the hostile markets in which new farmers find themselves. Voices are raised about the fact that people want land, but very little is said about wanting the kind of markets that will allow land-reform beneficiaries to make a decent living. I would propose that this is because of the official discourse on the matter, which largely ignores the fact that the terms of market access are critical to the success of these ventures. There is no protest because, in the popular imagination, there is not a problem.

And then there is the point of *why* people protest in the first place: the vast majority will only protest or resist something if they believe it can actually be changed. There is little point in protesting about the sun coming up in the east but there is a very good reason to protest your shoddy water supply – because, presumably, someone can do something about it. Perhaps the humiliation of publicly admitting you are hungry has effectively created a situation where people are not willing to stand up and demand their right to food. Perhaps the blame-the-victim discourse that pervades official discussions on food security and malnutrition has persuaded people that they have no right to demand these rights. The lack of *direct* resistance and protest around our food system seems to suggest that the vast majority of South Africans do not believe that anything can be done to change it, that the system we have is somehow *inevitable* or that there is no real alternative. This is because there is no national dialogue around our food system. If there were, it would show very quickly that *there is nothing inevitable about our agri-food system* at all, and that *there are actually hundreds of alternative approaches*.

You may have noticed that there is a small 'alternative' food movement in South Africa, reflecting trends in many other places, particularly Western Europe and the United States. In fact, you may be a supporter and/or participant in one of them. These alternative food movements tend to be focused on issues related to the environment and concerns about the health implications of much of our 'industrial' food. These movements are – in South Africa at any rate – almost the sole preserve of the wealthy. This alternative food is sold in smart farmers' markets and in the increasing number of organic food shops in the big cities. Take a short trip around the Internet and you will find a number of South African alternative food sites, extolling the virtues of organic and local food. Some of these express a high degree of opposition to the mainstream food system, citing environmental degradation, animal abuse and the serious health implications of the pesticides, herbicides and food additives routinely used in the production of our food. There is nothing wrong with these points – personally I prefer my food organic. But for me the most striking thing about this supposed 'resistance' to mainstream food is what it is *not* upset about. There is no mention of all the social justice implications of our food system, which I have discussed in the last hundred or so pages. Many people are upset about intensive chicken farming and the diet of these chickens (trust me, the details are nasty), but no one in these forums seems irate (or indeed, even to have noticed) that poor people are forced to eat reworked, brined chicken; that *they* have no alternative food options.

I see no reference on any of these websites to the plight of farmworkers. There is much discussion about issues like animal welfare, but nothing about the people who work on these farms. Do not get me wrong – I am a strong supporter of the agendas of organisations like Compassion in World Farming, but where is our anger on behalf of our fellow citizens, who are just as much the victims of our agri-food system? Don't they also count?

This obliviousness to the human impact of our food system (and thus that it is something worthy of our attention) is reflected in the conversation that I had with Gary Jackson, owner of Jackson's Food Market, a relatively new but rapidly growing organic food store in Johannesburg. I asked about the motivations of his customers for buying more expensive, but arguably healthier food. It is quite clear that, for almost all of them, the key motivations are *personal*, rather than communal. That is, people are choosing 'alternative' food because they believe that this 'clean' food is better for their health and that of their children. Some of his customers have indicated environmental concerns as a reason for choosing organic food, but none of them has ever indicated to him a concern about farmworkers or the ability of small farmers to earn a living. Save for the environmental issues, there is no *social* reason for them to want an alternative agri-food system, because they do not believe it is a problem for our society.

Do you remember the hopes for a new agricultural system expressed by the Kassier Committee back in 1992? '[T]hat the individual is a being in his/her own right and should be permitted to follow his/her own will within the limits set by society, rather than a situation where the individual is considered to be part of society.' Well, that certainly seems to have happened – our concerns around our food appear to be almost entirely individual. Most of us do not see that hunger, malnutrition and rural poverty are all fundamentally issues of *social justice* – of who we believe is entitled to rights – not of food.

When I tell people that I am writing a book about food, their first impression is that it is a recipe book. When I say that it is a book about food and social justice, almost every one of them asks, 'but what has food got to do with social justice?' And this, of course, is the main reason why there is no real resistance to the mainstream food system – most of us have no idea of what is at stake. I hope that by now you are beginning to understand that food has everything to do with social justice. And maybe you are also starting to believe that it is time for change.

PART 3

Time for change

If everything that you have read so far has convinced you that we cannot continue as we are, then the next logical question is – what can we do about it? And this is where things become difficult. Much as I would like to be able to say 'we need to do A, B and C, and in that order', in all honesty I cannot. In fact, I believe very strongly that this is one of the reasons why we have not been able to solve all sorts of socio-economic problems: all of us (politicians, the average South African and many of the so-called experts) have a strong preference for simple problem–solution narratives. We do not want to hear 'it is complicated and there are many possible options, and it will probably take a while for things to change'. We want a couple of lines telling us that the problem is this, and the solution is that. I am afraid that you are not going to find that in this book.

That is the bad news. The good news is that the evidence and analysis that I have presented so far actually puts us in a good position to make some informed choices about the kinds of actions and initiatives that are *likely* to generate better outcomes. After all, having a good idea of what is not working – and *why* it is not working – is a pretty good start to building something better. There are also hundreds of examples of successful agri-food systems built on principles of fairness and social justice in South Africa and across the world. We are certainly not the first to grapple with this problem, even if we face an extreme version of it.

I have started this part of the book with a discussion of how we could better understand the problem that we need to change. That is, what is it that is *fundamental* to where we find ourselves, because that understanding is what needs to underpin everything that we do. Thereafter I discuss possibilities based on some truly inspirational initiatives that are currently underway in this country and in others.

The first two parts of this book might have both saddened you and made you angry about the current situation. This part of the book aims to show that real change is really possible, and that we can think about our agri-food system in a very different way. Things definitely do not have to be this way.

Chapter 6

Getting to the heart of the problem: Power, morality and care

I shall start with some theory of change.[71]

Defining the problem

The way in which we understand the problem determines how we frame possible solutions. I know that I have written this before, but it is worth examining in more detail, because the process of 'understanding' the problem is far from simple, as the following examples will hopefully show.

If you understand that the problem is X, and that X is being caused by A and B, you would rationally allocate your efforts to fixing or changing or eradicating A and B. This seems straightforward enough, but there are many factors that could mean that you expend great effort for not much impact. What could go wrong? Well, firstly (and we have touched on this earlier), you might be *mistaken* in thinking that the problem is X. The problem might actually be Y; something altogether different. This happens when we confuse the *symptoms* of a problem with the actual problem. If you then put all your efforts into changing X, you are unlikely to fix the problem, simply because it *is not* the problem.

But let us say that you have been correct in your assessment that the problem is X. However, you may then incorrectly identify what is causing X, or you may identify only some of the factors that are causing

X. In this case you will still have only a limited impact on your problem, because you are not focusing on doing all the right things (or at least most of the right things) that are necessary to bring about change. To make things even more complicated, you may have correctly identified the factors that cause X, but then discover that you have little or no control over them. These are some of the issues that make identifying what needs to be done (and what can be done) so challenging.

How then could we proceed?

As a first step, how might I translate this little bit of theoretical thinking into what I have proposed so far in this book, and build on this? Well, the first thing I have proposed is that the problem is the dominant agri-food *system* rather than the food itself. The food and the issues around the food (that is, who has sufficient food and who does not; who eats well and who does not; who suffers from malnutrition and who does not) are the *outcomes* of the system. We can apply the same thinking to the incomes earned by those who grow our food and those who work on the farms: these outcomes are the result of the system rather than free-standing isolated problems.

Let us assume that you are in agreement – that the system is the problem. This means that we need to focus our efforts on changing the system so that it generates different outcomes – more affordable and nutritious food for more people, better incomes for more farmers and a better deal for farmworkers. And right away we have a problem: at least some of you will be thinking: 'and what about the environment?' or 'and what about animal welfare?' or 'and what about climate change?' or maybe all of these, plus a couple of other things. All of these issues have merit, but that is not what this book is about;[72] this is a book about food and social justice. This means that we are going to focus on social-justice outcomes, which I have defined as more affordable and nutritious food for more people, better incomes for more farmers and a better deal for farmworkers. It is necessary for us to focus on the outcomes that we want to change, if for no other reason than these are the measures that we shall use to decide whether or not we have been successful in our efforts to fix the problem.

So far so good, but the 'system' that we are talking about is very complicated, even if we have narrowed our focus to a limited number of the outcomes that it produces. It is made up of millions of participants, engaging in thousands of complicated transactions among themselves.

I have discussed many ways in which our agri-food system delivers social-justice outcomes that most of us would believe are undesirable, but this is only a snapshot of everything that goes on. Focusing on any of these individual issues (like bread-price fixing or nutrition education) may get us results in terms of *that* particular issue, but it probably will not do much to change the overall agri-food system.

It is important to guard against the temptation of these 'small picture' solutions. It is a natural tendency for humans to be overwhelmed by large and complicated problems and to prefer to focus on what appear to be manageable bits of the problem. If we do not have the big picture in mind, the chances of going off at a tangent are considerable. This is what I believe has happened with a lot of food-charity efforts; some kind of 'cannot see the food system for all the food parcels' effect. So we need to have a *framework* that we can use to understand and interpret the problem, and to make sense of *everything* that goes on in the agri-food system, not just a few things. A framework is also what we would use to assess our ideas about possible solutions – to test whether or not these are likely to move things along in the right direction.

Central to sharpening our understanding of the problem and developing such a framework is the notion of *causality*: we have (hopefully) agreed that the problem is the dominant agri-food system, but what is it *about* this system that generates the outcomes we would like to change? What are the crucial factors that drive who wins and who loses? It is at this level – the drivers of the system – that interventions are most likely to make a meaningful change. And the short answer to this is the distribution of power. Those who have power in the system are able to set the terms on which they transact with others; those who do not have power must generally comply with these terms, no matter how little they like them. Those who have power can extract value from others in the system; this is what makes them winners. Those who do not have power have value extracted from them, and that is what makes *them* losers. And so the outcomes of the system – who wins and who loses – are determined fundamentally by the distribution of power in the system.

But this is not where the causal chain ends or where we can stop our investigation: a particular distribution of power in a socio-economic system (which is what our agri-food system is) is not given, and it is not separate from our broader society. We did not all wake up one day and find that this particular agri-food system had magically materialised overnight, as if dropped on our collective doorsteps by aliens. An agri-food system in which a few big corporates have most of the power is not some kind of inevitable economic outcome; neither is it a reflection of who is most 'efficient' in the system and thus who 'deserves' to be a winner. This is the message of mainstream economics, but (as we shall discuss in more detail later) sometimes you need to pay close attention to the messenger when deciding on the credibility of the message.

The truth is that this is a system that has been *created*, through a great deal of conscious and unconscious effort, by a large number of organisations, institutions and ordinary people. None of these, of course, directly 'created' the system as it now stands, or consciously crafted the particular distribution of power that characterises it. However, what all of them have contributed to creating and (crucially) keeping in place is the *governance structure* of the agri-food system. These are the 'rules of the game' that are the real foundation of who has power and who does not. It is the details of the governance structure of our agri-food system that determine the distribution of power within it, and thus the outcomes of the system.

And it is this governance structure that is the *framework* – the big picture – we are looking for in order to think about where and how we can bring about change. This is the superstructure on which the agri-food system rests, and which determines why certain outcomes rather than others are generated. Interventions at the level of the governance structure therefore have a strong likelihood of generating change on the kind of scale we are looking for, since it operates across the system. We have already touched on issues of governance in the earlier chapters, now it is time for us to take a closer look.

Governance: Who sets the rules of the game?

We can think about governance as the rules of the game; the rules that determine who in the agri-food system gets to do what under which conditions. Key to having (and keeping) power is the ability either to write the rules to your benefit or to exert a strong influence on those who do. We have discussed how, based on the recommendations of the 1992 Kassier Committee and the thinking behind ANC agricultural policy, government largely withdrew from the governance of our agri-food system. This exit was formalised in the 1996 Marketing of Agricultural Products Act, which made it extremely difficult for government to intervene in the operation of agricultural markets, even in the interests of promoting food security or addressing rural poverty.

The result of this exit was that big corporates in the food sector were able to take much of the 'rule-making' authority for themselves. We can see this authority clearly illustrated in their ability to extract a range of preferential terms from farmers (this ability is greatly curbed in those countries that have different governance systems, as we shall discuss later).

In terms of being able to influence those who write the rules, we have also seen that the big food corporates generally have much more influence than other system participants, such as consumers or farmworkers or farmers. This is illustrated in who gets to make the greatest input into policy around issues like chicken-brining levels or agro-processing. It is also seen in who gets the most government support (direct and indirect) to grow their businesses, via all the policy decisions that we have discussed around land use, access to public space and food regulation. So we can see that a relatively small number of big corporates have much say – both directly and indirectly – in what our agri-food system governance structure looks like. This ability to write (or to heavily influence those who write) many of the rules to their own advantage is a central reason why they have most of the power in the system. But this is it not the only reason why they have power, and it is certainly not the main reason why they are able to *keep* power (that is, why the rules have not changed).

There is a third component to governance that is, in many ways, more important than the other two factors (namely, direct and indirect influence), and this is what has been termed 'governance by discourse'.[73] Essentially, what governance by discourse includes is all the ways in which a certain governance structure is seen as *legitimate* by wider society; all the generally held ideas and commonly held perceptions in a society that make one kind of governance structure more acceptable than others – even desirable. It is these ideas and social norms that underpin the kinds of policies that support corporate agri-food businesses, and that have created the current situation: where the vast majority of us – citizens and policy-makers alike – believe it is both *normal* and *appropriate* that our agri-food system is structured in this way. This is where the system winners derive their ability to keep power. And this is, I believe, the main reason why there is hardly any resistance to the dominant system – most of us believe that this is the way that things ought to be, or at least that it is our only real option.

This third component of the governance structure thus encompasses the general philosophy, the common social vision and the popular conversations (such as media reports) that give *credibility* to the written rules and regulations; the reason why we all (or at least most of us) accept the rules and regulations as *legitimate*, and why we all participate in the system without ever really questioning it.

Think about this for a minute: there are a lot of potential rules and regulations that government and/or the private sector could draft that we would (almost) all reject as illegitimate, such as if slavery were declared legal tomorrow. We would reject these because they are in conflict with our society's generally held ideas of what is acceptable and what is not. This is an extreme example, but it is a good illustration of the idea that what underpins a particular governance structure is some kind of commonly held idea or philosophy that we all buy into, and which stops us from questioning the existence of the system that it supports.

So what are these ideas, these norms that are so commonly held – and so closely held – that they have so successfully allocated and preserved power for the few in our agri-food system at the expense of the many? Contrary to what we might believe, government did not make these governance decisions because it *intended* to create a system where food was unaffordable for most South Africans, or where small farmers could not make a living, or where most farmworkers would be sentenced to a life of poverty. Instead, underpinning its decisions in respect of the governance of our agri-food system is a particular understanding of the kind of governance structure that would be in the best interests of the majority, and this is one based on free markets, free competition and economic efficiency. If you recall the debate in the early 1990s about what kind of agri-food system would be best for South Africa, there was a strong sense that free markets would work in everyone's best interests; that they would provide more and better market access opportunities for farmers, and cheaper and better food for all South Africans.

Or, to put it another way, our current agri-food system governance structure is focused on the goal of achieving economic 'efficiency' rather than social justice, *on the understanding that the former is the best way to achieve the latter*. This is the thinking that pervades almost all of government policy across a wide range of activities (not just food and agriculture); it is *also* how the majority of us understand what is 'best' for our country. Popular discourse and the media support this thinking. Almost every article on 'what needs to be done' to fix South Africa focuses on the need to grow the economy, and the general consensus is that this can be achieved only if we support businesses to grow. And so the growth of big corporates in the agri-food system, and the enormous power that they have over everyone else, is given legitimacy, to the extent that we very seldom discuss alternatives. The majority of South Africans believe that the current system is the best possible system, and *this* is where power really lies.

The food corporates themselves contribute significantly to maintaining this version of reality, through their insistence that they are keeping prices as low as possible and guaranteeing quality food, and doing all sorts of good works to support emerging farmers and hungry children. They spend much time and effort portraying themselves as the best, and the only viable, option for consumers to access food. This works very well because *we* believe it; and government officials believe it. And as long as everyone gives credibility (legitimacy) to the system through these beliefs, it will never change.

The strength of these beliefs (even among some of those who voice their opposition to rising food prices) is clearly illustrated by the fact that representatives of the Food Sovereignty Campaign (during their recent march in Johannesburg) talked about 'profiteering' and 'price fixing' as the reasons for high food prices. That is, they alleged that food (in this case bread) is unaffordable because of the *illegal* actions of certain companies, and they want the Competition Commission to investigate these. While I certainly cannot deny that there may be some kind of illegal activity underway in food markets, the fact of the matter is that almost all of the negative outcomes of our agri-food system, which I have described, are the result of the *normal* working of the system, rather than illegal activity. But we have all become so convinced that the current system is the best possible option that we are able to conceptualise negative outcomes only in terms of some kind of 'market failure', rather than being in the normal course of doing business. We just cannot get our heads around the idea that the system is *intentionally designed* to give more power to some than to others.

Inclusion, exclusion and adverse inclusion

To fully understand this issue, the work done by Professor Andries du Toit at the Programme for Land and Agrarian Studies (PLAAS) at the University of the Western Cape should be compulsory reading.[74] He writes about how we can misunderstand poverty (and thus the symptoms of poverty, such as low incomes for small farmers and destitute farmworkers) as being the result of *exclusion* from an economic system. The idea that people are poor because they are excluded from the 'formal' economy has been a popular discourse explaining how apartheid impoverished black South Africans. Thus, in 1994, ANC agricultural policy saw the inclusion of new black farmers into these formal markets (that is, as suppliers to companies like Pick 'n Pay, Tiger Brands and Clover) as the 'cure' for their poverty. But as thousands of (mostly ex) small farmers will tell you, getting a contract from one of these companies can be the crucial factor that puts you *out* of business. Because policy-makers do not see the system as the problem, they look for the reasons for failure in other places, like the shortcomings of these farmers themselves.

They are assisted in this by some academic research: I recently read a paper[75] about why dairy farmers go out of business. The short answer was that they are 'uncompetitive'; and the definition of 'competitiveness' they used was 'the ability to make a profit at the prevailing (very low) market price'. That is, if you are unable to make a living from dairy farming, it is because you are not a good farmer, not because the price that you are being paid is a declining portion of the retail price. The very idea that the prevailing price might be 'unfair' is not even considered, since this would require judging the legitimacy of the system.

As an alternative interpretation, Andries du Toit proposes the idea of *adverse inclusion* to describe all the ways in which the normal workings of an economic system can generate outcomes that perpetuate poverty. Adverse inclusion focuses our attention on the *terms* on which various people are incorporated into a particular system: winners participate on favourable terms and losers participate on unfavourable terms (such as the luckless dairy farmers described earlier). The *terms* on which you are included into a particular system (such as the fresh-milk market) are thus often more important to whether you succeed or fail than inclusion *per se*. The key point is that poverty can be (and often is) generated through the *normal* workings of a particular economic system, and not through what economists like to refer to as 'market failure'.

This adverse inclusion effect is exactly what is happening with our agri-food system, but it is very difficult for us to overcome our strongly held beliefs about the legitimacy of the system and to see this, so most of us still insist that bad outcomes are the result of *abnormal* behaviour, like price fixing. Or we believe that these outcomes can be explained as being the result of external factors, like unemployment and low household income, and not as the result of the normal workings of the system. Even those who suffer the most in this system – the hungriest families, farmworkers and the rural poor – often look somewhere else to find the reasons why they cannot afford to eat or to make a living from farming. This is the strength of our collective belief.

And so when people like me and activists like Nazeer Sonday from the Philippi Horticultural Area (PHA) Food and Farming Campaign and organisations like Oxfam talk about the terrible damage that the dominant agri-food system is doing to our society, the response from many is that we might not like these short-term implications but this is simply the way it has to be. We have to put up with a certain amount of collateral damage as the price of our generally 'efficient' system. We look to food charity to plug the holes made in our social fabric.

The generally held view is that no alternative to the 'free market' is as efficient or as effective in generating economic 'development'. Almost everyone who is considered to be an 'expert' on the economy (and thus whose views we hear or read about) promotes this version of reality. We need to remember, however, that very often these people have a vested interest in the status quo that they are promoting: they often work for banks and investment managers and stock brokers, organisations that stand to benefit from the growth of profits in the corporate sector. The radio journalist seldom asks a hungry person (whom we might legitimately consider an expert on the subject) for their view of the dominant agri-food system. All this is compounded by the fact that the average person (or business journalist) exercises very little imagination about possible alternatives to the current system. The common storyline goes something like this: 'you may not like all this hunger and malnutrition and rural poverty, but things would be much worse if the state owned the agri-food system.' For many South Africans, the choices are imagined as being only between rampant predatory capitalism or Soviet-style state control. This – as I hope to show quite clearly – is complete and utter nonsense, but these perceptions (and the ensuing conversation) are one of the reasons why the current structure keeps its power.

Let us challenge some of these perceptions and ideas: that the current agri-food system is actually working for us; that it is in all of our best interests to maintain the system as it is; and that it is contributing to 'development'. If we look around us, and see the effects of how our agri-food system has operated for the past 20 years, we could draw up a little imaginary set of accounts (using the terms 'plus' and 'minus').

PLUS	MINUS
Job creation in food manufacturing and retailing	Jobs lost in agriculture
Wealthy consumers can access a greater variety of food	Small farmers going out of business
Corporate profits increased	Land reform failing
	High levels of malnutrition in children
	High levels of public disease burden
	Declining social cohesion
	Increased rural poverty and unemployment
	Upward pressure on wage settlements due to high cost of food
	Increasing threat to domestic food supply
	Entrenchment of poverty and inequality
	Crime

This does not look so 'efficient' or 'developmental', does it? So why do we cling so strongly to the idea that it is? That if we wait long enough, this system will eventually work for all of us. That nothing else is possible.

Fred Block is an American sociologist who has written persuasively on this subject,[76] about how the supremacy of the ideal of economic efficiency (of the neo-liberal kind) has pervaded our thinking about almost everything in our lives. He proposes that this happens when we lose sight of, or no longer have, a vision for what kind of society we would like to be. But we cannot do without such a vision; we need something in which to anchor our everyday lives and decisions. And so what happens is that we substitute something else in its place –

a vision of what kind of *economic system* we would like to be. When that happens (as he proposed had happened in the United States in the last part of the 20th century), all of our important decisions are then made on the basis of what is good for the economy (which has become our vision of ourselves), rather than what is good for society. The substitution is complete when we are no longer able to think of our society without thinking immediately of our economy, *as if these were the same thing.*

I believe that this is precisely what has happened in South Africa over the past 20 years. If you do not believe me, try thinking about the kind of place you believe South Africa should be, and the kinds of policies the government should follow to get us there, without any reference to economics. For most of us this has become almost impossible and this is an indication of the extent to which this kind of thinking has pervaded every aspect of our lives.

And so, the destruction of natural resources like the PHA and the Cape Flats aquifer becomes justifiable because it is necessary for economic 'development', and the social impact is ignored. Education is no longer about creating people who will make a positive contribution to society, but rather about creating productive inputs for the economy. We talk about the economic costs of malnutrition via an increased public-health burden, but not about how it destroys children's lives. We calculate the costs of failed land-reform projects, but we never talk about how this entrenches racial notions of inferiority. We work out how much money companies have donated to food charities, but we never talk about the erosion of people's dignity through being forced to accept that charity, or the importance of their sense of self as equal persons. We justify not taking care of the most vulnerable in our society because it does not make 'economic' sense. And food is no longer about nourishment and life; it is about profit and efficiency and the effective allocation of resources. We can no longer think about 'value' without thinking about money.

And the worst part about this is that we actually do have a wonderful vision for the kind of society we would like to be – it is called *The Constitution of the Republic of South Africa.** Section 27 of our Constitution guarantees the right of every one of us to sufficient food. The last time I looked, it did not guarantee the right to corporate profit. I think it is time we stopped running our agri-food system as if it did.

---

* Thanks to Sasha Stevenson from Section 27 who pointed this truth out to me.

Society vs the economy: Truth and lies

If you have bought into the argument that I have presented, you would also have realised that the crucial first step in changing our agri-food system is to substitute an alternative vision for the one that currently underpins our governance structure. We need to replace the idea that one version of economic 'efficiency' and corporate 'success' are the most important benchmarks against which we measure social progress. An alternative vision is what we will use to determine the details of a new governance structure for our agri-food system, since it is through this governance structure that we will aim to achieve different system outcomes. This new governance structure will then determine and limit the relative roles of the system participants – government, food producers and food consumers.

If you believe that we need a new agri-food system because the current one is failing to deliver the social-justice outcomes our society needs,* it is time for us to start a conversation about morality – about right and wrong; and the place to start this conversation is the relationship (or perceived lack of relationship) between economics and morality.

First we need to have a brief discussion of economic theory, since it is the supremacy of a particular kind of economic thinking in our agri-food system that is our problem. And the thinking that dominates the mainstream and popular idea of what constitutes 'economics' in this country is neo-liberal economics, the kind made popular by Margaret Thatcher and Ronald Reagan. In a nutshell, this version of economics extols the merits of free markets, the benefits of reduced government regulation, the supremacy of the private company in generating economic growth, and the importance of economic growth in generating socio-economic benefits. It thus makes very strong claims about the relationship between supporting private (particularly big) business and increasing the common good. This theory about how an economy works has become so powerful that most of us cannot even imagine that there is a viable alternative way of thinking.

I am not going to present a detailed critique of neo-liberal economic theory here (it would take too long and there are already hundreds of excellent books on the subject), but it is important for our discussion to make two points by busting two myths. The first myth is that neo-

---

* If you do not, you should probably stop reading now – nothing from here on in is going to present a different message.

liberal economics represents an absolute truth about the way in which the real world works, in the way that one plus one equals two is a 'truth'. Despite all the fancy, incomprehensible mathematics and the way that most economists speak, neo-liberal economics is simply a *theory* of how the world works, and it is not a particularly good one. For example, let us look at the supposed relationship between economic growth, the growth of corporate profits and an increase in the common good that lies at the heart of this theory. (This supposed relationship is used as the reason for why our economic policy should focus on growing corporate profit – it is for our own good.)

Despite the fact that almost every economic commentator in the media maintains that there is a perfect and perfectly predictable relationship running from economic growth through corporate profits to the common good, no such thing exists. There is *no* – I repeat *no* – objectively verified empirical evidence which shows that if an economy grows by a certain amount and corporate profits grow by a certain amount, the common good will increase by a corresponding certain amount. If you do not believe me, ask an economist the following question: 'If the economy grows by 5.5 per cent next year, exactly how many new jobs will be created by the private sector and by how much will the average household income go up?' You will not get an exact answer; instead you will probably get something along the lines of: 'well, it is impossible to make such detailed predictions, but there definitely will be some kind of positive impact, unless there is not, in which case it is due to structural impediments.' We could translate this as, 'I have no idea, but I am still asking you to believe that my view on these matters counts more than anyone else's'.

This answer could be expected because there *is* no perfectly predictable and reliable relationship among these three factors – none at all. If there were, there would be no incorrect economic forecasts! It is quite possible for an economy to grow, and for corporate profits to grow, but for this to have no impact at all on the common good. As an example, companies often grow their profits by 'restructuring'; in other words, retrenching people. This is good for shareholders and the senior managers that remain, since they will inevitably get bigger bonuses, but it clearly is not very good for the rest of us. South Africa has experienced long periods of positive economic growth and improved corporate profits, but there were still more unemployed people at the end of the period than at the beginning.

The actual relationship between economic growth, corporate profits and the common good is extremely variable: it differs enormously from country to country, and is influenced by a wide range of factors such as the regulatory environment, existing demographics, consumer behaviour, trade relations and cultural priorities. All around the world, communities are experimenting successfully with models of human development that are linking improved well-being and quality of life with *lower* levels of economic growth (and lower corporate profits).

The fact of the matter *is* that there is a relatively strong relationship between economic growth and corporate profits in countries that prioritise the interests of private companies – which is exactly what we would expect. And this is also why corporates – and the economists who work there – tend to be keen proponents of neo-liberal growth policies. But the reality is that there is no guarantee at all that the rest of us will benefit to the same extent. The idea that we will benefit is simply a poor and inadequate theory of what actually goes on in the real world, heavily promoted by those who stand to gain the most from its acceptance. Rising corporate profits in the South African agri-food sector are clearly *not* positively correlated with an improvement in our common food position or the lives of those living in rural areas. In fact, the opposite is true, and this *can* be presented as empirical evidence that the assumptions of neo-liberal economics in this regard are incorrect. So that deals with the first myth – that these theories are an accurate reflection of reality and thus represent our best option on which to build an agri-food system.

The second myth is related to the first, and it has to do with the idea that neo-liberal theories of economics are politically 'neutral'; that a 'free market' of the kind represented by our current agri-food system is what happens when (bad) government withdraws from the economy and (good) 'market forces' are allowed to take charge. This is a complicated subject, but the bottom line is that the resulting market structure – the deeply exploitative system that we find ourselves stuck with – is presented as the logical outcome of these market forces, and the fact that some people are winners and some are losers is just the way it is. This kind of thinking underpins the blame-the-victim version of events. After all, if the overarching system is neutral and normal and inevitable, the failure of a small farmer *must* be the result of *their* shortcomings. This thinking is the main reason why we see so little protest against our agri-food system: almost everyone believes that this is the way it has to be – like gravity.

This, of course, is not true. It is the details of the current governance system that determine who has power and who does not, and there is nothing 'inevitable' about this since there are hundreds of forms that it could have taken. Government's withdrawal from the governance of our agri-food system did not create a 'neutral' outcome; it did not create the much-vaunted, level playing field that economists predicted it would. Instead, it created a situation in which those with the most power were able to entrench themselves at the expense of everyone else. Personally I cannot see much evidence of a 'free' market when a few companies have extraordinary power over thousands of farmers and millions of consumers. And government has not actually stayed out of the agri-food system. Instead, it continually makes decisions around land use, public transport and the allocation of retail space that benefit the winners. Of course the winners do not see any of this as government support. Instead, they continue to maintain that it is not desirable for government to 'interfere', by which they mean, unless it is to their advantage, in which case it is a great idea. They do not present it like this of course: instead, interventions to their benefit are termed 'good for the market' and those that are not to their benefit are termed 'bad for the market'.

Another way in which this narrative protects the interests of the few is by presenting an attack on corporate power as 'anti-market' (thus portraying anyone who criticises as some kind of Stalinist who favours Soviet-style authoritarianism). This is also nonsense: the kind of market in which big food corporates dominate everyone else is only one kind of market – the kind of market that benefits them. A 'market' is simply a term for a place of exchange and hundreds of market variations have been part of many human cultures for thousands of years. When you buy tomatoes from a street trader, you are engaging in a market transaction. When I buy milk directly from a dairy farmer, this is a market transaction. When you order meat directly from a small-farmer cooperative, this is a market transaction. When you swap your home-grown vegetables with your neighbour in return for his fixing your plumbing, this is also a form of market transaction, even though no cash has been exchanged. To suggest that encouraging these kinds of activities – and redirecting government policy to support them – is 'anti-market' requires an adjective stronger than 'ignorant'.

One of the triumphs of neo-liberal economics is its ability to present a governance system that is deeply biased in favour of one group of people as 'neutral', the fact that some people are winners and some are losers as 'natural', and the outcomes of the system as 'best' for all of us. The governance of our agri-food system is, of course, anything but neutral or in the best interests of the majority. It consistently allocates the bulk of the value created towards a few participants, by virtue of a consciously constructed framework that gives some participants a lot of power, rather than some 'invisible hand'.

The appeal of a narrative based on these two myths – that uneven rewards are somehow the normal and the best possible state of affairs, and that if we try to change these outcomes we are 'interfering' in this wonderful system – for the current system winners is very clear. It allows them to deflect accusations of unfair behaviour – such as making enormous profits while delivering inferior and over-priced food to poor South Africans – by presenting their own version of morality (that is, of right and wrong) to contest these. In other words, those who support the current system will often do so by presenting it as the 'best' option that is available, one that is to the overall benefit of society. In this way they are making a *moral* argument about the dominant system, about its *rightness*. We could refer to this as *economic morality*, to differentiate it from the other versions presented below. For this purpose, I would define *economic morality* as the idea that the growth of big business, and the corresponding rise in corporate profit, is a proxy for the greater good. It is on the basis of *economic morality* that food retailers present themselves as the best friend of the consumer, for example, by presenting themselves as the most 'efficient' way to supply our food.

This situation allows many economists and like-minded commentators to assert that there is no place for an *alternative morality* in economics, such as the values that most of us would prioritise in our own homes or the values that are prioritised in many religions. We could think about these as some kind of 'social' or 'human' morality, which leads most us to have strong views about ideas like 'fairness' and 'honesty' and taking care of the most vulnerable in our society, and to apply these in our dealing with our family and friends. Most of us believe that these values are usually more important than financial gain. We are constantly told, however, that we cannot prioritise this kind of morality in economic policy because 'this is not how the economy works'. Since we now know that this point of view – 'how the economy works' – is based on shoddy theory and vested interests, we can start to interrogate it.

The assertion that there is no place for an alternative morality (that is, one that prioritises *human* values over monetary gain) in economics is completely incorrect. An economy is not something separate from broader society, subject to its own independent set of rules over which that society has no influence (although neo-liberal economists would very much like you to believe that it is). As alternative economists from Karl Polanyi[77] to Raj Patel[78] have pointed out, an economy is deeply embedded in a society, and thus issues of *human* morality – what that society considers to be right or wrong – have always been important in determining what kind of economic activity is condoned and what is outlawed.

If that were not the case, slavery would still be legal, on the basis that it underpinned a vast amount of economic activity by reducing labour costs (which is an *economic morality* argument – lower input costs are 'good'). The abolition of slavery resulted in the collapse of many economic activities that relied on it (such as sugar and cotton plantations), but this was not seen as sufficient justification to continue a practice widely seen as deeply immoral by *human* moral standards. If we did not see a place for human morality in economic decision-making, the trade in women and children would be legal. There is demand and there is supply and there is plenty of profit to be made, but presumably none of us would think that these are good enough reasons to make it legal. The trade in all sorts of narcotics is illegal because we have collectively decided (and brought pressure to bear on policy-makers) that the collective interests of society are more important than the 'rights' of drug dealers to make a profit. The majority of South Africans are in favour of a total ban on the trade in rhino horn, even though this is a very profitable international business. They believe that society will benefit more from the conservation of the species than from the profits that could be made from trading its horns. The international ban on trade in ivory has been made with similar moral considerations around conserving wild populations of elephants.

Surely we should be making the same kinds of assessments about our agri-food system? After all, food is not the same as most other economic products. If you do not eat, you die. And as a society, we all stand to lose a great deal through the entrenchment of poverty, the erosion of individual dignity and the perpetuation of inequality that are the outcomes of the dominant agri-food system. Millions of South African children go to bed hungry each night: why do so many of us believe that the rights of a few corporates to make a profit are more important than they are? Why do we believe that there is no place for a human morality in our agri-food system?

Maybe it is time we changed our minds.

I would like to propose that we start to think about building an alternative agri-food system on the foundation of a *human* conceptualisation of morality – our collective social sense of right and wrong and fairness – rather than one of corporate power and *economic* morality.

Defining alternatives: Morality and the ethic of care

There are many ways in which we could define 'morality' and thus many possible notions of morality that could underpin an alternative agri-food system. 'Morality' does not mean the same thing to everyone; it is a term that carries a great deal of subjective and cultural interpretation across different communities in South Africa, with respect to both the production and the consumption of food. I do not want to get into a long debate about what and whose interpretation of 'moral' or 'immoral' could or should serve as a basis for a different vision to underpin our agri-food system. Instead, I would like to introduce you to the writing of Professor Joan Tronto, who has developed a compelling alternative paradigm of how we could organise our societies on a more equitable and moral way, based on her notion of an 'Ethic of Care'. She maintains that 'the world will look different if we move care from its current peripheral location to a place near the centre of human life'.[79] I believe that her notion of the Ethic of Care is a very good place to start rethinking some of our deeply held assumptions about how the world does, should and could work, and applying these to our agri-food system.[80]

In her 1993 book, *Moral Boundaries: A Political Argument for an Ethic of Care,* Tronto discusses the relationship between morality and *politics.* By now you will hopefully have realised that hunger and malnutrition in South Africa have very little to do with the production of food or consumer ignorance of correct nutrition, but instead are deeply *political* in nature and cause. By 'political' I mean that they are the outcome of who has power and who does not; of whose rights are considered more important than those of others; and of which persons are considered more valuable than others. In a similar manner, the poverty of farmworkers and the inability of many small farmers to earn a living is the result of political priorities – who gets to benefit from the system and who does not. The structure of the current system is thus the direct result of which group is deemed to have greater or more important rights than others and it reflects the elevation of the (non-existent) right to corporate profit over the (actual) right to food. And this is why a solution to hunger, malnutrition and rural poverty has to be based on an alternative *politics;*

on an alternative distribution of power.

One of the key points in Tronto's book is that 'moral arguments have a political context'.[81] That is, moral arguments (such as the assertion that it is 'inevitable' for one group to have more power than another) do not appear from nowhere, magically arriving fully formed on our collective doorstep one morning. They are the outcomes of the dominant political mores in a particular society and are legitimised by the social norms and values held by the average person. As Tronto puts it: 'Widely accepted social values constitute the context within which we interpret all moral arguments.'[82] Once we have accepted as the central vision for our society the type of economy we would like to be (as described by Fred Block), those 'social values' with which we make moral judgements are, in effect, *economic values*.

The relationship between morality, politics, economics and society has particular resonance in South Africa. It is not that long ago that opposition to apartheid on human moral grounds was squashed by arguments about political and economic necessity. One of the main reasons why black South Africans were dispossessed of their land was to promote the interests of the economy of white South Africa. This economy was held up as the 'reason' why we could not entertain too many moral qualms about the human cost of apartheid. Although apartheid represents one of history's extreme examples of drawing limits to human versions of morality, we should not forget where we have come from on our journey to somewhere better.

Tronto proposes that her concept of care can be used to rethink what she terms 'moral boundaries', that is, the boundaries in our society that determine the limits of morality, the *kinds* of morality we apply (or do not apply) in our society and whose version of morality we prioritise. These boundaries set *limits* to moralities, resulting in ideas such as 'there is no place for human moral arguments in determining what kind of food-marketing system is best'. These moral boundaries effectively determine who has power and who does not or, in our case, who gets to eat and who does not, and who does or does not get to make a living from producing food. In other words, these boundaries effectively include some in the winners group and relegate others to the camp of losers. They do so by *legitimising* a particular political arrangement (the distribution of power) and rendering alternatives *illegitimate*.

If we prioritise Tronto's notion of an Ethic of Care over, say, an Ethic of Power or an Ethic of Profit in how we see the world and (most importantly) in how we see others in that world, we would come to very different conclusions about the best – most *legitimate* – way to organise an agri-food system. If we saw the world differently, we would imagine very different limits to human morality in that system.

In her book, Tronto talks about three 'moral boundaries' that can be moved or changed or permeated when we start to think in terms of an Ethic of Care. The first is the boundary between morality and politics; the boundary that determines how we see the *relationship* between morality and politics and where we collectively believe the boundary between the two should be drawn. This is a critical point in our discussion about the role of morality in our agri-food system. Policy-makers do not believe that the question of 'is it fair to the most vulnerable?' can (or should) be taken into account when deciding on legislation in the agri-food system. This is precisely because of the way in which they (and, to be honest, most of us) perceive the boundary between human morality and economic morality. In other words, most of us would put that boundary very far on the side of economic morality (economic efficiency), effectively making human morality irrelevant in most economic decision-making.

What this means is that if we deem something to be economically efficient, then we generally designate it as 'moral' by virtue of being 'economically moral'. That is how we justify the poverty of farmworkers: that this poverty is 'necessary' so that farmers can stay in business. In this way, we are making a *moral* judgement about the living conditions of farmworkers, that it is acceptable ('moral') for them to live like this. If we started with the idea that a living wage for farmworkers was not negotiable (that is, if we radically shifted that moral boundary and now saw the poverty of farmworkers as 'immoral'), we would come to very different conclusions about how our agri-food system should be structured.

The second moral boundary is what she terms 'the moral point of view boundary',[83] which could be simply defined as the idea that 'morality' (and thus moral judgements) should be based on reason and be universally 'objective'. In this version of morality, there is no place for emotion, for a subjective sense of right and wrong and fairness in making moral arguments. And it is this kind of reasoned morality that should be the only kind that is permitted to have a place in politics or political debate. The moral point of view boundary thus serves to render daily accounts of hunger and deprivation effectively invisible, since they are the 'wrong' kind of morality. Stories of hungry children are deemed to be 'emotional' and thus irrelevant to the serious business of politics and economics.

The third moral boundary proposed by Tronto is that between public and private life. As a feminist scholar, Tronto is making the point here that there is a common understanding in many societies that there is a difference between public and private life, and that since many 'women's' activities are considered to be part of 'private' life, their input is not taken seriously in 'public' matters such as politics. I believe that this boundary is particularly relevant to our discussion of the South African agri-food system, since the way in which this system is structured is very much a reflection of who (or what) in our society we believe should have a place – a voice – in determining what that system looks like. This boundary thus sets limits to *whose version of morality* we consider valid, and whose we do not. This is a key issue in the South African agri-food system, where the points of view of 'experts' and representatives of winners are always accorded more value than those of the hungry themselves (or, indeed, any other of the system 'losers'). The vast majority of South Africans have no voice in this debate: and the poorer you are, the less you are deemed able to make a valid contribution. When someone like Nazeer Sonday tells me that the majority of people who live in Philippi and the surrounding areas of Grassy Park and Mitchells Plain understand very well that they have no 'value' in the eyes of those who have power in the City of Cape Town, he is articulating the ways in which some people are effectively considered (and treated) as 'less' than others.

Steve Biko referred to this state of affairs during apartheid as black South Africans 'living in a society where they are treated as perpetual under-16s'.[84] Biko's words resonate today and they remind us that what is really at stake in the battle for who controls our agri-food system is what type of society we aspire to be. And this depends critically on whose version of right and wrong – whose conceptualisation of morality – we prioritise, and whose voices we accord credibility.

So what does Tronto propose as an alternative way of thinking about how we organise our society? Her conceptualisation of an Ethic of Care is based on turning concern for others (and not only human others) into meaningful action: 'care implies a reaching out to something other than the self; it is neither self-referring nor self-absorbing'.[85] Care requires that we turn our attention from *ourselves* to those around us, and (most importantly) to those who are distant from us. This requirement to care for those who are outside our immediate family or circle of friends or neighbours is, to my mind, a critical part of thinking about 'care' in the South African context, and central to its transformative potential. Why? Because for so great a part of our history, we have been encouraged to do *exactly* the opposite – to think of our fellow South Africans as *other*, as *the others*. And very often this illusion of otherness was the basis on which it was excusable, acceptable even, to *not* care. Placing care at the centre of our actions requires us to fundamentally change this and to be concerned about those whom we would normally not give a second thought.

Tronto's conceptualisation of care has four progressive phases: Caring About, Taking Care Of, Care-giving and Care-receiving.

Caring About means that we notice a need (such as malnutrition in children) and then decide that something needs to be done about it. Very important here is the link between noticing the need and making this the basis for *taking action to address that need*. Tronto makes it very clear that saying something like, 'I care about hungry children in South Africa' but then not taking any action to do something about this means that this person does not actually 'care' about them.*

Taking Care Of is the next phase of care, and it requires that we in some way assume 'responsibility'[86] for the need that we have identified. This means that we believe that we *can* do something about the problem; that it is within our power to take action. If there is actually nothing that we can do, this phase cannot happen and we cannot 'care'. This underscores the importance of our sense of our own *agency*: whether or not we *believe* that we can make a difference. Many people are of the opinion that they cannot make a difference to our agri-food system because they are too poor, or because they have no political influence, or simply because the problem is 'too big'. Very often these are perceptions rather than an accurate reflection of reality: the consumer boycotts of the 1980s showed clearly that even the poorest communities could have a significant impact on local economic activity. But we must also acknowledge that our history has convinced many South Africans that they do not have agency and that they simply have to accept things as they are. These perceptions effectively prevent them from imagining something different. After all, our ability to imagine something is conditioned to a considerable degree by our experience.

These perceptions of not having agency underpin much of the lack of resistance to the dominant agri-food system (and, of course, it does

---

* Which hopefully puts into context all of those 'awareness-raising' campaigns which give people the opportunity to say that they 'care' without actually having to do anything to address the problem. Under Tronto's definition, this is not 'care'. It is just pretending to care.

not help that government regularly enforces this idea, that we must simply accept things as they decide they should be). The role of agency highlights the importance of *believing* that we can make a difference through our actions, as a first step to *taking* action.

Tronto acknowledges that the actual ability to act on one's concerns is limited by the real world in which we live – how much money we have, where we live, how much time we have and our access to resources. The requirement of 'action', therefore, is based on context and some people have a greater ability to act than others.

The third phase of care is **Care-giving**. Tronto is quite specific here that 'care-giving involves the direct meeting of needs for care. It involves physical work, and almost always requires that care-givers come in contact with the objects of care.'[87] She is also clear that just giving money usually does *not* qualify as 'care-giving'. This does not mean, in the context of the agri-food system, that engaging in a monetary transaction (such as with a small farmer) is not care-giving (as we shall discuss in chapters 7 and 8). What it does mean is that we cannot discharge our care duties by writing a cheque. Real care requires that we enter into personal relationships of a particular kind with others. I believe that it is through the constant elevation of this requirement to engage with each other that the notion of care has power to transform both our agri-food system and our broader society.

The final phase of care is **Care-receiving**. This is the 'feedback' phase of care whereby we can find out whether or not we have actually identified someone's needs correctly and whether we have taken the correct actions to fulfil them. Care-receiving requires that we pay attention to the point of view of the recipients of care, and not just to our own ideas of what needs to be done. It also means that we should constantly be open to revising our ideas of what constitutes good or appropriate care on the basis of those points of view.

Tronto is clear that we should understand her conceptualisation of care as a *practice*; that is, it requires the regular, daily *application* of care, rather than sitting around theorising about the idea of care. *Care as practice* emphasises the centrality of *action* in her notion of caring.

From the understanding of care as a practice, and based on the four phases of care discussed above, Tronto has developed her idea of an 'Ethic of Care'. These are the four elements that, she asserts, need to be in place for actions to be considered morally 'right'. It is in this definition of an Ethic of Care that I believe we can find a foundation for building an alternative agri-food system; one that prioritises the interests of the many (the greater good) over those of the few. The four elements of Tronto's Ethics of Care provide the guidelines that we can use to develop and test new forms of governance and action.

These elements are Attentiveness, Responsibility, Competence and Responsiveness. Each of these elements corresponds to one of the phases of care outlined in the preceding pages.

Attentiveness means that we pay attention to the needs of others – that we do not ignore them. When we close our minds to the suffering of other people, when we look away, when we are inattentive to others and focus only on ourselves, we are guilty of 'a form of moral evil'.[88] Attentiveness requires that we pay attention to both the direct *and* the indirect consequences of our actions (such as shopping with retailers who tacitly condone the abuse of farmworkers) and not look away. This notion of attentiveness as a moral good, and inattentiveness as a moral evil, is to my mind particularly relevant in the South African context. Apartheid survived for as long as it did in large part because of the *inattentiveness* of the privileged who chose not to see the needs of others, but focused on their own needs. It is the same kind of inattentiveness that has allowed our dominant agri-food system to become dominant. The remedy to this is greater attentiveness, but how do we differentiate between ignorance (that is, genuinely not knowing about the needs of others) and inattentiveness (choosing not to see the needs of others)? Tronto takes a hard line here, and I agree with her: we have a *fundamental responsibility* to notice other people, and in today's age of instant and all-pervasive media, we could say what is called 'ignorance' is almost always a form of inattentiveness. Most of us have so much information at our disposal that we could *choose* to know about the lives of others, but we *choose* not to. Most of us could have a real conversation (one where we listen) with a hungry person or a farmworker or a community gardener if we wanted to, and thereby gain insight into their worlds, but we *choose* not to. This is a moral evil.

Responsibility is a central feature of how we understand 'care', since caring requires that we take action, and taking action requires that we assume responsibility for meeting a particular need. Responsibility in the context of our agri-food system means that we understand the ways in which our actions (or our decisions not to act) have made *us* responsible for the outcomes of this system. We cannot simply blame government policy or corporate greed; we need to accept responsibility for the ways in which *we* have contributed to the current situation. This acceptance is a positive factor for change. Responsibility is strongly connected to agency – if we acknowledge that we have contributed to the current situation, we also acknowledge that we have the ability to change it.

Competence refers to our moral responsibility to provide *good* care. In the context of our agri-food system, I would link the moral requirement of competence not to some kind of technical expertise, but rather to our obligation to take note of what care is actually required. Being 'competent' means that we do our best to deliver *that* care and to meet people's actual needs, not what we assume to be their needs. The requirement of competence means that the actions of those who would like to give the impression that they are 'taking care' of the hungry (such as 'teaching' very poor parents how to feed their children) are exposed as immoral, since they reflect their self-interest.

Responsiveness requires that we pay attention to the ways in which the recipient of care responds. We need to pay attention to concepts such as inequality and vulnerability and be constantly aware of the possibility for abuse that arises out of the vulnerability of the recipients of care.

An Ethic of Care requires that these four elements are combined into a meaningful whole. In Chapter 7, I discuss the ways in which we could practically go about reworking the governance of our agri-food system to reflect this Ethic of Care. In Chapter 8, I present some of the ways in which we could establish a Practice of Care based on this ethic – how we could turn these ideas about human morality into a practice of everyday actions to transform our agri-food system.

Chapter 7

Building a new governance structure

In the previous chapter I proposed that we could build a new agri-food system on the philosophical foundation of a human morality and replace the economic morality that currently underpins the system. I suggested that as a form of this human morality, we could adopt the guiding principles of Joan Tronto's Ethic of Care. Now we get to the practicalities: how could we go about building a new governance structure for our agri-food system?

The overarching governance structure sets the rules of the game for the system – thereby determining who has power and who does not. It is made up of formal rules – like legislation and regulation – as well as a large number of informal 'rules', such as who gets to sit at the rule-making table and who does not. It is important to remember that a particular distribution of power is underpinned by these rules, but it is also supported by the actions of millions of consumers. We legitimise the current system through our spending decisions, allocating our money in countless 'yes' votes. We do so largely because of the third component of governance in the dominant system: governance by discourse. This discourse includes all the commonly held ideas and practices that have created the general impression that we *should* support the current system, either because we believe it is the 'best' one or because we cannot imagine anything different.

My goal in this chapter and the next is to show how we could build a new, different governance structure, one that will facilitate completely different outcomes. I have provided suggestions of how we could change the existing formal and informal rules of the game (such as different legislation and policy processes), and I have also tried to show that it is quite possible for us to aspire to something very different to what we currently have.

If we create a different governance structure – effectively replacing the structure that we have at present – the rules of the game will change. And then the distribution of power in the system among the main participants – farmers, food corporates and consumers – will also change. This does not mean, however, that a change in the governance system will result in the overnight eradication of the existing dominant system, and nor am I advocating trying to achieve anything so radical. Supermarkets and big food manufacturers in some form or another are here to stay, and will probably be an important (although hopefully not the main) source of markets for farmers and food for consumers for a while to come. I purchase quite a lot of my food from a supermarket – it is the current reality of my life. I am sure it is the current reality of most of you reading this book. This does not mean that we are not actively looking for and encouraging alternatives, but in the interim we do the best with what we have.

What I am advocating is that we create *space* for real alternatives built on the foundation of care; that government stops avoiding its constitutional obligations in respect of the right to food; that we curb the excessive power of the corporates; and that every food consumer starts to think about others in the food system from the perspective of an Ethic of Care. If we get all of this right, those alternative food and farming networks will thrive and grow, and over time become the dominant food system.

Right from the start I need to make myself clear on one point: unlike many people who have criticised our agri-food system, I do not believe that the existing food corporates (that is, the big supermarkets and the big food processors and manufacturers) can be part of an alternative system based on an Ethic of Care. Despite all the rhetoric about caring capitalism and the triple bottom line and corporate social responsibility, I do not believe that they can (or indeed want to) voluntarily migrate from being the problem to being the solution. Nor do I believe that we can effectively regulate them from being the problem to being the solution (without legislating them out of business, which is not, I think, a good idea). The real issue is that the most important motivating factor for these corporates – their only reason for existence (despite what all the cuddly adverts might suggest) – is the maximisation of profits. If they have to choose between 'fairness' or profits, they will always choose profits. This means that they are *fundamentally* at odds with the principles of human morality that I have spelt out, with the Ethic of Care. It is like expecting the people in charge of the rhino-poaching syndicates to be part of saving the species – it is not going to happen. We should just cross that off the list before we even start.

And to reinforce my point on this issue, these corporates *themselves* are clear that they cannot be part of a different, more caring and more humanly moral system that generates outcomes that are in the best interests of society. To almost every allegation of price fixing, or making excessive profits from the sale of food, the response of these companies is much the same: 'we do not make excessive profits; we actually make a very low margin; we are operating at maximum efficiency; there is no better way to manage our food supply'. That is, *by their own admission,* the companies that control the agri-food system could not make the system generate fundamentally different, better outcomes. Since we are hopefully in agreement that this system is not working for us, and that we urgently need to replace it with something significantly better, we can also agree that there is no place for the food corporates in 'that something better'. This means that we can legislate away (or bring consumer pressure to bear on) some of their worst excesses, but, by and large, meaningful alternatives must simply bypass them.

(The only way that this could change is if these companies came out and said, 'you are right, we make too much profit and our business model is not in society's best interests and we promise to take radical action to fix this'. I do not know about you, but I am not going to hold my breath.)

Let us consider now how we might go about writing some new rules of the game, starting with how government might go about meeting its responsibilities in terms of the right to food, land reform and rural poverty. The very first thing that has to happen in this regard, of course, is that government recognises that we have a problem that needs to be fixed, and the nature of this problem. It is the responsibility of all of us to work to ensure that hunger and rural poverty, and the real factors that cause these, are no longer marginalised in our public debates. As I am writing this book, the hotly contested 2016 local government elections have been held, with hardly any mention by anyone of these issues. If there is only one thing that you do as part of being an active citizen, it will be to bring these issues to the attention of the political party of your choice. Once the issue has been problematised – that is, once the powers that be recognise that there is a problem – how might they go about addressing it? Here are some ideas.

Organising to manage the problem

I have stated many times that one of the main reasons why we have such a disastrous agri-food system is because no one in government seems to be aware of the fact that it is a *system*. Instead, current policy efforts are broken up into random parts and distributed among the various departments and different spheres of government (national, provincial and local). The only way in which we are going to achieve meaningful change is if *this* changes; if policy and policy-makers start to look at the agri-food system in a very different way – a joined-up way. The underlying reasons for hunger and rural poverty will not become clear until policy-makers realise that the real issue is the food *system*. Getting this right will require two things – institutional change and a new set of guiding principles for policy-making and resource allocation that prioritise the *right* things across all departments and spheres of government. These two issues are interlinked: we need to build institutions that will facilitate the implementation of our guiding principles, and our guiding principles should determine what kind of institutions we have.

Let us start with the guiding principles. We could adapt the four components of Joan Tronto's definition of an Ethic of Care into the guiding principles for restructuring public-sector institutions around our agri-food system.

1. Attentiveness

The principle of Attentiveness requires that government pay a great deal more (that is, the most) attention to the voices and the needs of those who are most adversely affected by the current structure of the agri-food system. These are the people to whom they owe the greatest, not the least, duty of care. Policy-makers can no longer ignore or purport to speak on behalf of the hungry, the rural poor, small farmers, and those who cannot make a living from farming or farmworkers. In these circumstances, ignorance really is the 'moral evil' described by Tronto, since it arises out of a dismissal of people as less important than others, rather than any technical inability to collect information. The fundamental basis of an agri-food system centred on care is the prioritisation of the needs of the the current system losers – *as they articulate them*. And it is not only listening that is needed: attentiveness requires that the voices of these people are included and given adequate weight in every part of the policy-making process that impacts the agri-food system, and in the allocation of resources. Attentiveness requires genuine participatory decision-making, not simply some watered-down, after-the-fact right to agree or disagree with a policy written to benefit others.

2. Responsibility
The duty to care in this regard arises directly out of the rights of those in need, and cannot be seen as some kind of voluntary, charitable action. Government can no longer evade its constitutional Section 27 obligations in respect of the right to food. If the crafters of the Constitution were not convinced of the importance of equitable and universal access to food in our new society, they would not have included it in the Bill of Rights. This means that government has a clear responsibility to elevate this right over other claims, such as corporate profit (which, remember, is not actually a constitutional right). This responsibility is limited only by what government can realistically be expected do with the resources at its disposal.

3. Competence
The content of policies and the actions of officials need to be judged against a standard, the standard that has been set by the Constitutional Court in terms of government's obligation to deliver socio-economic rights. This means that every action that government takes, which impacts the agri-food system, needs to be constantly assessed against *this* responsibility to prioritise the right to food, by asking, 'Is this the very best that could be done under the current circumstances?' A key role of a new institutional framework will be to constantly ask this question of all responsible parties.

4. Responsiveness
Sadly, there are daily examples where government – whether it is the national Department of Agriculture or provincial agricultural extension officers, or a city that wants to turn farmland into middle-class housing – makes it quite clear that they are not interested in the responses to their actions by those to whom they owe a duty of care. This lack of responsiveness is not uniform: as a general rule, the poorer you are,

the less likely government is to actually care (as opposed to pretending to care) about your view of their actions. When people say to me, 'we know that we are not important in this city', they are articulating exactly this reality: their government's lack of interest in how they perceive the 'care' that they have received. A new institutional structure must ensure that this changes. True responsiveness means that we cannot continue to prioritise programmes (like homestead vegetable gardens) that clearly do not address the underlying problems, simply because we cannot be bothered to think of anything better.

On the basis of these four guiding principles we could start to think about institutional arrangements – how could government be better organised to deliver more appropriate governance outcomes? Despite the attractiveness of some kind of Ministry of Food operating along the lines of wartime Britain, it is probably not the best way to deal with the issues, certainly not at a national level. It would be very difficult to restructure all the existing departments and lines of authority in this way without extreme disruption to the daily business of government. Despite the severity of the challenges that we face in our food system, we are not actually at war (which is a great thing for motivating radical change), and thus the challenges of getting everyone to buy into a drastically different system would be considerable. These problems would probably be great enough to prevent such a ministry from ever really getting going.

An appealing alternative is some kind of *Agri-Food Policy Council*, structured along similar lines to the many food-policy councils that have been established in many other countries. This Agri-Food Policy Council would have oversight over (at least) the departments of Agriculture, Rural Development and Land Reform, Social Development, Health, and Trade and Industry with respect to legislation and policy relevant to the agri-food system. This council would have the right to propose (and draft) relevant new legislation and/or policy to the included departments, and it would also have some kind of veto right over legislation and policy proposed by these departments. In this way, departments could get on with their existing activities with the minimum of disruption, but slowly the activities across all of these would be more focused and synchronised to address the underlying problems around the governance of our agri-food system.

In order for this proposed policy council to work, three things would have to be in place. Firstly, it must have *real authority* and this requires true commitment from the people that have real power in government.

If, for example, the Department of Agriculture is allowed to simply ignore the recommendations of this policy council, it will very quickly become another ineffective and largely pointless government entity, like the hapless National Agricultural Marketing Council (NAMC), doing the best it can while nobody pays it any attention.

Secondly, this council must have real resources at its disposal. It must be able to undertake innovative and meaningful primary research that incorporates a wide group of people. It must be able to draft effective policy in a genuinely participatory manner, and it has to be able to exercise meaningful and critical oversight over several other departments.

Thirdly, it must pay full service to the notion of Attentiveness. This means that in its composition, its information gathering and its decision-making, it must prioritise the input of those who have been neglected to date. We cannot create another entity that simply prioritises the input of big business and a handful of 'experts', and repackages this as a policy priority. Yes, the corporate food sector is a stakeholder that requires a place at the policy table, but only one place and certainly not at the head of that table. Nor should this policy council be an organisation that does public consultation in the manner that has, sadly, become the norm in this country: getting a group of 'experts' to do all the analysis and prepare all the recommendations, and then convening some kind of rent-a-crowd 'workshop' to give the illusion that they have incorporated the input of 'the people'. This is precisely what happened with the drafting of our current national food-security strategy, and is the main reason why it is so disconnected from reality.

Legitimate representatives of farmworkers, of small farmers, of hungry communities, of health workers, of landless people's movements, of land-reform beneficiaries, of consumers, of the rural poor and of other groups that have traditionally been marginalised in our policy formulation should make up the majority of those who are consulted by the Agri-Food Policy Council. And this 'consultation' should cover all aspects of policy-making and the drafting of legislation, from inception through to approval. We need to stop confusing poverty with stupidity. We need to understand that those who daily experience the negative impact of the current agri-food system are in a particularly good position to offer insights about what needs to change. The role of technical experts is to provide technical expertise, not to speak on behalf of any of these groups, or to decide on their behalf what should be done. With respect to such technical expertise, it would probably be useful for this policy council to have a close working relationship with the NAMC.

One of the key activities of an Agri-Food Policy Council, and where its greatest potential lies, is to generate a comprehensive view of all the various participants in a food system, and to make decisions about how to manage competing goals, such as: how can we manage the trade-off between better incomes for small farmers and lower prices for consumers in a way that will benefit the greater good? These trade-offs – and the potential role for government in altering these – will become apparent only when one institution is given the specific responsibility to identify and investigate them.

What are the priorities on which the Agri-Food Policy Council could focus? The short answer is – a great deal of things, given the current state of policy-making in this area. However, we could narrow this down to a few priority areas, focusing on the most problematic legislation and policies. In my assessment, these are the Marketing of Agricultural Products Act, the current National Policy on Food Security and Nutrition Strategy, social-grant administration, and current policy towards small farmers. It is not my intention here to propose a detailed list of policy initiatives, as some kind of 'expert' input. This work needs to be done by this policy council in proper consultation with affected parties. My goal here is simply to make some suggestions about where that work could commence, and to highlight particularly important issues that I strongly believe can no longer be ignored.

As we have already discussed, the Marketing of Agricultural Products Act is the main reason why government is unable to intervene in agricultural markets to facilitate a more equitable distribution of power in the system, and thus more socially desirable outcomes. In many respects, this Act appears to drastically limit government's ability to meet the constitutional right to food: the vast majority of people access their food through *markets*, and thus it is through markets that the right to food will be realised practically. As the central piece of legislation in this regard, and by preventing government interventions in almost all or any circumstances (including in the interests of advancing food security), the Act functions as a very effective impediment to achieving this Section 27 right. This Act needs to be reviewed urgently, and either amended as required (obviously keeping in mind South Africa's international trade obligations) or completely rewritten. Specifically, the conditions under which government may intervene in markets, and the tools that they have at their disposal to do so, need attention.

We have also discussed the dismal National Policy on Food and

Nutrition Security. This is a sad example of how the moral evil of inattentiveness can be translated into inappropriate, even damaging, policy. Preferably, the entire thing should be binned and something new put in its place – something based on the lived reality of those who have to deal with food insecurity and malnutrition every day. If the formulation of a new food security and nutrition policy were drafted under the four guiding principles of the Agri-Food Policy Council, it would be much more likely to take account of the real drivers of food insecurity. It would be more likely to consider the many ways in which there are opportunities to create new kinds of relationships between the producers and the consumers of food that will benefit the majority of South Africans.

Social grants – which currently amount to some R140 billion each year – are effectively propping up a system that is fundamentally anti-poor. In many ways, this money represents a transfer from taxpayers to the corporate food sector. This is not because there are no alternatives, but because no one in government believes that this money could be a powerful force for change. In several other countries (and in complete contrast to what is happening here), schemes have been put in place to encourage social-grant recipients to spend their money with local small farmers, thereby using government funds to leverage additional poverty alleviation. This could be done in various ways, including a 'spend plus' scheme which would, say, allow a grant recipient to receive R100 worth of goods by spending R95 at a designated trader. Or loyalty card schemes, which give successive discounts for prioritising grant spend at designated traders. But we cannot decide which of these options would work best until government accepts that there is a problem that needs solving.

Current policy in respect of small farmers is both undermining rural development and ignoring the reality of the potential of small (and very small) farmers, not just to create rural livelihoods, but also to provide high-quality and reasonably priced food. The general assessment by policy-makers is that small farmers have no real role to play in a 'successful' agri-food system, but this is more of a reflection of how they define 'success' than any reality. As a result of this misinformed (inattentive) and dismissive attitude, small farmers are actively being disadvantaged and undermined by current policy, which often forces them into abusive market relationships and generally makes it very difficult for them to earn a living.

The vast majority of small farmers do not receive any public-sector support *at all* in many of the areas where it is most critical, such as transport or access to processing and storage facilities. Where they do receive assistance (such as with some inputs or access to irrigation), this is often delivered in a manner that is so bad and devoid of care that it makes it quite clear that the government officials in charge of these programmes have no real interest in supporting small farmers. One group of small farmers, with whom I spent time a few years ago, had their (relatively new and government supplied) borehole pump break down in the middle of a hot and dry summer. It was almost 10 days before the local extension officer* could rustle up the time to come past and take a look (which had to happen before he would authorise someone to come and fix it). At no point did he offer any apology to the group or, in fact, appear as if he thought these people were entitled to something a little better from their government. This was not an isolated incident.

Remember the land reform beneficiary whose tenant was told by Minister Xingwana: 'Do you know who I am? I am the Minister of Land Affairs and this is my house. Pack your bags and get out of my house right now'? The woman in question alleged that the main reason why the farm was not operating properly was because none of the promised support from the Department of Agriculture had actually materialised, despite her waiting two years for this. In addition, because she did not have the title to the land (under the new rules, most beneficiaries are given only the right to lease the land), she was unable to borrow money against it to self-fund her operations.** I have seen variations of this situation replicated over and over again, all across the country, as government officials fail to deliver what was promised (or deliver it too late, which is much the same thing in farming) and small farmers go out of business as a result. This failure is often seen as 'evidence' that small-scale farming is inherently unsustainable and that small farmers are inherently incompetent.

Every gathering of small farmers that I have ever attended has highlighted the shocking state of agricultural extension services, and has made that issue very clear to whichever government official was in attendance. But nothing changes. It is hard to escape the conclusion that no one in authority is really interested in supporting these farmers. The moral evils of inattentiveness and avoiding responsibility have seldom been so clearly evident.

---

* The provincial official directly in charge of managing (or mismanaging) support to farmers.

** She eventually won a legal battle to have her access to the farm reinstated.

This is precisely why we need to place a truly representative Agri-Food Policy Council in a position of authority over these officials. The only way to stop this cycle of abuse is by elevating the beneficiaries of land-reform programmes to a position where they are genuinely able to oversee the work of the public servants whose job it is to provide them with quality services.

In sharp contrast to the disdainful dismissal of smallholding as a viable production model, many of the small farmers with whom I have spent time are extremely productive. There is no doubt in my mind that they could provide a solid foundation for a new food system, if only anyone in government would pay a little attention. Shadreck Mahlanga is a good example. He farms on 1 000 square metres of land (a small plot of about 35 by 30 metres) near Hartebeespoort Dam.* The plot – Reed Farm – is a model of efficiency and produces high quality (I have eaten some of it) certified organic produce the whole year round. Shadreck Mahlanga sells most of his vegetables through a cooperative that has a regular stand at the Bryanston Organic Market in Johannesburg, and he receives about 60 per cent of the final selling price (which is a far better deal than most vegetable farmers in this country get and he does not carry the risk of unsold produce). He also has some customers to whom he supplies directly, and he does so at a very competitive price. He is a prime example of an alternative food system.

He works full-time on his plot, employs another person full-time, and gets some additional part-time input from his son and wife, Thoko. In keeping with his organic methods, he makes his own compost and saves most of his own seed for replanting. He pumps water through a highly efficient (self-installed) irrigation system from the nearby river. As a result of these factors, his farm operates on a very low-cost basis. Despite the fact that he is getting only 60 per cent of the final selling price for most of his produce, his annual turnover is close to R95 000. On a per hectare basis, this puts him very close to the most productive, big organic farmers in the country.

A similar story can be told about Mosima Pale,** who farms a small plot in the Philippi area and supplies organic vegetables to a number of restaurants in Cape Town. He operates an extremely productive small plot of land, producing high quality produce (once again, I am speaking from experience). Also in Cape Town, Sibongile Fityedi heads a group

---

* About 50 kilometres north west of Johannesburg

** You can find him on Facebook – Wynberg Organic Urban Farm.

of four people who run a wonderful organic mini-farm in the grounds of Gugulethu Comprehensive School (across the road from Nyanga Station.) His group sells most of their produce through the Harvest of Hope initiative (which falls under the NGO Abalimi Bezekhaya),[89] and they receive 50 per cent of the selling price of the produce. The plot is a model of efficiency, producing a wide range of high-quality vegetables (yes – if you are wondering – I have eaten these as well). They are comparable to the best that is available in a supermarket.

One of the goals of the Philippi Horticultural Area (PHA) Food and Farming Campaign is to demonstrate the viability of a peri-urban smallholder model, to counter the City of Cape Town's assertion that small-scale agriculture cannot be considered as an option for the PHA. They are developing an organically farmed plot at the campaign headquarters, operating in a way designed to replicate what would be possible for a small farmer with limited resources at their disposal. They are keeping careful record of production, income and expenses, and operating it as a demonstration farm, a living example of what is possible when we start to pay attention and to take responsibility.

All of these small farmers – and there are many, many more like them – represent a solid foundation on which to generate sustainable incomes and create employment. They also have significant potential to form the basis of more equitable food systems that will benefit both producers and consumers. In sharp contrast to the profit-at-any-cost model of corporate food, almost every one of the small farmers with whom I have been in contact expresses a strong sense of 'fairness' as their guiding business principle. None of them are wealthy people – some of them would certainly count as poor – but they are clear about their desire to prioritise equity and fairness in their business activities. That is, they have a strong sense of their *duty of care to others by virtue of their position as producers of food*. Most of them donate produce to local charities (such as an orphanage) whenever they are asked to do so. They will regularly charge a lower price for their produce for customers that they know cannot afford to pay more. They will make up special-sized items (such as a R2 bunch of spinach) to accommodate their poor neighbours. This duty of care is prioritised, I believe, because of the fact that their producer–consumer relationships are intimately *human*, rather than resolutely economic. That is, they are firmly located in a sense of community, and thus take decisions based on a *human* morality, rather than an economic morality. This is the kind of food system we could build if we wrest it away from corporates and hand it back to human beings.

On the basis of their proven productivity and preference for equitable transacting, we would imagine that small farmers would be a prime target for government support, and that policy would prioritise the replication of smallholder models. Rather unsurprisingly, but still depressingly, this is not the case, despite the fact that a successful smallholder model could dramatically improve land-reform outcomes, and give many more people access to land-based livelihoods. Where government is interested in such small farmers, it is either to insist that they must be 'scaled up' into 'commercial' farmers, or to provide small amounts of irrelevant and/or shoddy support.

To the first issue: what seems to have escaped the attention of policy-makers is that Shadreck Mahlanga, Mosima Pale and Sibongile Fityedi are already *commercial* farmers: that is, they sell what they produce, and they are in farming to make a living, not as some kind of weekend hobby to fill up their spare time. In fact, they are relatively successful commercial farmers, with high productivity and access to reasonable markets, although all of them would like to achieve more. The assessment of them as 'non-commercial' is an indication of the ignorance (inattentiveness) and bias of the government officials in question, rather than reflecting any reality.

They do not need to be 'scaled up' into some big farming operation where their cost base will increase exponentially, and they will go out of business supplying vegetables to a big supermarket. (This is exactly what such 'scaling-up' policies aim to do.) Instead, policy-makers need to recognise that they are *commercial smallholders* (this will be a new phrase in the official language) and that what they need is not 'scaling up' into some made-for-failure model, but targeted support of a particular kind to allow them to improve – on their own definition of 'improvement' – on what they are already doing. What is the support that these farmers actually need, as opposed to what policy-makers have negligently assumed they require?

Some of these small farmers would like to have more land, but it is usually a very modest amount that they have in mind, such as an additional few thousand square metres. Sometimes they would like that extra land in order to add on a higher-value product to their existing farm, such as free-range chickens or exotic fruits such as berries. What they really require is guaranteed access to perennial water of suitable quality* (where they do not already have it) and small amounts of

---

* Water quality is a critical issue for those farmers hoping to get organic certification.

capital (that is, cash) to spend where *they* believe they need inputs or infrastructure. In our current 'poor people cannot be trusted to spend money wisely' models, it is government officials who get to decide what goods these farmers 'need'. These decisions are often wrong. The resulting waste of resources is generally far greater than it would be if a few small farmers misspent their cash allocations.

These small farmers also need technical support to obtain the kind of market access options they *actually* require. One example is transport: Shadreck Mahlanga is the farmer who faced huge transport challenges until he was able to save enough money to buy himself a car. Sibongile Fityedi's group has no access to their own transport. They are aware that there are potentially lucrative, direct markets within a few kilometres of their smallholding, but they have no cost-effective way of regularly transporting their produce there. None of these farmers (or the thousands like them) has access to the kinds of processing and storage facilities that they require. Because they do not have access to *and control over* such facilities, many farmers are forced to sell their produce at a very low price to big food processors that then take the enormous margin between farm gate and processed-food item. These facilities are critical to the ability of small farmers to increase margins (that is, to get a higher share of the retail price of food), to reduce waste and to access higher-value markets. Smallholder livestock farmers need access to low-cost and accessible slaughter and storage facilities that will allow them to sell small quantities of meat into local markets at a significantly higher price than they would get from a local abattoir (but still a cheaper option for local consumers). Vegetable farmers like Sibongile Fityedi need access to low-cost processing facilities to enable them to store excess produce, and to be able to monetise produce that is not suitable for direct sale (for example, a hail-damaged butternut, which is perfect for making into high-value baby food).

There are literally thousands of examples of successful interventions in this area from around the world, which have radically altered the terms on which small farmers participate in agri-food systems. What we need is for those in charge of smallholder policy to take notice of these successful ventures. But this is not going to happen as long as they are inattentive to the actual requirements of those whom they profess to be assisting.

A policy council, such as the one I have described, would fill a big void at the national policy-making level and also influence what happens in agricultural and rural development policy at a provincial level; but this would still leave a gap at the local government level, and this gap is considerable. Some of the most important decisions that influence the distribution of power in our agri-food system are made at the local level. Local municipalities – and particularly the big metro areas, which are home to the majority of hungry people in South Africa – have considerable power over issues such as land use and access (including what kind of retail dominates), policy around public space and informal trading, the regulation of fresh produce and other agricultural markets, transportation, infrastructure like water and electricity, and the prioritisation of local economic development (LED) projects. In many respects, local government is falling even further short than national in its responsibilities to ensure the right to food and the prioritisation of the needs of the poorest citizens in this respect. This means that the work to create a new governance structure for our agri-food system must incorporate what happens at local government level, if it hopes to succeed.

Local government: Planning for human-centred food systems

Local government in South Africa has a wide range of development responsibilities in terms of our Constitution. The reason for this is that local government, by virtue of its proximity to citizens, is presumed to be in a good position to determine accurately the needs of those citizens and to provide services that respond to these needs. Well, that is the theory anyway. In the area of food security (including relevant urban and small-scale agriculture), local government has fallen so far short of its obligations that most municipal officials are not even aware that such obligations exist.

Let us start by getting ahead of them and looking at what these are.

The Local Government Municipal Systems Act 32 of 2000 (the MSA) introduced the requirement for every local municipality to have an Integrated Development Plan – the generally well-known and often-cited IDP. IDPs are prepared for five-year periods (to coincide with the term of office of a particular local council) with annual reviews to update or revise as is deemed necessary. The IDP was envisaged by the writers of the MSA as the most powerful tool at the disposal of local government to undo apartheid-era planning and resource allocation. Under the latter, the majority of South Africans were largely ignored and resources were allocated almost entirely for the benefit of the white population. The MSA envisages a planning and resource-allocation environment that prioritises equity, democracy and participation.

To this end, chapter 5 of the MSA makes it mandatory for each municipality to produce an IDP, which is intended to reflect 'the municipal council's vision for the long-term development of the municipality with special emphasis on the municipality's most critical development and internal transformation needs'. This requirement results in a pretty long to-do list: if any of you have ever read through your local municipality's IDP (and you really should), you will know that these are very considerable documents. They often run to hundreds of pages, covering a wide range of municipal activities, from basic service delivery through to detailed plans for local economic development. In the metropolitan areas, these documents are even longer and more detailed, reflecting the increased responsibilities of these councils. The IDPs for these cities, together with supporting budgets and implementation plans, can run to nearly 1 000 pages.

In fact, the only thing that does not seem to make it into any IDP in any meaningful way is food. Looking through the City of Johannesburg's 2012–2016 IDP, I found a very limited number of references to food, mostly stating that food security is a problem for many people in the city (they estimate that more than 40 per cent of all households are food insecure) and that this represents an undesirable state of affairs. OK – so what is planned in response? I got a little excited when I saw the following:

IDP sub-programme: Food resilience and food security
The City is committed to promoting and providing access to safe, affordable food citywide, with targeted support to the extremely food insecure.

I got unexcited again when I saw that this actually implied some charity food and food parcels for those close to starvation, and that old standby, homestead vegetable gardens, for everyone else. This is how the City of Johannesburg interprets being 'committed' to addressing food insecurity.

It is much the same story everywhere else – inattentiveness cuts across all party–political lines. Take a look at the City of Cape Town's IDP and you will find even fewer references to food security. So what is their main (actually, only) plan in this respect? You guessed it – backyard vegetable gardening. This is not because the City is unaware that it has a problem: research that *it* commissioned indicated the severity of the problem. In some of the poorest areas of Cape Town more than three-quarters of all households can be classified as hungry. Their approach does not, therefore, reflect real ignorance – it reflects a total absence of caring.

But does local government actually have an obligation in respect of food? If we look at what issues the IDP is supposed to address (the MSA is quite clear) – it should place 'special emphasis on the municipality's most critical development and internal transformation needs'. If hunger does not count as a 'critical development need', then I am not sure exactly what does. Local government prioritises the provision of all the basic necessities of life – shelter (housing), water, electricity, healthcare, public transport, infrastructure, safety and security, social security and transport – except for food. Against this backdrop of legislated planning to address developmental needs, it is a most peculiar omission. Does local government not know that the right to food in included in the Bill of Rights? Are they unaware that there are significant numbers of hungry families living under their jurisdiction? Have they not noticed that 20 years of food-garden projects has not made an impact?

We might think that local government has not paid proper attention to food because they see it as something that is provided through the private market, and is thus not a 'proper' point of intervention for government. But this argument does not make sense. Many of the other goods and services that government provides – like housing and healthcare and education – also have big, private-market components. The presence of a sizeable and profit-driven market in something like healthcare is not seen as a reason why government should not get involved in planning for and providing healthcare. In fact, the opposite is generally true: government justifies significant expenditure and complex programmes for supplying services, such as subsidised healthcare, free education and cheap public transport, precisely because the private sector is *not* providing these services at an affordable rate to low-income households. So why do we not apply the same thinking to food?

Think about this for a minute: if government applied the same reasoning to housing that it does to food, local housing policy for the poor would look something very much like this:

> We have noticed that 60 per cent of the population cannot afford to buy a house from a private developer because they do not have sufficient income. As a result, thousands of families are

homeless and living on the streets. This is a serious problem for our city and we need to address it. In our 'Address Homelessness' IDP Programme, we will be distributing 200 free bricks, five bags of cement and a pamphlet on how to build a house to 500 needy households every year. In this way your city will be resolving homelessness and its associated social evils.

Can you imagine if you read this nonsense in your IDP, presented as your city's 'developmental' housing policy? I would put money on it that there would be a riot, even a light stoning of the mayor's office. But this is exactly what local government is presenting as its food policy, and none of us are even vaguely upset.

What makes this sorry situation even worse (and I bet you thought that it could not get worse) is that there are thousands of examples of successful local-level food planning all around the world.[90] In many cities, the importance of the right to food is generally accepted. As an official from the Brazilian city of Belo Horizonte (a leading example of what can be achieved through focused food planning) put it:[91]

> There is a pervasive attitude that this is not the role of the state. And we challenge this: Why is this not the role of the state? Because the state is saving banks, constructing highways – why not save lives through food?

The obligation of local government to engage explicitly in comprehensive food planning is generally accepted around the world, as illustrated by the following: In a 2009 editorial for a special edition of the journal *International Planning Studies*, Kevin Morgan (from Cardiff University) referred to what he termed the historical 'puzzling omission' of food planning from the wider planning agenda. His conclusion was that 'this "puzzling omission" is now a matter of historical interest only because, for the foreseeable future, food planning looks set to become an important and legitimate part of the planning agenda in developed and developing countries alike'.[92] This, written *seven years ago*, illustrates that this academic believed that planning policies that neglected food had been relegated to the dustbin of history. This is how far out of step our supposedly world-class cities are with what is going on in that world they aim to emulate.

Food planning requires that local municipalities *prioritise* (not just recognise) the right to food, and align all other policies – such as land use and access, infrastructure development and social services – to achieving universal access to food. In practice, this means that local government needs to focus on supporting the growth and development of the alternative, human-centred agri-food systems described in Chapter 8. They need to stop prioritising the desires of a few corporates over the rights of the rest of us. They need to stop talking and start listening.

We can achieve these goals only by putting in place – and empowering – institutions similar in nature to the national Agri-Food Policy Council described earlier. In such an environment, the City of Cape Town's plans to rezone and build over high-value agricultural land in the PHA and the Cape Flats aquifer could not happen, because city planning would have to prioritise the right to food over other possibilities. And this would mean that the city would be forced to plan for how the area could contribute to a more equitable and accessible food system, rather than being allowed to shrug its collective shoulders and refuse to even consider the idea. The City of Johannesburg would have to prioritise the rights of small food traders to public space and to new retail developments. All cities would have to give careful consideration to how small peri-urban farmers can store, process and transport food to consumers. Nazeer Sonday's and Sheryl Ozinsky's* vision of a farmers' market within walking distance of every inhabitant of Cape Town would be adopted and made real by the city itself. Half-hearted, uncaring programmes around food, which are there only to give the impression of doing something, would properly be relegated to the dustbin of history.

Rural municipalities, where hunger rates are highest and where the possibility of earning a living from farming becomes more remote every year, could do even more. Many of the small towns in the Free State – where tens of thousands of families go hungry and ex-farmworkers with no employment options populate informal settlements – are surrounded by hundreds of hectares of high-value agricultural land that *belongs to the municipality*. This municipal commonage is made up of two kinds of land: that which historically formed commonage land for use by the town's residents, and that which has been purchased by government since 1994 (the latter making up the majority). The aim of this acquisition policy was to make land available for agricultural activities by low-income households in the municipality.

---

*   From Oranjezicht City Farm – you will get a full introduction to Ozinsky in Chapter 8.

We are talking about sizeable amounts of land: about 113 000 hectares just in the Free State.[93] If mathematics is not your strong point, this is *1 130 square kilometres* or almost 70 per cent of the area covered by the entire Johannesburg metropolitan area. And much of this land is of reasonable or good quality agricultural value. It represents a significant capital outlay by government, paid for under the land-redistribution programme. It also offers an excellent basis on which to build an alternative local food system. The commonage land is located right next to tens of thousands of consumers of food. Although these people are poor (sometimes very poor), they spend money on food (they have no choice). When we start to think about a settlement of 3 000 households (which represents one of the *smaller* Free State towns) and we apply the estimate of how much the poorest households in South Africa spend on food each year – R4 868[94] – we can get a rough estimate of an annual food spend of about *R14.6 million* by that community. If only 20 per cent of that went to local food producers, it would represent an income opportunity of almost R3 million each year. And the food produced by those small farmers could contribute significantly to the nutritional status of the community, by making quality food available at a significantly cheaper cost than they can currently purchase it. Achieving this goal, however, will require a rather different approach from that currently employed by the majority of those municipalities that own this land.

What is the current approach? The words that spring to mind are 'neglect' and 'indifference'. If you think I am exaggerating, I suggest you take a drive to one of these commonages and see for yourself what a pitiful sight they are. Fences are almost non-existent because they have never been repaired. Water (and thus the possibility of irrigation) is almost always a problem because infrastructure has either not been installed or never maintained. Inherited farming infrastructure has either fallen into disrepair or been stolen. Very few of the appropriate by-laws with respect to maintaining the commonage (such as preventing illegal dumping) have been enforced. Where some local residents are attempting farming activities, they generally receive no meaningful government support. There is zero investment in any kind of infrastructure – storage or processing – that would allow these farmers to increase their incomes, or facilitate better access to better food by the local community. Instead, charities hand out plates of food to ragged children. Nowhere is the moral evil of inattentiveness – of wilful blindness to the needs of fellow citizens – more apparent.

Regulating the corporates: Competition and market power

To close off, let us take another look at our food corporates and how they do business. As I stated at the beginning of this chapter, I do not think that there can be a meaningful role for these corporates in an agri-food system based on an Ethic of Care. Any new, alternative system that aims to prioritise human morality will simply have to pass them by, as if they did not exist. This does not mean, however, that it is not in our collective best interests to curb their worst excesses and abuses of power: most of them will be in operation for the foreseeable future. There are a number of ways in which government could do a whole lot better than it currently does in this regard, and many of these areas of potential improvement relate to competition legislation.

The regulation of competition (and thus any anti-competitive behaviour) in South Africa is governed largely by the 1998 Competition Act. This Act states the following as its goals:

- To provide all South Africans equal opportunity to participate fairly in the national economy
- To achieve a more effective and efficient economy in South Africa
- To provide for markets in which consumers have access to, and can freely select, the quality and variety of goods and services they desire
- To create greater capability and an environment for South Africans to compete effectively in international markets
- To restrain particular trade practices which undermine a competitive economy
- To regulate the transfer of economic ownership in keeping with the public interest
- To establish independent institutions to monitor economic competition
- To give effect to the international law obligations of the Republic

This means that government is empowered to investigate and to take action against companies that it believes are abusing their market power or colluding to abuse their potential combined market power. The legislation also gives government the right to veto any proposed merger which it believes will create a company with so much market share that it will be in a position to enter into abusive practices. The key institution through which the Act is enforced is the Competition Commission.

The Act lists a number of 'prohibited practices', dividing these into 'Restrictive Practices' and 'Abuse of a Dominant Position'. In terms of the former, it makes a further division – between 'horizontal practices' (that is, practices among firms that are supposed to be competing with each other) and 'vertical practices' (which refers to the relationship between suppliers and buyers, that is, up and down a supply chain). The bread price-fixing agreement of 2006 entered into by the major baking companies fell under the first kind – prohibited horizontal practices. It is these kinds of activities that come to mind for most people when thinking about why food prices are so high.

Restrictive vertical practices essentially prevent an agreement between parties that are in a vertical relationship (such as a flour miller and a bread baker) if that agreement 'has the effect of substantially preventing or lessening competition in a market'. An example would be if the flour miller agrees with the bread baker to sell flour to all the bread baker's competitors at a price 20 per cent higher than it charges the first bread baker. (It is a little confusing – they might actually do this, but it is the existence of an *agreement* that makes it illegal, rather than if it just turns out that way.)

The part about abuse of dominant position is a little more complicated: a firm is *automatically* determined to be dominant in a market if it has at least a 45 per cent share of that market. It *may* be determined to be dominant if it has between 35 and 45 per cent of the market and *cannot prove* that it *does not* have market power. And it *may* be determined to be dominant if it has less than 35 per cent of the market if someone else can prove that it has market power. (Just read this again ... all will become clear.)

Once it has been determined that a firm qualifies as dominant, there are a number of things that it is prohibited from doing, such as charging excessive prices to consumers. The Act also lists a few practices that dominant firms are not allowed to engage in with respect to their suppliers, such as 'requiring or inducing a supplier ... to not deal with a competitor'. You may recall that in his 2009 report investigating the dairy industry, Professor Kirsten suggested that milk buyers are, in fact, engaging in this prohibited practice, by punishing farmers who sell milk to anyone else. Kirsten's report also listed a number of other ways in which milk buyers (retailers and processors) were, in his opinion, abusing dairy farmers, and that this abuse was a factor pushing these farmers out of business. It was also a factor that he alleged was preventing new farmers from entering the industry. I have pointed out my own opinion: that abusive treatment of suppliers in the dominant agri-food system threatens our domestic food supply and greatly limits the ability of new black farmers to make a living.

What is the Competition Commission planning to do about this? The short answer is very little, not because it is not committed to prosecuting those that break the law, but because often they *have not* broken the law. The real problem is that our competition legislation does not really allow for firms to be investigated for abusive practices towards suppliers unless they are determined to be dominant firms, and this is a fairly hard thing to prove in the absence of a 45 per cent market share.

In 2008, the UK Competition Commission published the second report arising out of its investigation into the supply of groceries in the UK market.[95] Its findings are relevant for South Africa because the level of market share of supermarket retailers is similar in both countries, and supermarkets in both countries follow similar business models with respect to the management of their supply chains. They thus tend to have similar practices around how they treat their suppliers (or at least they did until recently). The UK Competition Commission investigation found that a supermarket needed only an 8 per cent market share to be able to impose a wide range of abusive practices on its suppliers. These included many of the practices recorded by local investigations such as Professor Kirsten's: last minute changes to the terms of an order; delayed payment; and making suppliers carry a range of extra costs that should really be for the account of the supermarket.

This 8 per cent threshold is much lower than the threshold set in our Competition Act, and it suggests that all of our Big Four supermarkets may have sufficient market share to be able to abuse their suppliers. Certainly, this is exactly where much of the evidence is pointing. There are also a number of processors that could be deemed to be in an effectively dominant position with respect to their suppliers. Companies like Tiger Brands, Premier Foods, Pioneer Foods and Clover all hold significantly more than an 8 per cent market share in many basic food items. There is no reason to suppose that they are not also in a good position to implement an abusive relationship with their suppliers (and certainly, Professor Kirsten's investigation into the milk market suggested that this was the case).

The problem, of course – and as I am sure many of you are thinking right now – is drawing the line between an 'efficient' business practice and an 'abuse' of power. One of the key guiding principles of being a profit-making corporate is to increase your market share *precisely* so that you can exercise power over your suppliers. Being able to squeeze a good deal from your suppliers is how you can increase your margin and your profits. That is exactly what your shareholders want and what will guarantee the CEO a good bonus. This is a good example of *economic morality*: we reward and congratulate business managers that are able to achieve exactly that outcome – it is generally considered to be a 'good' thing. And it may be good in many industries but it is not such a good thing in our agri-food system. We might be able to accept some abuse of suppliers if the outcome of all that squeezing was lower food costs for consumers, but we now know that this is most definitely not the case. Instead, the benefits accrue to a relatively small group of winners.

Our Competition Commission has taken an interest in some of the indirect ways in which corporate food companies use their market power to exclude competitors. In June 2015, the commission gazetted a proposed Terms of Reference for a *Grocery Retail Sector Market Inquiry*. The proposed scope of this market inquiry is the following:

- The impact of the expansion of the large supermarket chains on smaller and independent retailers
- The impact of exclusive long-term property leases entered into by large supermarket chains on market competition
- The dynamics of competition between local and foreign-owned, small and independent retailers
- The impact of various regulations (including local spatial planning regulations) on small and independent retailers
- The impact of buyer groups on small and independent retailers
- The impact of certain value chains (the gazette does not stipulate *which* chains) on the operations of small and independent retailers

In May 2016, the chairperson of this enquiry indicated that it was anticipated that it would be completed by the end of May 2017. Although this enquiry will – hopefully – highlight some of the ways in which food retailers are entrenching their market position and shutting out competitors, this is only a small part of how market abuse takes place.

I think we could make a good case for arguing that we need some kind of differential competition legislation with respect to food, on the basis of its position as a fundamental necessity of life. It is not like most other goods and services – if you cannot access food you die. This, together with the inclusion of the right to food in the Bill of Rights, suggests to me that it may be appropriate to hold corporates in the food sector to a higher standard of behaviour – something that incorporates ideas of human morality rather than just economic morality.

And there are international examples for adopting such an approach: following the 2008 report of the UK Competition Commission enquiry into the operation of the grocery retail sector in that country, a Code of Conduct was implemented in 2010. It applied only to the biggest firms (those with an annual turnover greater than £1 billion sterling) and took the form of a set of compulsory terms to be included in all contracts between retailers and their suppliers. This included a prohibition on making suppliers responsible for shrinkage (that is, product being spoiled or damaged); a prohibition on retrospective changes to the terms of the agreement; the necessity to conclude all agreements in writing; and the implementation of the principle of 'fair dealing' as the guiding principle for these contracts.

The Groceries Code Adjudicator was established in 2013 specifically to exercise oversight over the relationship between supermarkets and their suppliers. It oversees the implementation of the Code of Conduct, investigates (confidential) complaints and arbitrates in disputes. Given how much more serious the impact of corporate abuse of suppliers is in South Africa than in the United Kingdom, perhaps it is time that we investigated similar remedies.

More drastic solutions may also be useful, particularly in increasing transparency and highlighting exactly who in our agri-food system is winning and who is losing. In 2011, the Farm Gate to Plate Bill was proposed in the Australian parliament. It was never passed – it faced extreme opposition from food retailers – and lapsed in 2013. But it contained an interesting proposition: it would have required retailers to display, 'in close proximity', the producer price and the retail price of fruit and vegetables. It would also have imposed penalties for failing to do so.

I would bet that I am not the only person who thinks this would be a fantastic idea right here in South Africa.

Chapter 8

Consumption as care: Solidarity and ethical food citizenship

You and I, and every other South African, are the most important participants in our agri-food system, and thus have the greatest capacity to effect change. Some of us fill dual-participant roles in this system, being farmers or farmworkers, or food traders or food manufacturers, but we are *all* food consumers. And it is in our roles as *food consumers* and as *citizens* that we have the ability to enforce meaningful change in the current system, and to create and sustain completely new systems that will be to the greater benefit of us all. However, to achieve real change, we need to start thinking about ourselves and those around us in a very different way. We need to realise the power that we *actually* have in the system, as opposed to what we have been led to believe. We have to re-imagine ourselves as a collective of *ethical food citizens*. We need to embrace the four components of Joan Tronto's Ethic of Care as the guidelines for how we participate in the system, how we make decisions, and how we allocate our resources. Every one of us – no matter how poor – has the ability to effect this change. It is not always going to be easy, but it is not always going to be difficult either. Once again, we can draw inspiration from thousands of communities around the world (including in South Africa) who are doing exactly this – building themselves new, people-centred food systems from the ground up.

Taking action: The power of the collective

Becoming an ethical food citizen requires that we do a number of things: the first is that we use our collective *political power* as voters to get food onto the priority political agenda and to make sure that it stays there. That is our role as *citizens*. We should no longer tolerate having some of the most important social issues of our time swept under the collective carpet as if they never existed. We should no longer tolerate local government avoiding its constitutional obligations to plan comprehensively – and properly – for an equitable, local food system. We should no longer allow rural municipalities to look away from their obligations towards municipal commonages. We should no longer tolerate the government we voted for acting as if a few big corporates have more rights than all the rest of us put together. We should no longer tolerate the absence of Attentiveness and the avoidance of Responsibility and the lack of Competence and the zero Responsiveness.

We also need to make our voices loud and clear in our local, integrated development plan (IDP) processes, so that the meaningless nonsense that passes for 'food-security policy' or 'small-farmer support' is deleted for good. I know that this can be a particularly frustrating and thankless task. I have participated in writing lengthy documents setting out a community's objections to an IDP, only to have it (very politely mind you) put in the bin. I sometimes get the distinct impression that no one in power really cares what the average South African thinks or wants. But as I am writing this book, there seems to be a different mood in the country: local government elections have shaken some of the established power bases and power relations, and this seems to me to be a good time to start putting pressure on our elected officials to give food the attention it deserves.

There is another issue that we cannot ignore for much longer in this country, and which needs to be part of that priority political agenda. The overarching agri-food system is a critical success factor for land-reform beneficiaries, since it is the terms of their inclusion into that system that is the most important determinant of their ability to make a living from farming. This point is seldom, if ever, included in the debates over land restitution. The EFF (Economic Freedom Fighters) is South Africa's newest notable political party and, although it has put land at the forefront and centre of its economic agenda, it has had little or nothing to say about the overarching agri-food system into which new landowners will be dropped, despite the fact that this is almost a guarantee of their failure. Unless the system changes fundamentally, no amount of land transfer will make a meaningful impact on poverty. Instead, it will merely contribute to the popular discourse that black South Africans are not as good at farming as their white contemporaries. This is not how we should be going about building an equitable society.

As citizens, it is *our* responsibility to ensure that these issues are placed at the top of the political pile, and that our fellow citizens – all of them – have equitable access to their rights. It is our moral obligation not to look away, no matter how frustrating or annoying the process. Failing to do something because it seems like a lot of hard work is a form of evading Responsibility; of failing in Taking Care Of. Tronto writes specifically of the conceptualisation of care as some kind of burden – it is not meant to be effortless.

The second part of being an ethical food citizen is to make good use of one of our greatest powers to effect change – our money. We really do live in a material world, and, although it seems paradoxical, we can make our economy more *human* through the way in which we choose to spend our money. I should point out that Joan Tronto did not believe that *giving* money generally qualified as caring. She was referring to giving money to someone *instead* of taking care of them, insisting that genuine care involves *doing* care. I do not believe that this idea means that *monetary transactions* cannot be the basis of a caring agri-food system. This is not the same as giving someone money; entering into a transaction with someone is not *giving* them money.

The agri-food system is different from the care-giving on which Tronto based her analysis. This system is fundamentally a monetary, transaction-based one. Our goal in creating a human-centred system based on an Ethic of Care is to change the basis on which those transactions are made, for the greater good, rather than to abolish them entirely. As we shall discuss, the basis of ethical transacting is reciprocity, in other words, that we deal with each other as equals in an environment of mutual respect. This is very different from charity and involves both giving *and* receiving value.

The basis on which we make monetary decisions, and with whom and on what basis we transact, can be a powerful force for change. Money (or money as we know it) is not the *only* basis on which we can create new kinds of networks around agriculture and food, but it is certainly one of the most powerful ways of doing so. In addition, money-based alternative networks form a good foundation for building money-free or alternative-money networks, since we are all familiar with the act of exchanging our rands for goods or services.

Although we are often made to feel powerless in our agri-food system – to believe that we have no real agency to effect change – we actually wield considerable power as a *collective* of consumers. One of the main reasons, of course, why we *feel* so powerless to initiate change is because the entire system (reflecting neo-liberal economic theories) is focused on making us feel like individuals, rather than a collective. We are encouraged to think of ourselves as 'unique', and to express our 'individualism' through our shopping. Nonsensical advert-speak such as 'there is only one you' and 'be more you', and 'good for you' is designed to make us feel that we stand apart (or should strive to stand apart) from everyone else. Even the term 'collective' conjures up some nasty Soviet-style conformity, with all of us dressed in matching pyjama outfits. There is method in this madness of course: as individual shoppers chasing our own unique selves, we have no power in the system. As individuals we effectively hand over our real power to the big corporates, trading it in for some imaginary sense of self. As a collective, things are very different.

Thinking of ourselves only, or foremost, as individuals 'apart' from those around us, is fundamentally opposed to Tronto's definition of care: 'care implies a reaching out to something other than the self; it is neither self-referring nor self-absorbing'.[96] The first part of the Ethic of Care – Attentiveness – requires that we pay attention to *others*, and that we take note of both the direct *and* the indirect consequences of our actions. It is important to ask yourself, 'what am I facilitating or supporting by engaging in this transaction with this supermarket?' and then take Responsibility (the second part of the Ethic of Care) for those outcomes. There can be no hiding away behind the excuse of, 'but what difference does my little bit of money make to how things work?'

The very foundation on which to build a human-centred, a people-centred agri-food system is the recognition of, and the prioritisation of, our *interdependence*, not our isolation. And so we need to start embracing the notion of the collective: after all, what is so bad about standing together with our fellow South Africans to get something done? Some of our best recent memories as a nation have been those very occasions when we have been a collective: our mutual flag displays in the 2010 Football World Cup; our standing in line together to vote every couple of years; our shared grief at the death of our Tata Madiba. Surely we are up for a little collective shopping in the interests of the greater good?

The consumer boycotts of the 1980s – where entire black communities (many of them very poor) stopped shopping in white-owned stores as a means of applying pressure to the apartheid government – provide an excellent local, historical example of what can be done as a group. Even the poorest communities wield significant collective spending power on food, much of it concentrated on a few basic food items. It is through our collective shopping that we can enforce change in the most unacceptable parts of our existing agri-food system. The obvious example that springs to mind is farmworkers. Even those farmworkers who do get paid the mandated minimum wage (it is R2 778.83 a month at the time of writing, or a daily rate of R128.26) cannot afford to feed their families adequately. Much worse off are those farmworkers whose employers still do not pay the legislated minimum wage (and there are more of them than you would think). And at the bottom of the misery pile are those who are made to live in sub-human conditions, and are subjected to regular abuse from their employers.[97] In these latter two instances, employers are simply ignoring their legal and moral obligations, because they believe that no one can make them act differently. It is time to put this notion to bed.

These farmworkers deserve our attention. Looking away will make each of us guilty of the moral evil of inattentiveness. And there is plenty that we could do. Although not all farmers sell into supermarkets or the big food processors, a significant number of them do (the other main market access points are the municipal fresh-produce markets and direct sales). As I have discussed at length in Chapter 7, most of the supermarkets and processors probably exercise significant power over their suppliers. Until now they have used this power for the sole purpose of increasing shareholder profits. It is up to us to use *our* power to insist that they use *theirs* in a way that is beneficial to the greater good.

How could we do that? A Code of Conduct for agri-business corporates (that is, including both processors and supermarkets) with an annual turnover of, say, more than R1 billion would be a good start. That Code of Conduct would require these businesses to audit the employment practices of their suppliers, and to refrain from doing business with those who do not comply with a set of employment standards, including the minimum wage and the living conditions of farmworkers. If these businesses are able to audit the temperature at which their supplier stores the vegetables and a whole host of other private standards, I am sure that auditing labour practices would be a relatively simple matter. To make things a little more transparent, we could think about appointing an NGO like Women on Farms to check compliance. We would have to think of some practicalities – like how to exempt small farms using family labour and community cooperatives – but the general idea is not complicated. And how could we enforce this? We should refuse to shop at supermarkets that cannot prove that they comply and we should refuse to buy the products of those companies that do not comply. This is exactly the way in which the anti-apartheid boycott of South African produce worked. It really is that simple.

If you are a person who is deeply concerned about hunger in this country, but do not know where to start doing something – this could be exactly the initiative that you have been looking for. Certainly, you will impact the lives of many more hungry people this way than by doling out food at a soup kitchen. And you will be doing this in a way that is mindful of their rights and their dignity.

We could also be putting pressure on agri-business in respect of particular products, like milk, where the local industry is under threat of going out of business because of excessive profit-taking by corporates (but poor consumers cannot afford to buy the product). If you recall, dairy farmers are getting paid about R4.50 a litre, while you and I are paying close to R13 a litre. At the time of writing this book, there is rising consumer dissatisfaction with a very similar situation in Australia, where dairy farmers have had the price that they receive unilaterally cut by processors. As a result, many of them face bankruptcy and have had to apply for emergency government relief. Consumers are responding by purchasing only those milk brands that they know pay farmers a higher price. They are avoiding house brands of supermarket milk, on the basis that these brands are associated with the lowest prices for farmers.

There is also a growing movement in the United Kingdom protesting the low prices that are paid to dairy farmers, which is threatening the entire dairy industry. In 2015, dairy farmers organised protests against those processors and supermarkets that were paying the lowest prices, and asked consumers to boycott certain stores. And there are many other similar actions and campaigns that we could initiate and be involved in, if we started to get organised and if we started to throw around our own power.

Although we can certainly force some changes to make our existing agri-food system a little more focused on the needs of human beings rather than on corporate profits, I need to restate here my belief that there is a limit to what we can achieve in this regard. (And a limit to what can be achieved by all the recommendations I made in Chapter 7 about government policy regarding the regulation of these companies.) There are only so many concessions that these companies are willing and/or able to make, before their entire business model starts to show cracks. The reality is that this is where most of us will get the majority of our food in the foreseeable future, but if we want real change, we will have to start building new systems, not keep applying Band-Aids to the existing one. In fact, the more we believe that we can change the existing system into something genuinely ethical, something that prioritises the greater good rather than the interests of the few, the more time we will be wasting, which we could be using to build real alternatives. We need to move on. Now.

And so the third part of being an ethical food citizen is the most powerful: our ability to organise ourselves to build and grow completely new agri-food systems; systems built on an Ethic of Care, which prioritise human morality rather than economic morality. The good news is that we do not generally need anyone's permission or political approval to do this – very often we can simply go out and take charge and get it done. How? In many, many ways, some of which I am going to discuss here, and some of which you will discover yourself as you begin to embrace the notion of *solidarity* with your fellow citizens.

The solidarity economy

A solidarity economy is one that gives practical meaning to an Ethic of Care; it is the daily *practice* of care in the economy or, in this instance, our agri-food system. There are many different definitions of a 'solidarity economy', but I prefer those interpretations that do not insist on a bounded definition – a solidarity economy is this or that and nothing else. I particularly like Ethan Miller's definition of a solidarity economy as analogous to 'making the road by walking',[98] since it talks to ideas of community sovereignty – that it is up to individual communities to decide what kind of economic (or agri-food) system they want, and to develop it by doing, by making it up as they go along. This is very different from what we have now – a situation in which communities (and particularly poor ones) are deemed to be too ignorant to understand their own problems or to make meaningful input into their own solutions. And so others must do it for them, through the IDP or through national development strategies that take no notice of their lived realities or their own priorities. A solidarity economy is one in which these communities are involved in all the talking and the doing, and are not just passive listeners; the grateful recipients of the largesse of others.

There are some things, of course, that make a solidarity economy uniquely a solidarity economy, rather than anything else. Most importantly, these are economic systems that are firmly located in *human morals*, motivated by growing the greater good, rather than generating benefits that accrue to only a few. A solidarity economy is based on *mutual respect*, notions of fairness and shared decision-making. A solidarity economy specifically incorporates goals of *social justice*. There is no place in a solidarity economy for poverty-stricken farmworkers existing alongside billionaire supermarket owners. Why? Because this is not fair and it is not just.

It is in forming relationships of solidarity that we build a *practice* of care; that we exercise care in our everyday lives by reaching out to others in mutually respectful relationships. There are thousands of examples of solidarity economy movements around the world, from community credit associations to free mobile-phone apps written by people who simply want to provide a useful service, to community provision of social services, to worker cooperatives, to open-source free software. Many solidarity economy movements have focused on agriculture and food: it is a universally consumed item and many people have grave concerns about the social, environmental and human health consequences of the dominant agri-food system.

It is important at this point to note the difference between an 'alternative' agri-food system and a 'solidarity' agri-food system, given how much has been written about alternative food. 'Alternative' means just that – different from the mainstream. But some food systems can be 'different' without embracing notions of solidarity and social justice. For example, many of the people who shop at the new organic food stores and farmers' markets in South Africa are looking for 'alternative' food; that is, certified organic, free from chemical additives and produced in an environmentally friendly and/or humane way. They may also be getting it in an alternative way, such as supporting locally produced food or buying directly from a local farmer because they believe that this has a reduced environmental impact. These agri-food networks are 'alternative' because they are not the mainstream (which is generally associated with 'industrial' food that involves lots of chemicals and processing and big supermarkets).

But there may be nothing 'solidarity' about these alternative networks at all. In fact, there often is not, particularly in South Africa. My research suggested that the majority of people who shop at organic stores have little or no interest in social justice or the welfare of farmworkers, or the fairness of the food system or how their purchases might contribute to any of these goals. Instead, they are motivated largely by wanting food that is good for *them* and only good for them (with the odd nod towards the environment). Many of the people who buy Shadreck Mhlanga's produce at the Bryanston Market do so because they want to buy quality organic food, not because they want to be sure that the farmer who grew it received a fair deal.

There is, of course, nothing wrong with these 'alternative' food systems, and many of them – particularly those based around organic production – are better for the environment *and* for the people who work on these farms, since they are not exposed to large amounts of toxic chemicals. Many farmers' markets provide an attractive outlet for small farmers who might otherwise not have such a good option (like Shadreck Mhlanga). In my opinion, this pro-small farmer bias counters criticism that these markets are targeted at wealthier consumers. They may in this manner be contributing to improved social equity outcomes. So alternative food networks are basically good things, in many ways better than the dominant corporate model.

But they are not solidarity networks. Although 'alternative' food networks (like farmers' markets) *may* also be solidarity networks, or they may have potential to become solidarity networks, they are not *automatically* solidarity networks. We need to be mindful of the difference, since the real power of transformation of our agri-food system lies in solidarity, not in alternative.[99] Solidarity implies a particular intention and purpose, a desire to fundamentally change the world around you for the benefit of others as well as yourself, and to act on this basis. Without that clear intention, any change that does occur will simply be coincidental.

'Solidarity' implies thinking beyond the self and incorporating the needs of others in our economic decision-making. It means embracing care for others in a mutually respectful manner. It means thinking of all the ways in which your decisions about what to feed your children could impact someone else's ability to feed *their* children.[100] It means making connections with your neighbours, with your community, with your fellow South Africans in order to effect change. It thus also implies thinking very differently about how you get your food and who you get it from, and how you pay for it. It means taking *responsibility* for changing the outcomes of our agri-food system. Solidarity networks are the key to revolutionising our agri-food system, for the benefit of all of us.*

There are all sorts of ways in which we can embark on 'making the road while we walk' towards a solidarity economy. Many of these will represent only a small fraction of your monthly food budget. But over time, each of these actions will accumulate. And that is how we build a new system – by walking one step at a time. My purpose in the remainder of this chapter is not to provide you with a point-by-point guide on how to build a solidarity agri-food system (and I am sorry to disappoint you if that is what you were expecting). The very notion of a solidarity economy is to develop something that works for *your* community, from the ground up, based on shared learning and shared experience. And so my goal is to share with you some stories about how other people have gone about doing this, to give you an idea of what is possible and to spark your imagination.

Building a solidarity economy is not meant to be a solitary pursuit. It is fundamentally about rebuilding our economy as a *collective,* as a place where we celebrate our interconnectedness and mutual dependency. It stands in direct contrast to the me, me, me culture that sits at the heart of neo-liberal economics, with its insistence on the solitary, utility-maximising person who values an extra unit of money above all else. That is, it is based on a more accurate version of how human beings actually behave and their potential when they work together.

The solidarity purchase groups of Italy – the *gruppi di acquisito solidale* or *GAS*[101] – provide a fascinating example of the power of the collective. A GAS is a kind of collective provisioning scheme, that is, members purchase as a group. These groups focus mainly on the collective purchase of food, although some groups do purchase other items as well. It is estimated that almost one in five Italians are involved in some kind of collective provisioning of food, although not all of this takes place via a GAS. They are an interesting example for South Africa because they are made up primarily of middle-class and lower-middle-class families, thereby effectively dispelling the common perception that non-supermarket food is only for the rich.

The economic and political context of contemporary Italy – which

---

* OK – maybe not the CEOs of the supermarket chains in the short run, but even they will eventually benefit from a more equitable and caring society.

has provided the impetus for the growth of these groups – also has interesting parallels with South Africa. The global economic crisis has put many Italian families under pressure, including their ability to afford food as prices rise and household income comes under pressure. There is growing disenchantment with what is seen as corrupt government that favours the interests of the few over the many. There is also growing unhappiness with Mafia control of a significant part of Italy's agriculture, not just because of the involvement of organised crime in this production, but also because these farms are often worked by migrant labourers who live in appalling conditions and are paid very low wages. These are all important issues for GAS members, who prioritise social justice issues in their food-purchase decisions over considerations such as whether or not the food is organic. (Grasseni's study showed that labour conditions on farms were the *most* important factor for GAS members in making purchases.)

GAS are thus *fundamentally* about putting into practice notions of care for others, and many GAS members see their actions as overtly *political*, in that they have the clear intention to effect social change. GAS members understand very well that how you choose to feed yourself and your family is not politically neutral: your decisions will either entrench one form of power distribution in an economy or facilitate something different, hopefully something better. This awareness – and choosing to act on it – is the critical difference between membership of an organisation like a GAS, and choosing the pack of organic vegetables on the supermarket shelf.

This is (basically) how a GAS works: a group decides to get together on the basis of shared ideas about food provisioning – that is, how and (critically) from whom they should buy it. GAS vary in size, from a few families to more than a hundred. The group works on democratic principles, based on face-to-face discussions within the group. Grasseni made the interesting point in her book that almost none of the GAS ran a Facebook or similar social-media platform as a means of facilitating communication within the group. Instead they placed a high premium on personal interaction. This highlights the importance to these groups of building *personal* relationships, no matter how much more time and effort they might require. This *reconnection* with our neighbours and with our communities is a critical part of a solidarity network. This is in stark contrast to the lone shopper making her solitary way up and down the supermarket aisles.

The GAS decides what products it would like to buy collectively, and how much of each it will purchase each year. Getting to this point requires that each GAS member makes a commitment to the group – you cannot say that you will buy 120 litres of milk in the next year – 10 every month – and then pull out after three months. And this is the second feature of a solidarity network – commitment. Change requires that we make commitments and stick to them to the very best of our ability. Once again, this implies a very different approach towards our food provisioning from the one we currently have, where we can purchase something whenever the fancy takes us, and make that purchase wherever it is most convenient for us. Collective-purchase schemes require that we rethink our definition of 'convenience' with reference to more than just our own interests: is it really 'convenient' to be able to buy an excessively processed and overpriced pack of food produced in a way that promotes rural poverty just because you can do it on a whim at 7 pm?

At this point you may be thinking that a GAS-type arrangement sounds like a lot of hard work and commitment, and may not be a very good idea. You may need to think again: although a GAS-like arrangement is not for everyone, Grasseni reported that most GAS members enjoyed the sense of community that came from being part of a committed group. GAS meetings often involve the sharing of meals and represent enjoyable social occasions for members. Closer relationships with food producers (described later) give GAS members and their children the opportunity to spend time on farms and with farmers. Finally, a GAS enables members to access high-quality food at a price that is generally cheaper than in a supermarket.

A GAS is a *direct* purchase group. Once the GAS has a commitment from members on what and how much they will purchase in the following 12 months through the group, they then decide what their priorities are in selecting the farmers (or manufacturers if they have an item like bread or pasta on their list) from whom they will buy. The group decides these priorities based on their personal concerns and ideas. They may decide that farmworkers' living conditions are their priority, or supporting small, local, urban farmers or purchasing from black farmers. Issues like organic production may also be a concern for the group. In reality, the GAS will produce a *list* of issues deemed important by the group. They may not always find farmers or manufacturers who meet all of these requirements, in which case they have to find a basis on which to make compromises. For example, they may decide that the working conditions of employees (whether farmworkers or bakery employees) is not negotiable, but that they are willing to compromise on whether or not that farmer is strictly local. They may decide that the quality of the produce (determined by eating it) of a small urban farmer is more important than whether or not it is certified as 'organic'.

Once this prioritisation process has been completed, the group will start to look for farmers (or food manufacturers) from whom they can purchase directly the items on their list. Within the group, individual members are allocated the responsibility for certain products, such as vegetables or meat or flour, and then it is up to them to find produce that meets the group's requirements. This could prove to be a tricky task in South Africa, where we are so used to buying our food from supermarkets that we cannot imagine how to do anything different. You will, however, be pleasantly surprised at how many options are available once you start to look around.

In terms of vegetables, there are hundreds of options in and around our cities: for instance, there is Sibonigile Sithole and his group in Gugulethu (and no – you will not get mugged, or at least I have not been), or Shadreck Mhlanga at Reed Farm, or the Khulisa Social Services Streetscapes garden in Roeland Street in Cape Town, or the PHA Food and Farming Campaign's demonstration farm, or Siyavuna in Durban, or the many people all around South Africa who are growing food on their own small, urban vegetable plots. Look on the Internet, speak to people, visit a farmers' market or simply drive around. Take a trip to Genadendal and meet the farmers there. Make a visit to your local municipal fresh-produce market. You will be inspired and astonished at what you find.

Other products, such as meat and dairy products, may not be as easy to locate, but they are there. Ask at the local organic shop, visit a farmers' market, talk to your local butcher and wander around the Internet.

Once we start thinking in a different, more mutually beneficial way, it is not hard to see how a different vision of the PHA in Cape Town could support a large solidarity agri-food system, to the mutual benefit of thousands of city residents. If land in the PHA was prioritised for the use of small farmers, such as the Vukuzenzele Urban Farmers Association, these farmers could form the core of a city-wide, solidarity agri-food system that could fundamentally transform access to food in the city. But this will not happen unless the city starts to prioritise food and livelihoods over their narrow definition of 'development'.

Once potential farmers have been identified by the GAS members, and initial discussions have indicated how much they are able to supply of each product and at what price, the GAS member who is 'in charge' of a particular product will present their recommendations to the group. These recommendations will take account of the group's priorities in selecting farmers, as well as practical considerations such as how far away the farmer is and how delivery will take place. The group then decides on a short list of potential suppliers, based on the factors that the group deems important. Most GAS groups do not neglect the issues of price and food quality alongside social considerations, like who is going to benefit from their purchase. It is customary for the entire GAS group to visit the short-listed farmers (or manufacturers), to meet the people who will be producing their food. These visits provide everyone in the group with the opportunity to ask questions and to start building the personal relationships between food producer and food consumer that are the hallmark of a more equitable agri-food system.

The group also has to decide who will deliver the produce to individual members, since this has cost and practical implications. In the case of many small, urban, vegetable farmers in South Africa, who do not have access to their own transport, the group would have to collect the produce and work out a way of getting it to members. Meat could be delivered to a central point every couple of months by a farmer, and then someone in the group could be designated to get it to the other members, or members may have to collect it. There may be a central storage facility that the group could use. These are all practical arrangements to be negotiated and decided by the group.

Once the group has selected the suppliers (and there may be more than one in any particular category), each one concludes a written agreement with the GAS. This agreement commits the group to buying a certain amount of produce, at a pre-determined price, at regular intervals. In the case of vegetables, this may be a weekly transaction. For items such as meat, it may be quarterly (every three months). The important thing is that this represents a commitment by the GAS members. This buyer commitment is critical for the suppliers – they know that they have a guaranteed customer at a pre-determined price for the following 12 months. GAS members cannot pull out of their commitment because they are bored with eating their weekly allotment of vegetables.

The agreement also requires a commitment from the supplier.

Farmers have to understand that they cannot drop out of their agreement if someone else comes along and offers them a higher price. But it is an agreement based on mutuality and working together: GAS members have to understand that things can go wrong in farming – a bad hailstorm could wipe out a vegetable crop which would mean no deliveries for a couple of weeks. Farmers need to understand that sometimes consumers cannot stick to an agreement, due to circumstances beyond their control. Farmers and GAS members are thus in a particular kind of *committed* relationship, one that emphasises their interconnectedness and mutual respect. This is very different from the consumer–supermarket relationship, which requires zero commitment on your part.

Seasonality is another factor that members have to get used to – you cannot have fresh aubergines from your farmer all year round. All this does not mean that GAS members put themselves in an inconvenient position by participating in these collective provisioning systems. On the contrary – Grasseni's research shows that they generally access high quality food at a cheaper price than in the supermarkets. They also benefit in other ways from this connection with their food suppliers. Yes, participation in a GAS-type system does require more commitment than the supermarket model. You may have to learn to cook a lot more ingredients and accommodate less of a variety of goods than you may have at your immediate disposal in your local supermarket, but these are opportunities to share experiences and skills with fellow GAS members.

GAS members usually make regular visits to 'their' farmers, taking a personal interest in how their food is produced. Over time, the relationships between the GAS and their farmers may develop into very interconnected ones: many GAS members like to refer to themselves as 'co-producers', referring to how deeply they are involved with their farmers. They may ask a farmer to cultivate a particular variety of vegetable and share the costs and benefits of doing so. They may agree to pay a higher price for a product if the farmer receives organic certification. Grasseni records an instance in which a GAS even organised a loan for their dairy farmer, to support him through a difficult period (such as we might do if 'our' farmer was feeling the pressure of the drought). These are all things that mark the difference between solidarity economic relationships ('we are all in this together') from mainstream economic relationships ('I am the only one who matters').

It is also important to remember that you don't have to jump into the provisioning deep end: you do not have to commit your entire monthly food purchases to a GAS (and it probably is not a good idea to do so at the start). Maybe start by getting together with some like-minded people and find three or four products that you would like to purchase as a collective, and see how that goes. Very few GAS members purchase all their food through the group, and many reported that they still shopped at supermarkets. The idea is to enter into an arrangement that is beneficial – for you and for others – not to engage in some kind of self-punishment.

There are other, less difficult (but also less revolutionary) ways of participating in agri-food systems that are different from the dominant corporate model. Shopping at a farmers' market is one of these: ask questions of the farmers who sell their produce there. How do they treat the people who work for them? How do they produce their food? Ask them if you can visit their farm. You may very well find a producer (or more than one) who ticks all your social-justice boxes, and you can support them without having to enter into the kind of GAS-like commitment you may not be quite ready for. You could also support an initiative like Cape Town's Harvest of Hope, which packages and sells the produce of the urban farmers of Abalimi Bezekhaya in a weekly box subscription scheme; or the similar Kumnandi initiative of Siyavuna in Durban.

If you are feeling more ambitious, you may decide to start your own community food initiative, like Sheryl Ozinsky did in Oranjezicht in Cape Town. She was mugged in the street shortly after moving to the suburb several years ago. Her response was not to move, but to do something about it (she is definitely a 'do something about it' kind of person). She pushed for the establishment of a neighbourhood watch, not just to directly address crime in the area, but to address what she identified as the real underlying cause of the problem: the distinct lack of a community spirit.

After the neighbourhood watch was established, Sheryl noticed that there was a 'problem' property in the suburb: a neglected and overgrown plot of land – quite a sizeable piece – which was home to the local drug dealers and various other undesirables. After a bit of investigation, she discovered that the property was part of the original Oranjezicht farm, one of the first food farms established in the Cape colony. In the 1960s, the City of Cape Town had decided to demolish the original homestead and turn it into a municipal bowling green.* This had later been abandoned, the city lost interest and the property slowly fell into disrepair. Based on its history, Sheryl decided that it would make a great city fruit and vegetable garden and set about raising funds and marshalling volunteers to get it up and running – as the Oranjezicht City Farm.**

Once the garden was up and running, she started a weekly market selling its produce to raise money to fund the ongoing operations of the garden. This proved extremely popular and rapidly outgrew the available space. Today the market is housed at Cape Town's waterfront, attracting about 3 000 people at a time. The weekly market sells much more than just vegetables from the original farm, and includes farmers and food producers from all over Cape Town and the surrounding areas,[102] providing an important market access point for small food producers. In addition, there is a monthly 'pick-your-own' day at the farm in Oranjezicht, which gives people the opportunity to select and harvest organic vegetables at a reasonable price.

This farmers' market has been criticised because it caters mostly to higher-income households, but this is precisely why it offers such an attractive opportunity for smaller farmers. And Sheryl is very aware of this: she buys the boxes of vegetables that Harvest of Hope is unable to sell and resells them at the market, thereby reducing Harvest of Hope's financial risk and contributing to the sustainability of the initiative. She also has ambitions way beyond the Waterfront market; ambitions to build more solidarity-type food networks in the City of Cape Town. She would like to see an affordable food farmers' market on every street corner in Cape Town, but has identified two key obstacles to achieving this. The first is what she sees as the general lack of interest in solidarity food networks by the average South African. This means that they are often not prepared to make an effort and change their food provisioning habits in the interests of the greater good. The second is the City of Cape Town itself; its administration does not seem that interested in supporting these kinds of food networks. Like Nazeer Sonday, she sees the city's determination to destroy the PHA as evidence of this lack of interest. 'Cities are not focused on food, they are focused on development,' she tells me. The real problem, of course, is that the city's administration would think of these as two different things. Her sentiment is reflected in the words of a PHA farmer, who

---

* Unbelievable, I know

** If you have not visited Oranjezicht City Farm I would urge you to do so. It is marvellous.

asked, 'what is the point of building tens of thousands of houses in the area if there is not going to be any food on their tables?'

If food were a priority for the City of Cape Town (or in fact any other South African city), they would be thinking along the lines of the initiatives undertaken by Philadelphia, as part of its Greenworks programme to develop the decaying industrial city by making it 'the greenest city in America'. Food is a priority area in Greenworks, via the Philadelphia Food Policy Advisory Council.[103] Tellingly, the city's food plan falls under the Equity Programme of Greenworks, highlighting the social-justice implications of more equitable access to food. It set a goal of giving all Philadelphians access to affordable, healthy food within walking distance of their homes, by supporting urban agriculture *and* markets at which that produce could be sold. In the first five years of operation, the programme had facilitated an additional 84 farmers' markets, urban gardens and urban farms. They did this through a variety of initiatives, including making it easier to establish urban farms on public land, and streamlining the process for setting up farmers' markets. This is somewhat different from the approach of our own city planners.

I discussed earlier the absurdity of the criticism that being opposed to the dominant, corporate agri-food system is somehow 'anti-market'. All of the solidarity economy options that I have presented here are market transactions: the difference is in who benefits from these market transactions. A cityscape that is dominated by small food markets supplied directly by farmers (particularly small farmers) is a market system that works for the majority.

It is the markets envisaged by Sheryl Ozinsky and Nazeer Sonday and many others that are critical to the success of urban agriculture and new agri-food systems. They provide the income-generation opportunities that farmers like Sibongile Fityedi require through direct sales to consumers, and they will bring more affordable food closer to consumers, by cutting out the middleman. Nor should these markets be confined to higher-income areas – they offer a real prospect of bringing quality, affordable food to everyone in a city.

In rural areas these markets offer even greater possibilities for increasing access to food and creating rural livelihoods, which then also contributes to addressing food insecurity by raising household incomes. Currently we have a situation where government spends money on developing local agricultural projects, almost always with the express purpose of getting them to sell their produce to supermarkets or processors. Given that these customers are generally looking for high volumes, this encourages monoculture – the growing of only one or two products. As we now know, the farming margins for these items are usually very low, as most of the value accrues to processors or supermarkets or both.

At the same time, these project participants and their neighbours are buying almost all of their food from the local supermarket, at a much higher price than it is being produced *right there*. Sadly, no one has taken note of this. Instead of getting hungry people in these towns to grow food for themselves, and the agricultural project participants to grow for the supermarkets, they should be growing food to *trade* in their local communities. If local development officials took the time and effort to work out the food spend of a particular community, they would see that this is a considerable potential market. If local farmers were equipped to produce a range of food items that their neighbours buy, they would be able to take advantage of that to earn a much better living. In turn, their neighbours would have access to cheaper food. All we really need is a bit of imagination and a genuine commitment to doing those things that are really in the best interests of the majority.

Some final thoughts

Although this is a book supposedly about food, now that you have come to the end of it you know that it is not just about food. This is because food is not really just about food. It is much more than a combination of calories and nutrients and national production calculations. Food is not just central to whether we live or die; it is also central to our personhood, our place in society and our fundamental notions of who we are.

Food is a focal point of our social life: all of life's most important transitions – birth, marriage and death – are marked by food. Food plays a pivotal role in our celebrations and in our memories. We offer food to comfort one another. The sound of a crying baby is most often met with the comment, 'is she hungry?' Food is solace; food is kindness; it is how we show our love for our children and our friends and our family. Food is care on a plate.

Not having food is not really about not having calories or micro-nutrients or any other material thing. It is about being denied comfort and kindness. It is about hearing your children cry because they *are* hungry and not being able to do anything about it. It is about being denied the opportunity to care for those you love, and to feel unloved yourself. It is about living a life without comfort or solace. It is about being a lesser person in the way that it matters the most.

And so 'an empty plate' is not just about the absence of a meal. It is about the absence of care, the absence of dignity and the absence of kindness. These are the real moral evils of our food system.

Acknowledgements

Only when I started writing these acknowledgements did I realise how many people had helped me in the research for this book. Any errors that I have made are, of course, entirely my responsibility.

The first 'thank you' must go to all the people who took time out of their busy lives to talk to me and share their experiences. They had no motivation to do so, save for good will, and without them this book could not have been written. Nazeer Sonday and Susanna Coleman at the PHA food and farming campaign not only answered endless questions and drove me around, they also participated heavily in marketing the book and gave me a wonderful platform on which to speak about these issues. Given the demands on their time made by their day jobs and their commitment to the campaign, I really have no way of thanking them enough.

Brian Joffin at the PHA Campaign farm has always been unfailingly welcoming, and happy to spend time in debate and answering my questions.

Shadreck Mahlanga and his wife Thoko welcomed me into their home, and took several hours out of their working day to show me their farm. They also gave me some fabulous vegetables. Sibongile Fityedi's enthusiasm never fails, even when I phone to ask yet another question. Mosima Pale has been just as generous in answering my questions, despite my having just pitched up at his farm with no introduction. Khotso – Mosima's assistant the day I visited – patiently showed me around and gifted me with vegetables. Thanks also to Joseph (Boetie) Bantam and

Johannes Arendse in Gendendal. These farmers deserve your support.

Sheryl Ozinsky had no reason to take time out of her incredibly busy life to chat to an unknown author, but she did so with what I suspect is her trademark enthusiasm. Thank you Sheryl.

A special mention to Annamarie Grobler from GIZ, who made it possible for me to attend a two-day workshop on PGS for small farmers, which gave me the opportunity to meet and talk to them. Thanks to everyone there (some already mentioned plus the people from Siyavuna) who shared their experiences with me.

Thanks also to Rob Small at Abalimi Bezekhaya/Harvest of Hope, to Janet Gracie at PGS, and to Gary Jackson from Jacksons Food Market.

Audrey Wainright at the Bryanston Organic Market introduced me to many of the people who helped me with this book, and was unfailingly helpful and encouraging.

Particular thanks to those who agreed to read the book in advance and helped to get it noticed: Dr Jane Battersby is a leading academic in her field, and her generosity in this respect is remarkable.

The South African Food Sovereignity Campaign and Andrew Bennie – thank you for providing me with insights for my research and for doing an advance review.

Sasha Stevenson at Section 27 is another busy person who always had time for me, and I am indebted to her for making a number of good points about the Constitution.

Ishtar Lakhani very generously agreed to let me use the research contained in her Masters' thesis. Her work is remarkable – she really should write a book!

A big thank you to Glenda Younge for doing a great editing job.

Thanks to everyone at Jacana, particularly Bridget, who agreed to publish this book without having read a word I had ever written. I hope she thinks it was worth it!

Thank you to Samantha Yeowart, who read an early version, provided input and never tires of trying to improve the world.

Thanks to my father – John Ledger – for unfailing support, a steady flow of news articles and whose name I shamelessly dropped whenever I needed someone to take me seriously.

And most of all, thanks to my partner, Hein. He never doubted that I could write this book, even when I did. He read everything I asked him to, sometimes several versions of the same pages, and always gave me good advice. Without his generosity, insight and support this book truly would never have been completed.

Endnotes

1. www.groundup.org.za/article/de-doorns-farm-workers-strike-after-wages-dropped_375.
2. ibid.
3. BFAP, *Farm Sectoral Determination: An Analysis of Agricultural Wages in South Africa*, 2012, p vi.
4. Based on a 42 per cent household allocation to food expenditure.
5. First quarter of 2013, using prices from StatsSA's published consumer-price index data.
6. Wylie, *Starving on a Full Stomach: Hunger and the Triumph of Cultural Racism in Modern South Africa*, 2001.
7. Wylie, *Starving on a Full Stomach*, 2001.
8. ibid., p 85.
9. RSA, *Report of the Committee of Enquiry into the Marketing Act*, 1992.
10. NDA, *White Paper on Agriculture*, 1995, p 5.
11. NDA, *Agricultural Policy in South Africa: A Discussion Document*, 1998, p 20.
12. ibid., p 20.
13. Section 2(1) of the 1996 *Marketing of Agricultural Products Act*.
14. Vink & Kirsten, *Deregulation of Agricultural Marketing in South Africa: Lessons Learnt*, 2000.
15. ibid, p 29.
16. www.namc.co.za.
17. NAMC, *Report on the Investigation into the Effect of Deregulation on the Diary Industry*, 2001.

18. NAMC, *Report on the Investigation into the Effect of Deregulation on the Red Meat Industry*, 2001.

19. NAMC, *Section 7 Committee Evaluating the Deregulation Process: The Wheat-to-Bread Value Chain*, 1999.

20. NAMC, *Report on the Section 7 Committee Investigation into the Wheat-to-Bread Value Chain*, 2009.

21. Comments contained in a speech released to the media in March 2013. Available at: www.news24.com/SouthAfrica/News/Use-it-or-lose-it-20090313 (accessed on 16 July 2016).

22. Wegerif, Russell & Grundling, *Still Searching for Security: The Reality of Farm Dweller Evictions in South Africa*, 2005.

23. The official national statistics office.

24. Shisana et al., *South African National Health and Nutrition Examination Survey*, 2013, p 39.

25. Tathiah et al., 'South Africa's nutritional transition', 2013.

26. 2016/17 budgeted expenditure.

27. US$2 545 and US$5 090, respectively, as at date of writing.

28. As at 31 May 2016.

29. Hendriks, 'The potential for nutritional benefits from increased agricultural production in rural KwaZulu-Natal', 2003.

30. You can find them at www.namc.co.za.

31. PACSA, *PACSA Monthly Food Price Barometer: May 2016*, 2016

32. The size of the average South African household.

33. Calculated by StatsSA.

34. PACSA, *2015 Annual Report*. Available at: www.pacsa.org.za (accessed on 12 July 2016).

35. Available at: www.pacsa.org.za (accessed on 12 July 2016).

36. Jacobs, 'Identifying a target for food security in South Africa', unpublished report, 2009.

37. Lakhani, 'Food for(e) thought: Strategies of the urban poor in Johannesburg in achieving food security', unpublished Masters' thesis, 2005.

38. Oxfam, *Hidden Hunger in South Africa*, 2014.

39. Battersby, The state of urban food insecurity in Cape Town, 2011.

40. Said-Mohammed et al., 'Has the prevalence of stunting in South African children changed in 40 years?', 2015.

41. Referenced in Tathiah et al., 'South Africa's nutritional transition', 2013, p 721.

42. This refers to the consolidated groups. So, for example, Score is part of Pick n Pay, and Checkers and U Save are part of Shoprite.

43. Pereira, *The Future of South Africa's Food System: What is Research Telling Us?*, 2014.

44. You can find these at www.namc.co.za.

45. Kirsten, *The Impact of Market Power and Dominance of Supermarkets on Agricultural Producers in South Africa*, 2009.

46. MPO, *Lactodata*, 2009; MPO, *Lactodata*, 2016.

47. Clover Limited, *Annual Report 2013*, 2013

48. ACB, *GM Contamination, Cartels and Collusion in South Africa's Bread Industry*, 2014.

49. Clover Limited, *Annual Report 2015*.

50. ACB, *GM Contamination, Cartels and Collusion*, 2014.

51. www.timeslive.co.za, 23 April 2016.

52. In her September 2013 speech at the inauguration of the advisory committee on the future of payment grants in South Africa.

53. ANC, *ANC Agricultural Policy.*

54. RSA, *The National Policy on Food and Nutrition Security for the Republic of South Africa*, 2014, p 4.

55. ibid., p 7.

56. GDARD. *Gauteng Department of Agriculture and Rural Development Strategic Plan 2010 – 2014*, 2009, p 1.

57. www.abalimi.org.za.

58. www.khulisa.org.za.

59. www.siyavuna.org.za.

60. People in North West province, who achieved a mean score of 4.65, with almost 25 per cent of respondents falling into the 'low knowledge' group

61. Shisana et al., *South African National Health and Nutrition Examination Survey*, 2013, p 178.

62. Poppendieck, *Sweet Charity?*, 1999.

63. Pioneer Foods, *Integrated Report 2015*, 2015, p 45.

64. 2014/15 financial year, as per the company's annual report.

65. Based on the assumptions that wages make up 10 per cent of farming costs, a wage increase of 50 per cent and a farmer share of the retail price of 40 per cent.

66. Mauss, *The Gift*, 1967.

67. Lakhani, 'Food for(e) thought', p 74.

68. Gibson, *Fanonian Practices in South Africa*, 2011.

69. In May 2016, 13 schools were burnt down in Limpopo province for exactly this reason.

70. Congress of South African Trade Unions – South Africa's largest organised labour federation.

71. My theory. Sorry to disappoint you if you were expecting some famous thinker!
72. Each of these topics is worthy of its own book, and many have already been written. One of my motivations for writing *this* book is that I believe that the issue of food and social justice has not received the attention it deserves. In addition, the idea of social justice indirectly includes many environmental issues.
73. From Clapp & Fuchs, 'Agrifood corporations, global governance and sustainability', 2009.
74. See Du Toit, Forgotten by the highway, 2004 and Hickey & Du Toit, 'Adverse incorporation, adverse inclusion and chronic poverty', 2007.
75. Du Toit & Ortmann, 'Impact of market deregulation on the competitiveness of commercial milk producers in East Griqualand', 2009
76. Block, *Postindustrial Possibilities: A Critique of Economic Discourse*, 1990.
77. His book, *The Great Transformation: The Political and Economic Origins of Our Time,* written in 1944, is probably the best known of his works in this regard.
78. Patel's 2009 book, *The Value of Nothing,* focuses on this subject.
79. Tronto, *Moral Boundaries: A Political Argument for an Ethic of Care,* 1993, p 102.
80. This idea is related to the analysis proposed in Kneafsey et al., *Reconnecting Consumers, Producers and Food: Exploring Alternatives,* although I am asking different questions and approaching the issue of alternative food systems from a different starting point.
81. Tronto, *Moral Boundaries: A Political Argument for an Ethic of Care,* 1993, p 6.
82. op cit.
83. Tronto, *Moral Boundaries,* 1993, p 9.
84. Biko, *I Write What I Like, 1978* p 21.
85. Tronto, *Moral Boundaries,* 1993, p 102.
86. ibid., p 106.
87. ibid., p 107.
88. ibid., p 127.
89. www.harvestofhope.org.za.
90. Google 'urban food planning'.
91. Ariana Aranha, Special Assistant to Belo Horizonte's Food Security Programme and Brazil's Zero Hunger Strategy.
92. Morgan, 'The Rise of Urban Food Planning', 2013, p 341.
93. Buso, *Municipal Commonage Administration in the Free State Province,* 2003.

94. I did this calculation in Chapter 2, based on the 2010/11 Income and Expenditure Survey undertaken by StatsSA.

95. UK Competition Commission (2008), *The Supply of Groceries in the UK Market Investigation*, 2008.

96. Tronto, *Moral Boundaries: A Political Argument for an Ethic of Care*, 1993, p 102.

97. I would encourage you to familiarise yourself with the NGO, Women on Farms. You can find them at www.wfp.org.za.

98. Miller, 'Solidarity economy: Key concepts and issues', 2010.

99. For example, in Italy some Mafia-owned farms produce organic food, using exploited migrant labour. As Italian consumers rightly point out, consuming this organic food is hardly going to advance the interests of social justice.

100. Grasseni, *Beyond Alternative Food Networks*, 2013.

101. Most of what I have discussed about GAS comes from Cristina Grasseni's 2013 book, *Beyond Alternative Food Networks*. I can highly recommend it to anyone who is interested in the details of how these groups operate. It includes detailed accounts of how various groups were established and how they dealt with the inevitable problems they encountered.

102. Look at www.ozcf.co.za for more details.

103. www.phillyfpac.org.

References

ACB. *GM Contamination, Cartels and Collusion in South Africa's Bread Industry* (Johannesburg: African Centre for Biosafety, 2014)

ANC. *ANC Agricultural Policy*, 1994. Available at: www.anc.org.za (accessed on 14 December 2015)

Banerjee, AV & Duflo, E. *The Economic Lives of the Poor* (Cambridge, Massachusetts: Massachusetts Institute of Technology, 2006). Available at: www. economics.mit.edu/files/530 (accessed on 23 January 2012)

Battersby, J. The state of urban food insecurity in Cape Town. Urban Food Security Series No. 11 (Kingston and Cape Town: Queen's University and AFSUN, 2011)

BFAP. *Farm Sectoral Determination: An Analysis of Agricultural Wages in South Africa* (Pretoria: Bureau for Food and Agricultural Policy, 2012)

Biko, S. *I Write What I Like: A Selection of His Writings* (London: The Bowerdean Press, 1978)

Block, F. *Postindustrial Possibilities: A Critique of Economic Discourse* (Berkley and Los Angeles, California: University of California Press, 1990)

Buso, N. *Municipal Commonage Administration in the Free State Province: Can Municipalities in the Current Local Government Dispensation Promote Emerging Farming?* (Pretoria: Human Sciences Research Council, 2003)

CBH. *Integrated Annual Report 2013* (Johannesburg: Country Bird

Holdings Limited, 2013).

Clapp, J & Fuchs, D. 'Agrifood corporations, global governance, and sustainability: A framework for analysis', in Clapp, J & Fuchs, D (eds). *Corporate Power in Global Agrifood Governance* (Cambridge, Massachusetts: Massachusetts Institute of Technology, 2009)

Clover. *Annual Report* (Johannesburg: Clover Limited, 2013)

Clover. *Annual Report* (Johannesburg: Clover Limited, 2015)

CompCom. *Terms of Reference: Grocery Retail Sector Market Enquiry* (Pretoria: Competition Commission, 2015)

Du Toit, A. Forgotten by the highway: Globalisation, adverse incorporation and chronic poverty in a commercial farming district. PLAAS Chronic poverty and development policy series; no.4. (University of the Western Cape, 2004)

Du Toit, JP & Ortmann, GF. 'Impact of market deregulation on the competitiveness of commercial milk producers in East Griqualand: A unit cost ration (UCR) analysis: 1983–2006,' *Agrekon,* 48, no. 2 (2009), pp. 146–170

Food Ethics Council. Food ethics. Newsletter 8, no. 4 (Brighton: Food Ethics Council, 2013)

GDARD. *Gauteng Department of Agriculture and Rural Development Strategic Plan 2010–2014* (Johannesburg: Gauteng Department of Agriculture and Rural Development, 2009)

Gereffi, G. *A Commodity Chains Framework for Analysing Global Industries.* Mimeo, Duke University, 1999. Available at: www.eco.ieu.edu.tr/wp-content/Gereffi_CommodityChains99.pdf (accessed on 6 May 2010)

Gibson, N. *Fanonian Practices in South Africa: From Steve Biko to Abahlali baseMjondolo* (Durban: University of KwaZulu-Natal Press, 2011)

Grasseni, C. *Beyond Alternative Food Networks: Italy's Solidarity Purchase Groups* (London: Bloomsburg Academic, 2013)

Hendricks, SL. 'The potential for nutritional benefits from increased agricultural production in KwaZulu-Natal,' *South African Journal of Agricultural Extension,* 32 (2003), pp. 28–44

Hickey, S & Du Toit, A. 'Adverse incorporation, social exclusion and chronic poverty,' CPRC Working Paper No. 81 (Manchester: Chronic Poverty Research Centre, 2007).

Jacobs, P. 'Identifying a target for food security in South Africa', unpublished report, Centre for Poverty Employment and Growth (Pretoria: Human Sciences Research Council, 2009)

Kneafsey, M, Cox, R, Holloway, L, Dowler, E, Venn, L & Tuomainen, H. *Reconnecting Consumers, Producers and Food: Exploring Alternatives* (Oxford: Berg, 2008)

Kirsten, J. *The Impact of Market Power and Dominance of Supermarkets on Agricultural Producers in South Africa: A Case Study of the South African Dairy Industry* (Pretoria: National Agricultural Marketing Council, 2009)

Lakhani, I. 'Food for(e) thought: Strategies of the urban poor in Johannesburg in achieving food security', unpublished Master's thesis, University of the Witwatersrand, 2014

Mauss, M. *The Gift: Forms and Functions of Exchange in Archaic Societies* (New York: Norton, 1967)

Miller, E. 'Solidarity economy: Key concepts and issues', in Kwano, E, Masterson, T & Teller-Elseberg, J (eds). *Solidarity Economy 1: Building Alternatives for People and Planet* (Amherst: Centre for Popular Economics, 2010)

Morgan, K. 'The rise of urban food planning,' *International Planning Studies*, 18, no. 1 (2013), pp. 1–4

MPO. *Lactodata, May 2009* (Milk Producers' Organisation, 2009)

MPO. *Lactodata, May 2016* (Milk Producers' Organisation, 2016)

NAMC. *Section 7 Committee Evaluating the Deregulation Process: The Wheat to Bread Value Chain* (Pretoria: National Agricultural Marketing Council, 1999)

NAMC. *Report on the Investigation into the effect of Deregulation on the Dairy Industry* (Pretoria: National Agricultural Marketing Council, 2001)

NAMC. *Report on the Investigation into the Effect of Deregulation on the Red Meat Industry* (Pretoria: National Agricultural Marketing Council, 2001)

NAMC. *Report on the Section 7 Committee Investigation into the Wheat-to-Bread Value Chain* (Pretoria: National Agricultural Marketing Council, 2009)

NAMC. *Food Price Monitor: May Issue* (Pretoria: National Agricultural Marketing Council, 2016)

NAMC. *Food Basket Price Monthly: June Issue 6* (Pretoria: National Agricultural Marketing Council, 2016)

NDA. *White Paper on Agriculture 1995* (Pretoria: National Department of Agriculture, 1995)

NDA. *Agricultural Policy in South Africa: A Discussion Document* (Pretoria: National Department of Agriculture, 1998)

Oxfam. *Hidden Hunger in South Africa* (Johannesburg: Oxfam, 2014)

PACSA. *PACSA Monthly Food Price Barometer: May 2016.* Available at: www.pacsa.org.za (accessed on 12 July 2016)

Patel, R. *The Value of Nothing* (London: Portobello Books, 2009)

Pereira, LM. *The Future of South Africa's Food System: What is Research Telling Us?* (Cape Town: SA Food Lab, 2014).

Pioneer Foods. *2015 Integrated Report* (Cape Town: Pioneer Foods Limited, 2015)

Polanyi, K. *The Great Transformation* (Boston: Beacon Press, 2001 [1944])

Poppendieck, J. *Sweet Charity? Emergency Food and the End of Entitlement* (London: Penguin Books, 1999)

RSA. *Report of the Committee of Enquiry into the Marketing Act* (Pretoria: Republic of South Africa, 1992)

RSA. *Constitution of the Republic of South Africa, Act 108 of 1996* (Pretoria: Republic of South Africa, 1996)

RSA. *Marketing of Agricultural Products Act, No 47 of 1996* (Pretoria: Republic of South Africa, 1996)

RSA. *Competition Act, No 89 of 1998* (Pretoria: Republic of South Africa, 1998)

RSA. *The National Policy on Food and Nutrition Security for the Republic of South Africa.* Government Gazette, 22 August 2014 (Pretoria: Republic of South Africa, 2014)

Said-Mohamed, R, Micklesfield, LK, Pettifor, JM & Norris SA. 'Has the prevalence of stunting in South African children changed in 40 years? A systematic review,' *BMC Public Health*, 15 (2015), p. 534

Shisana, O, Labadarios, D, Rehle, T, Simbayi, L, Zuma, K, Dhansay, A, Reddy, P, Parker, W, Hoosain, E, Naidoo, P, Hongoro, C, Mchiza, Z, Steyn, NP, Dwane, N, Makoae, M, Maluleke, T, Ramlagan, S, Zungu, N, Evans, MG, Jacobs, L, Faber, M & SANHANES-1 Team. *South African National Health and Nutrition Examination Survey (SANHANES-1)* (Cape Town: HSRC Press, 2013)

StatsSA. *Income and Expenditure of Households 2010/2011.* Statistical release P0100 (Pretoria: Statistics South Africa, 2012)

Tathiah, N, Moodley, I, Mubaiwa, V, Denny, L & Taylor, M. 'South Africa's nutritional transition: Overweight, obesity, underweight and stunting in female primary school learners in rural KwaZulu-Natal, South Africa,' *South African Medical Journal*, 103, no. 10 (2013), pp 718–725

Tronto, JC. *Moral Boundaries: A Political Argument for an Ethic of Care*

(London: Routledge, 1993)

UK Competition Commission. *The Supply of Groceries in the UK Market Investigation* (London: United Kingdom Competition Commission, 2008)

Vink N & Kirsten JF. *Deregulation of Agricultural Marketing in South Africa: Lessons Learnt* (Johannesburg: Free Market Foundation, 2000)

Wegerif, M, Russell, B & Grundling, I. *Still Searching for Security: The Reality of Farm Dweller Evictions in South Africa* (Johannesburg: Nkuzi Development Association and Social Surveys, 2005)

Wylie, D. *Starving on a Full Stomach. Hunger and the Triumph of Cultural Racism in Modern South Africa* (Charlottesville: The University Press of Virginia, 2001)

Index